D1072448

Twenty-seven Contemporary Essays

Twenty-seven Contemporary Essays

EDITED BY

 Walter Brownsword

CHAIRMAN OF ENGLISH DEPARTMENT
RHODE ISLAND JUNIOR COLLEGE

Charles Scribner's Sons, New York

A–4.67[V]

PRINTED IN THE UNITED STATES OF AMERICA
Library of Congress Catalog Card Number 67-17871

Acknowledgments

The editor is indebted to the following authors, publishers, and other holders of copyright for permission to use the selections reprinted in this book.

Charles W. Cole for his article, "American Youth Goes Monogamous," published in *Harper's Magazine,* March 1957, copyright © 1957 by Harper's Magazine, Inc.

Collins-Knowlton-Wing, Inc., for "Public Schools Are Better Than You Think," by Sloan Wilson, published in *Harper's Magazine,* September, 1955, copyright © 1955, by Harper's Magazine, Inc.

Condé-Nast Publications, Inc., for "Meihem in ce Klasrum," by Dolton Edwards, reprinted from *Astounding Science Fiction* (now Analog Science Fiction–Science Fact); copyright © 1946 by Street & Smith Publications, Inc.

Cornell University Press for "Out for Stars: A Meditation on Robert Frost," originally published in *The Atlantic Monthly,* May, 1943, copyright 1955 by Cornell University. Used by permission of Cornell University Press.

Norman Cousins and the *Saturday Review* for Mr. Cousins' article, "The Desensitization of Twentieth-Century Man," from the *Saturday Review,* May 16, 1959.

Otto Friedrich for "There are 00 Trees in Russia," copyright 1964 by Otto Friedrich. Originally published in *Harper's Magazine,* October 1964.

Grosset & Dunlap, Inc., for "Comedy's Greatest Era," by James Agee, from *Agee on Film,* Vol. I, copyright © 1958 by James Agee Trust. Reprinted by permission of Grosset & Dunlap, Inc.

Harper & Row, Publishers, Inc., for "Will Strunk" (Turtle Bay, July 15, 1957), with postscript, from *The Points of My Compass,* by E. B. White, copyright © 1957, 1962, by E. B. White. This piece appeared originally in *The New Yorker,* in 1957, in a slightly different version as part of a larger essay; as the Introduction by E. B. White to *The Elements of Style,* by William Strunk, Jr., and by E. B. White (The Macmillan Company, 1959); also as part of the essay "Will Strunk" in *The Points of My Compass,* Harper & Row, Publishers, 1962.

Harper & Row, Publishers, Inc., also, for "Walden" (June 1939) from *One Man's Meat,* by E. B. White, copyright 1939 by E. B. White, and for "The Retort Transcendental" from *The Second Tree from the Corner,* by E. B. White, copyright 1942 by E. B. White, which originally appeared in *The New Yorker.* Reprinted by permission of Harper & Row, Publishers.

Gilbert Highet and *The New York Times* for "Teaching Not Facts, But How to Think," by Gilbert Highet, which appeared in *The New York Times Magazine,* February 25, 1951, © 1951 by The New York Times Company. Reprinted by permission.

Look Magazine for "Who Cares," by Leonard Gross, which appeared in the September 8, 1964, issue of *Look.*

Los Angeles Times Syndicate and *Newsweek,* for Walter Lippmann's column, "Kennedy at Mid-term," from *Newsweek,* January 21, 1963, copyright *Newsweek,* Inc., January 1963. Reprinted by permission.

The New York Times for "What Was Killed Was Not Only the President, But the Promise," by James Reston, from *The New York Times Magazine,* November 15, 1964, © 1964 by The New York Times Company. Reprinted by permission.

Penguin Books, Ltd., for Chapter XIII, "British and American English," in *Our Language,* by Simeon Potter, Penguin Books, 1950, 1966.

Charles S. Plotkin for permission to reproduce "Here's to Dear Old . . . ," the Atlantic prize essay, 1948–1949 contests for college students. Reprinted by permission.

Publishers Newspaper Syndicate for "Stanley Woodward," by Red Smith, which appeared in the New York *Herald Tribune* for November 30, 1965.

Helen Thurber for "Here Lies Miss Groby," copyright © 1942 James Thurber, from *My World—And Welcome To It,* published by Harcourt, Brace & World; originally printed in *The New Yorker.* For excerpt from "The Perilous Labor of Prince Thag," copyright © 1945 James Thurber, from *The White Deer,* published by Harcourt, Brace & World. For sections 1, 2, and 5 of "The Ladies' and Gentlemen's Guide to Modern English Usage," copyright © 1931, 1959 James Thurber, from *The Owl in the Attic,* published by Harper and Row; originally appeared in *The New Yorker,* and reprinted by permission of Harper & Row, Publishers.

Dr. Mortimer J. Adler and the *Saturday Review* for "How to Read a Dictionary," by Mortimer Adler, from *Saturday Review* for December 13, 1941.

Norman Podhoretz and *Harper's Magazine* for "In Defense of Editing," by Norman Podhoretz, from *Harper's Magazine,* October 1965, copyright © 1965, by Harper's Magazine, Inc. Reprinted by permission of the author.

Time, Inc., for "The Great Sir Laurence," by Richard Meryman, published in *Life,* May 1, 1964. For "In His Talent, Shakespeare Summoned Up," by Kenneth Tynan, in *Life,* May 1, 1964. For "Two Most Eminent and Strikingly Different Columnists," by John K. Jessup, in *Life,* May 7, 1965. All copyright Time, Inc.

The *World Journal Tribune* for "Stanley Woodward," by John Rogers, which appeared in the New York *Herald Tribune,* November 30, 1965. For "One Strike Is Out," by Stanley Woodward, which appeared during 1947 in the New York *Herald Tribune,* copyright 1947, New York *Herald Tribune.*

Preface

This book purposes to provide an introductory selection of essays on a variety of modern topics, topics related to students and to the world we all know. The ideals, the ideas, the problems, the successes, and the sheer good fun of life will all be found here. It is the hope of the editor that students will, through the use of this text, come to enjoy and appreciate the essay as a form, the realm of ideas as a source of great satisfaction, and good writing as a desirable goal.

To help both teachers and students, three types of study guide material have been provided with each essay.

The headnotes to the essays have been kept deliberately brief. Biographical details have been included only when a knowledge of them would be an aid to understanding and appreciation. More importantly, each headnote provides information, questions, and provocative suggestions to make the reading of the essay more desirable, more stimulating, and more rewarding.

Another feature of study material is the section entitled "For Greater Insight" that follows each essay. These sections include observations, comments, questions, and suggested assignments that will guide and direct the thinking of the student. There has been a deliberate attempt to avoid factual recall questions. There has been an equally deliberate attempt to include items that will require rereading, thoughtful comparison, and often, an examination of the reader's own ideas and convictions.

Whether reading is called "intensive," "in depth," or "study" reading, it should give the reader insights, relationships, and intellectual stimuli. Such reading cannot be the "once-over-lightly" type. It may be fast, but it must be thoughtful, and more than one reading may be called for. If these essays and accompanying study materials require such reading, this text will have accomplished one of its many objectives.

The whole section called "For Greater Insight" has been planned to cover a wide variety of teacher aims and class needs. If understanding of style is to be emphasized, then some questions will be more important than others. If stimulation of class discussion is the need, a different selection of questions is necessary. While no text can be all things to all people, the questions and suggestions have been designed to bring about that most necessary aspect of good reading—a thoughtful analysis of material read in relation to oneself and the world in which one lives.

The Word List completes the study material for each selection. The importance of growth in the ability to use words intelligently and to appreciate the value of such use is well known. However, stimulating that growth is not easy and the Word Lists can be helpful.

The words chosen here are essential for a thorough understanding of the particular essay in which they appear. Probably no one should say, "Look up in the dictionary all the words in the Word List," although a very few students might find the task beneficial. The lists should find their most effective use when attention is called to them to arouse an awareness of their importance for full comprehension, to create a personal dissatisfaction with one's own vocabulary, and to awaken an interest in precise expression of meaning.

Choice of the essays has not been dictated by any single criterion, unless that criterion is the belief that the subjects of the essays have a recognizable relation to the lives of students; that the styles of writing, though varied, are all admirable for some quality; and that the essays are in themselves interesting and provocative.

To a very real extent, the essay by Mr. Plotkin is the introduction to this book, and the editor hopes that no student will read the rest of the essays until he has first read and thought about "Here's to Dear Old . . ."

To Mr. Plotkin's ideas can be added only this—that education is not something done to or for anyone, but something which takes place within the person himself. It is a reaction, a developing, an awareness. It is vital and necessary, and it is a miracle of the mind and spirit.

I am indebted to Stuart C. Sherman, Librarian of the Providence Public Library, and many members of his staff, to Mrs. Elizabeth Daneker, on the staff of the John D. Rockefeller, Jr., Library of Brown University, to Miss M. Jane Allaire, Librarian at Rhode Island Junior College, to Frank O. Stred, Alumni Secretary at Bates College, and Charles H. Abbott, a Bates alumnus and an old friend, to Robert O. Anthony, who made available his files and catalog of Walter Lippmann material, to my son Dr. Alan W. Brownsword, to Francis B. Armington, and to John Gibb and Alex Begley, of Clapham College, London, England.

My most heartfelt thanks go to Paul L. Millane, of Charles Scribner's Sons, whose ideas, attitudes, criticism, and encouragement have been given with a warm generosity that has made working with him a pleasure.

Further, I owe a great debt to my wife and family for their patience and understanding; I have not seen as much of them as I would have liked during the past year!

WALTER BROWNSWORD

Contents

YOUTH, EDUCATION, AND EDUCATORS

STAGE AND SCREEN

LANGUAGE AND LITERATURE

LITERATURE AND VALUES

Introductory

Here's to Dear Old . . .

Charles S. Plotkin

When Mr. Plotkin was a senior at Bates College in 1949, he wrote the following essay as part of his course work. It was submitted in the Atlantic Monthly Essay Contest, and was awarded first prize. Bates College published the essay in their *Alumnus* for May 1, 1950, suggesting in their headnote that the essay was worth the reading of "every Bates graduate—and every high school student looking ahead to college."

There is much in the essay to think about, particularly in the section beginning "Shall I say that college has revolutionized my beliefs . . ." The student who reads the essay with the care it deserves will learn something about what to expect from his education, and something about attitudes he should take toward his education.

The extract beginning "This is the way my schooling ends . . ." is a paraphrase from T. S. Eliot's "The Hollow Men," and the extract at the end is from William Wordsworth's "The Prelude, or Growth of a Poet's Mind, an Autobiographical Poem," Book IV, lines 333–335.

Sometimes after an engrossing evening, a bridge game or a bull session, I lie awhile in bed too tense with recollections to sleep. As all kinds of curiously related thoughts ramble through my mind, I stop to wonder, now that my formal education is over, whether or not my canceled checks and paid semester bills . . .

Have all the hours of preparation for tests been worth while? Grind grind grind study memorize; facts facts dates formulas names events; learn learn—and go forth educated! Biology—I remember a long, yellowish worm with a nauseating stink. Cut it open, find this and that. Let's see now, there must have been some good reason why Professor Pomeroy wanted us to cut open that worm. Something about reproductive organs? Four hours a week for a whole semester and you don't even remember why old Pom wanted you to cut a worm open! Speech—required subject . . . must be good . . . needed . . . essential to well-rounded individual. Let's see, introduction, body, conclusion, be interesting, get variety in voice. Didn't you memorize that in high school anyway, only you called it beginning, middle, and end? Freshman English—remember anything from that? Irony! That's it! Irony, irony, irony, irony.

So the years pass in review. Like a general I stand on the reviewing platform, catch a glimpse of a few passing individuals, and soon forget their faces. Five years from now shall I even remember the parade?

> This is the way my schooling ends
> This is the way my schooling ends
> This is the way my schooling ends
> Not with a bang but a whimper.

What a waste! You light several little fires that glow merrily awhile and then leave gray ashes. Hour after hour, week after week, month after month, semester after semester—watch the flames dance and die. Such fitful dreams as rack the soul! The green-faced inquisitor stands on a desk in hell and shouts horrible questions: You went to college—What three things is 1776 memorable for? You are educated—How many years between Agincourt and Shakespeare? College graduate?—Al C + H O equals what? Trace Pericles' oration, compare Aquinas, analyze. The leering incubus jumps frantically up and down on his flaming desk laughing and laughing. Equals what? Ha, ha, ha. College educated, ha, ha, ha. Equals what, then? Tell me, equals what?

Morning brings coherence. But reason wants to know whether these phantoms of inefficacy represent the true state of the educated mind. What can be said for hours of painfully noted facts that vanish like a thousand separate shadows? They tell us, at the end of our four years, that we are educated—and give us a degree to prove it. Educated? For what?

For what purpose does a young man tell his employer he's collected his last thirty-five dollars, kiss his mother goodbye, and set off for New Haven, Waxahachie, or Rochester? Perhaps so that he can return to Littleville, kiss his mother hello, and demand seventy-five dollars a week. Such a man is a fool. He could have remained in Littleville, kissed his mother every day, and, by dint of hard work, soon made one hundred dollars a week. For proof one need inquire no farther than of the nearest businessman who probably quit high school and found himself a job sweeping floors.

A working woman whom I know was convinced that college offered something other than pecuniary success. When I told her of my planned return to school, her face became an ecstatic smile. "Gee, I wish I could have gone to college," she said. "Dances, parties, singing!" This woman sees the movies every Wednesday night, not only for the opportunity to enjoy college life vicariously, but because Wednesday night is door prize night.

If we discard financial and social considerations, we must demand again, "Why do I come to college?" More than one well-meaning acquaintance has answered my question for me somewhat as follows: "Well, you'll always have something that no one can take away from you." Usually my friends repeat this platitude with a practical inflection which implies that they neither know what this "something" is, nor would desire to take it away if they did. Yet this generality, I believe, conceals the truth as surely as do such other parroted assertions as "I am an American" or "I am a Christian." Americanism and Christianity and burglar-proof education require only personal clarification to become foundations of life rather than underlined topics: *Principles of Ethics*, page 106.

This "something" that my friends speak of is the abstract essence of education: understanding or wisdom. And understanding is more than an inalienable possession. It is a wordly approximation of God.

Understanding is also more than knowledge: the concise lists memorized for examinations. These unrelated facts are learned and forgotten. They wear off, like the specious wisdom of educational phonograph records that reiterate, "Je suis un élève; je parle française; répétez." Nature kindly purges the mind of such spurious stuffing.

And yet, from all the facts, from the worm and the microscope of Biology 111, that "something" remains: a conviction that life is ineffably sublime. If I was at one time certain that man, with all his Daedalian proficiency, would some day realize Dr. Frankenstein's dream, now I feel that the creation of living men lies beyond the scientist's greatest expectation. If I have forgotten how many layers make up this skin, I have not forgotten how humble I felt before the unfathomable complexity of a single cell of a pickled earthworm.

Should I say that college has revolutionized my beliefs, solidified my unformed conceptions, shaped my character? How strange and true a thought! When did this happen? After what course did I become aware of God's influence? What lecture taught my heart to break at the piteous wail of Shostakovitch's eerie violins in his Sixth Symphony? Which course in philosophy or psychology or English or chemistry made me know that I could no longer condemn because my understanding was too limited? On which doodle-filled notebook page did I record my new awareness of Shakespeare's perspicacity? During which yawn-stifling economics lecture did I learn that Republicans are not all good and Communists all bad? Which assignment set me to observing the idiosyncracies of others rather than fretting over my own? After how many hours did I open my ears to the music of Milton's crashing iambs? Which discussion made me see that there was a good case for Catholicism too?

There is no answer. Many things have affected and changed me; I know not when nor how. No one can say when a stream of water wore away this cavern or that cliff. A mother looks at her child and sees him a man. "But he was only a baby yesterday!" When did he change? When did he grow? When did he attain manhood? Imperceptibly, adding ideas one by one, college has made a new sum of life.

Like many others who have entered college, I came unsure of the future and of my interests in life. I was vaguely aware that I respected college graduates as profound beings. I had read that they carried fatter pocketbooks than high-school graduates; society set great store on education. I am now aware that some Ph. D.'s lack both profundity and pocketbooks. No matter. One day you see us as freshmen singing "Buffalo Gals" loud enough to scare away homesickness and trepidation—and all the girls in Buffalo. But look again; there we are chasing and grubbing like determined ants from one classroom to another. Now look again; we've found some palatable course, something that suits our taste and fills our minds. We've found a major, perhaps in some field we'd never dreamt of. And now look again; we still seem the same. But we have changed while you weren't noticing and while we had our attention focused on something else. Now we know, each one of us in his own way, in which endeavors lie our interest and hopes for consummation.

Has the trip to New Haven, Waxahachie, or Rochester been worthwhile? I know now that an educated man must understand himself as a man among men; that he must love life enough to strive for his own perfection; that he must be his brother's keeper. What good has college done me? It has taught me that the books I have studied, the lectures I have heard, the emotions I have discovered, are debts I owe, debts that I can discharge only by disseminating what I have taken. For hoarded wisdom, like buried money, rots unless one puts it into circulation.

Above all, I have been taught to read the road map of life. The city of satisfaction, success, balance, fulfillment, lies ahead. The route is charted.

> . . . I made no vows, but vows
> Were then made for me; bond unknown to me
> Was given, that I should be, else sinning greatly,
> A dedicated spirit.

Public Affairs

Two Most Eminent and Strikingly Different Columnists

John K. Jessup

The image of the newspaper writer as a trench-coated, hat-on-the-back-of-the-head, brash, flip, daring, adventurous young man has been so deeply ingrained in us by Grade B movies that it is hard to erase the false and recognize the true.

The real newspaper columnist—using rich resources of memory; devoting hours of time to reading, interviewing, and study; exercising his analytical intelligence—has come to be one of the most important newspaper writers in our contemporary world.

Mr. Jessup, Chief Editorial Writer for *Life,* wrote this essay for the issue of May 7, 1965, to introduce pictures and further descriptions of Walter Lippmann and James Reston.

As you read, note that the essay is clearly divided into beginning, middle, and end, and that the middle is divided into two sections. (The "line breaks" or extra spaces, used to break up a magazine article, and reproduced when reprinting it, may or may not correspond to the actual thought divisions.)

Note also that although Jessup analyzes the two men and their work he does not give any feeling that he believes one to be more effective than the other. He keeps his writing completely objective.

The two men pictured on these pages are the most influential columnists in Washington, and therefore perhaps the most im- ¶1 portant political writers in the world. They are important not just because their syndicated columns are read several times a week by a lot of people—30 million in Walter Lippmann's case, up to 15 million in James Reston's—but also because they are regarded as must reading by makers of policy and opinion in the capital. At the Metropolitan Club, where Lippmann and Reston usually eat lunch (often with each other), the distinguished diplomats, bureaucrats and politicians at the other tables are more than likely to be salting their conversation with a reference to what Lippmann or Reston said in the paper earlier. So, quite often, does the President.

¶2 Lippmann and Reston arrived at their eminence by strikingly different routes. Lippmann has been an influence on American public life and thought for more than 50 years. The only son of wealthy and cultivated parents of German-Jewish origin, he was an outstanding member of the outstanding class of 1910 at Harvard, where philosophers William James and George Santayana were rivals in shaping his mind. He helped Santayana teach for a year after graduation, but was later to call James "the hero of my life." In his youth he was also a friend and fan of Theodore Roosevelt, who reviewed his second book, *Drift and Mastery*, and called him "the most brilliant young man of his age in all the U.S." He spent four months as an aide to the Socialist mayor of Schenectady and during the First World War he served as a brain-truster to Woodrow Wilson's brain-truster, Colonel House, and was a source of ideas for Wilson's "Fourteen Points."

¶3 But since 1919 Lippmann has eschewed public service and close ties with public figures. Instead he has deliberately kept his keen mind engaged in ideas and events but aloof from movements and causes. He exemplifies perfectly what Emerson called "Man Thinking," the disinterested but concerned intellectual.

¶4 "I have lived two lives," he once said. "One of books and one of newspapers. Each helps the other. The philosophy is the context in which I write my columns. The column is the laboratory or clinic in which I test the philosophy and keep it from becoming too abstract." Before starting his column in 1931 in the New York *Herald Tribune* he had been a founding editor of *The New Republic* and later the editorial chief of the New York *World.* In recent years he has also mastered another medium in his annual hour-long interview for CBS-TV. Meanwhile he has written more than two dozen books—notably *The Good Society* and *The Public Philosophy*—some topical, some permanent contributions to American political thought.

When two admirers produced an anthology of Lippmann's ¶5
best writing a couple of years ago (*The Essential Lippmann*, Random House) they extracted more than 200,000 words from a total yield which they reckoned at "more than 100 million words of opinion and advice to the American public." More impressive than the amount is its high quality both of form and content. His thoughts, whether right or wrong, are always lucidly expressed and are always the disciplined and "inner-directed" thoughts of a civilized sage.

Lippmann is one of the few Washingtonians, Reston has ¶6
written, "who never complains that he cannot find time to think." This is partly because he guards and rations his time and orders his day, and his year, according to plan. By 9 o'clock, on the mornings he has a column to write, he has already read the newspapers. Then he sits down and writes for two or three hours; if it is a column, it is always typed, checked and retyped in time for a 12:30 deadline. Then he goes to the Metropolitan Club for lunch. Afternoons are for relaxation or reading; dinners are for conversation with the great. Reston once wrote with a touch of envy: "His life is not commanded by events. He is up to the minute with the news, but he keeps his news ticker and his television in a closet."

Reston's has been a harder life than Lippmann's. The son ¶7
of an immigrant mechanic, he was raised in frugal and pious sur-

roundings, first in Scotland, then in Dayton, Ohio. His first ambition was to be a preacher, his second to be a professional golfer. Far from sitting under James and Santayana, he flunked philosophy at the University of Illinois and graduated without honors in 1932. But he married a Phi Beta Kappa ("I married above me," says "Scotty" Reston) and developed his own intellect, as he had his golf game, with a built-in Calvinist drive. He worked as traveling secretary for the Cincinnati Reds before landing a job covering sports for the A.P. In 1937 he was transferred to London where he also covered the Foreign Office. At the time he knew nothing about diplomacy, but his energy and enterprise soon mastered the subject and propelled him to the *New York Times* in 1939 and ultimately to its Washington bureau in 1944. Covering the Dumbarton Oaks rehearsal for the United Nations conference, he scored a major scoop by getting his hands on all the leading Allied position papers and won a Pulitzer Prize for his reporting of the conference. He has been in the thick of top-level political reporting ever since, both as the *Times'* Washington bureau chief (a demanding administrative as well as writing job) and more recently as associate editor of the paper.

¶8 In preparing his column Reston remains an insatiable digger, especially by telephone, for news and ideas and regards himself as a reporter rather than a pundit. He prefers to pick the brains of deputies or under-secretaries who do most of the work of government, rather than take up the time of the very top people. He reads books only for information and while he knows something about virtually everything, his former boss, Arthur Krock, does not consider him a cultivated man. He retains the ex-sportswriter's common touch and can write comic and elegiac pieces as well as what the *Times* calls "News Analysis." His column is usually a highly intelligent summary of what policy makers are thinking or worrying about; Reston does not so much argue for or against their policies as clarify them with a readable prose style and stamp them with his own healthy and hopeful point of view. He is not above flying kites in the guise of reporting when he thinks they are useful, as when he recently wrote from Rome that President Johnson is considering exchanging envoys with the Vatican. But the quality of his reporting remains the key to his influence, and he wouldn't want it otherwise. He has never systematized his own political philosophy and has written only one book.

Thus Lippmann, the born mandarin, can be said to have brought philosophy down from its mountain to the sweaty forum of public events; whereas Reston, moving in the opposite direction, has elevated cityroom journalism into political and social criticism of a high order. Reston has written of Lippmann that "he has given my generation of newspapermen a wider vision of our duty." Plenty of younger reporters feel the same way about Reston, who has a passion for educating beginners in his trade, and who continues to set higher standards in his own writing from year to year. ¶9

Which, then—the mandarin or the reporter, the brain or the brain-picker—has better served the public? Which has given it the fewer bum steers? Lippmann has been writing much longer than Reston, likes to stick his neck out farther, and has therefore made more mistakes. He regards it as his duty not just to criticize policy but to propose alternatives. Moreover his criticisms are likely to be "contracyclical," or deliberately unfashionable, as they are right now with his "neo-isolationist" opposition to the war in Vietnam. Reston, who knows more details about the reasons and motives for any given policy, is less likely than Lippmann to oppose it. ¶10

Among Lippmann's errors, as hindsight usually counts them, were his somewhat petulant support of Landon in 1936, his opposition to the rearmament of Germany in the late '40s and early '50s and his advocacy of U.S. military disengagement in Europe. He is a leader of the Morgenthau-Kennan "realist" school in diplomacy, which assumes that national interest will sooner or later ¶11 determine what statesmen will do, including Communist statesmen. But when U.S. policy and opinion get too "realist," Lippmann can be relied on to preach a more evangelical form of democracy. If these are intellectual inconsistencies in his career, he has more than balanced them by the quality of the national debate on public issues which he has nurtured for 50 years, a debate he has "saturated" with true philosophy.

¶12 Reston has a Scottish capacity for indignation which showed during the newspaper strike of 1963. He wrote a column urging his employers to break the strike (they not only rejected the advice but killed the column). As Murray Kempton once observed, Reston "is not so much a man of the left or right as he is a man of the *Times.*" He and Lippmann both resist easy classification as liberal or conservative. Between them they are sturdy foes of emotional or stereotyped thinking—and critics of U.S. democracy because they are also its staunch friends.

For Greater Insight

1. Why should diplomats, bureaucrats, politicians, and even the President, read Lippmann and Reston? For the same reason?
2. What do you think Jessup tries to do in his first paragraph? Does he succeed? Explain.
3. How do you know that the second paragraph has a different purpose from the first? What is its purpose? In what sentences are you told of the change in purpose? Comment on the transitional value of these sentences.
4. Explain what is meant, in the next paragraph, by "engaged in ideas and events, but aloof from movements and causes." Explain also "disinterested but concerned intellectual." Can a person be both disinterested and concerned? Should he be? Explain and illustrate.
5. What outstanding quality characterized Lippmann's daily routine? Explain the quotation from Reston at the end of Par. 6.
6. What is the transitional sentence that tells you that the author is now speaking about the second columnist?

7. The sentence just referred to is a topic sentence. How does the paragraph illustrate the claim made in that sentence? In what respects does it contrast Reston's life with Lippmann's? What order of events is followed in the paragraph? In each case, explain your answer.
8. What do you think is meant by "flying kites in the guise of reporting"? What would be the value of such an action?
9. Par. 9, beginning "Thus Lippmann, the born mandarin . . ." is an interesting example of both parallel construction and contrast and comparison. Point out examples of each.
10. Why should Reston know "more about the reasons and motives for any given policy"?
11. Sometimes a writer deliberately mixes careful, proper, formal language with words and phrases which are informal, slangy, and colorful. In which paragraph do you find examples of such mixing? Identify them and explain their meaning and their effect.
12. At the very end of the essay, in what two ways does Jessup say Lippmann and Reston are alike?

Word Study

salting their conversation:
served as a *braintruster*:
eschewed public service:
kept his mind *aloof*:
He *exemplifies* perfectly:
some *topical*, some permanent:
lucidly expressed:
in *frugal* surroundings:
an *insatiable* digger:
reporter rather than a *pundit*:
can write *elegiac* pieces:
Lippmann, the born *mandarin*:
his "*neo-isolationist*" opposition:
petulant support of Landon:

Kennedy at Mid-term

Walter Lippmann

This essay, surveying President Kennedy's accomplishments and prospects at "mid-term," first appeared in the January 21, 1963, issue of *Newsweek.*

It would be difficult to find an essay which illustrates more clearly some of the qualities Jessup points out in Lippmann's thinking and writing. You should watch for evidence of well-informed analysis, thoughtful organization, and some tendency toward prophecy.

The step-by-step orderliness of Lippmann's writing is very clear. While you read, notice the way in which he identifies his sections and helps you move with him from one idea to another.

¶1 Now that we have the benefit of hindsight, we can compare the world as it looked to the candidate and the world as it has turned out to be for the President.

¶2 When we reread the key speeches from the 1960 campaign, we are reminded of three main themes. The military power of the United States is falling behind that of the Soviet Union: we are on the wrong end of a missile gap. The American economy is stagnating: we are falling behind the Soviet Union and behind the leading industrial nations of Western Europe in our rate of growth. The United States is failing to modernize itself: the public services, education, health, rebuilding of the cities, transportation, and the like, are not keeping up with a rapidly growing urbanized population. So Mr. Kennedy promised the voters to restore the balance of military power, to get the economy moving again, and to bring about reforms and innovations in the public services.

The past two years have shown, I would say, that the candi- ¶3
date was overconfident about what the President would be able to do at home. On the other hand, in foreign affairs, he could not foresee that the over-all balance of forces had begun to turn in favor of the West.

The outcome of the election itself cast a dark shadow upon ¶4
the promise to open up New Frontiers. We can now see that the promised innovations and reforms would have been politically workable only if the voters, feeling that they were in a great crisis, had turned the Democratic gains of 1958 into a landslide in 1960. To do what he promised to do, Mr. Kennedy needed the kind of power which Franklin Roosevelt possessed in the 1930s.

The Hard Facts

But Mr. Kennedy was elected by the narrowest margin, and ¶5
in the 1960 Congressional elections, the Democrats lost some twenty seats. Mr. Kennedy is a great respecter of the hard facts. As soon as the election returns were in, he began to shape his Administration accordingly. Since almost as many people had voted against him as had voted for him, since almost certainly General Eisenhower could have defeated him, the President-elect began to put together—particularly in the field of high policy—a bipartisan Administration.

This was not, I imagine, altogether uncongenial to him. For ¶6
while he is a highly skilled professional politician who fights elections to win them, in matters of high policy, and by temperament and instinct and association, he has never been a partisan Democrat of the Roosevelt or the Truman persuasion.

¶7 The key positions in the field of high policy are State, Treasury, Defense, Central Intelligence, Federal Reserve, and, we may add, the White House itself.

¶8 For the State Department he chose Dean Rusk, a Georgia Democrat who worked for John Foster Dulles and who had never been in active politics. Except for Rusk, Mr. Kennedy chose Republicans for the key posts: Douglas Dillon for the Treasury, Robert McNamara for Defense, John McCone for Intelligence. William McChesney Martin Jr., who if he is not a Republican can pass for one, was encouraged to remain on as chairman of the Federal Reserve Board. The management of our international payments problem was entrusted to Republicans. For a long time the President tried to find a Republican to manage foreign aid. He has put General Eisenhower's Secretary of State, Christian Herter, in charge of tariff negotiations under the new Trade Expansion Act. And at the center of high policy-making in the White House itself, he put McGeorge Bundy, the biographer of President Hoover's Secretary of State, Col. Henry Stimson, and a lifelong Massachusetts Republican.

¶9 Mr. Kennedy reached out further still for Republican support. To a critical degree he did so in matters of fiscal policy. This is the field where Republicans have always contended they hold the sound views, and the Democrats the unsound ones. During his first year and well into his second, there were no sharp differences in fiscal matters between President Kennedy and General Eisenhower. The President made a few speeches, notably the one at the Yale commencement in June 1962, which General Eisenhower regarded as horrifying and heretical. But in his actual measures, the President stayed within the bounds which were acceptable to Eisenhower Republicans. For he felt himself constrained not only by his narrow majority but also by public opinion, which on most issues was a great deal closer to Eisenhower than to his own campaign speeches.

The Necessary Majority

In short, if President Kennedy was going to do what he said ¶10
he would do, he had first to win over a popular majority. The majority had to do more than like him. They had to follow him. Unless he could bring that about, he must lay aside, or at least tune way down, the promises to promote economic growth and to carry out innovations and reforms. As a result, during these two years the economy has been growing at an embarrassingly slow rate.

Until the current session of the new Congress adjourns, we ¶11
shall not know how successfully the President has been able to make converts to his principles and his plans. Thus far, the Congress, which is controlled by a coalition of Republicans and Southern Democrats, has refused to open the New Frontiers. In this refusal Congress has, I believe, reflected the opinions of the majority. Thus, while there is much sentiment in favor of the domestic innovations and reforms, the sentiment, by and large, is passive and diffuse. The people are not passionately excited about education, medical care, conservation, and urban development. Under these circumstances the opposition of the highly organized political groups—the Roman Catholic hierarchy, the American Medical Association, and the farm lobby—has been very effective.

Further, more people are angrily opposed to the high taxes, ¶12
especially the highly visible income taxes. Yet they have believed that to open the New Frontiers they must either reduce their private spending in order to pay higher taxes or have their money lose value by inflation.

Thus, the Administration was caught in the dilemma of ¶13
private versus public spending. The official view of this dilemma is that it should not exist. It can and should be dissolved by taking measures to induce the economy to operate at full capacity. If this were done, the country could produce something like $30 billion to $40 billion more wealth annually. And this would be

quite enough to pay for more public services, also to lower taxes, and at the same time to maintain a rising standard of private life.

¶14 During his first two years, however, the President did not think that he could convince Congress or a majority of the people that economic growth can be promoted deliberately. He knew he would be charged with quackery, with attempting sleight of hand, and his Administration would be impugned as unsound and rather disreputable. In fact, though the economists have been preponderantly on the side of the Administration, General Eisenhower and the mass of the people have been against it.

¶15 The Administration has, of course, had some legislative successes, notably the passage of the Trade Expansion Act. But it has not yet been able to win for itself a general understanding of its purposes. We must wait to see if it can do this. We have yet to find out whether the country can be converted by persuasion at a time when business is fairly good and there are only scattered pockets of unemployment. Although President Kennedy is very popular, he has not yet been able to carry the country with him. He has not yet won over the minds of the people. This may be because he has not yet conquered their hearts by opening his own.

A Gross Miscalculation

¶16 During the campaign of 1960 almost nobody was aware that the tide of world affairs was turning. In fact, in 1960 things looked worse than they were. In the main, this was due to an accident. The country was the victim of a gross miscalculation of Soviet and American nuclear power. This professed to prove that the United States was on the wrong end of a frightening missile gap, and that it would soon be wide open to a knockout in one cataclysmic salvo.

¶17 Nobody would listen to President Eisenhower's denials and assurances. Not even Vice President Nixon really denied the

Democratic charges, and Governor Rockefeller was believed to support the charges. In this fog of hysteria nobody would have dared to say, even if he had discerned the fact, that the global tide was turning. Moreover, with the Soviet intervention in Cuba, it certainly did not look as if the tide was in fact turning in our favor. As a result, it was not until the second Cuban affair in October 1962 that it really began to be believed that the nuclear balance was in our favor, and that the general balance of ideological and economic power was less favorable to the Soviet Union than it had been thought to be during the campaign of 1960.

Until recently, the Administration acted on the notion that ¶18
we are, so to speak, the underdog in the cold war. The first beginning of a change of mind showed itself in February 1961 when Secretary McNamara, after a few weeks' investigation in the Pentagon, let it be known that there was no missile gap. Not long after, thanks to the acceleration and enlargement of the Eisenhower program, it began to transpire that the United States had and was enlarging a considerable margin of superiority in nuclear weapons. In October 1961 the Deputy Secretary of Defense, Roswell Gilpatric, confirmed this officially.

A Fresh Perspective

From this new appraisal of the balance of power has come a ¶19
renewal of self-confidence. We dare to see things in a fresh perspective. Thus, it became apparent that the Soviet Union broke the moratorium and resumed nuclear testing in the hope of closing the missile gap. Very probably the madcap Soviet gamble with missiles in Cuba also originated in a desperate attempt to close the nuclear gap. In any event, in the confrontation over Cuba, Chairman Khrushchev recognized the facts of the situation. He has continued to recognize them in regard to Berlin, and he has emphasized them most spectacularly in resisting the Chinese warhawks.

¶20 The military balance of forces has not only ruled out military action to change the general situation, it has allowed other favorable developments to take on new energy. The improved sense of military security has played a big part in the rapid revival of Western Europe. The revival has exceeded anything that Communist thinkers thought was possible and anything that most Westerners expected to see.

¶21 The revival in Europe has vast significance for the future. It is already exerting great influence in the present. In 1948 when the Marshall plan was proposed, Western Europe seemed about to fall to the Communist parties. Today, the West European Communist parties, notably the big French and Italian parties, have no prospect whatever of taking over power. They have become parties of protest and dissent, rallying points against reaction around a dwindling and softening Leninist core. Moreover, the success of the West European economy, which is a mixture of free enterprise and state socialism, is now a powerful magnet of attraction upon Eastern Europe. The day can be foreseen when the European economy will reach beyond the Iron Curtain, perhaps, as General de Gaulle has often predicted, to the Ural Mountains.

¶22 The industrial success of Western Europe and the agricultural abundance in the Western world make a strong contrast with the economic troubles of the Communist nations. Few can argue any longer that the Communist countries have mastered the problems of economic progress while the West has no solution to the problem of poverty. For there has now become visible, because it is actually in successful use, a way, which is not totalitarian, to overcome poverty and backwardness. Thus, of the 45 new countries which have emerged from the old colonial empires during the past seventeen years, none is openly and avowedly Communist. What has happened in Cuba has not happened in Africa and Asia; the control of Cuba by a Communist regime is an exception to the general movement of human affairs.

Finally, there is the great schism between Moscow and Peking, a schism comparable, it may be, to the division of the Roman Empire between Byzantium and Rome. This historic schism is demonstrating that the Communists are not a band of brothers unaffected by nationalism, imperialism, power, self-interest, and the other propensities of the human animal. ¶23

When Mr. Kennedy took office there were few who foresaw that he would be dealing not with one Communist brotherhood but with two rival Communist empires. ¶24

It would be a grievous mistake, however, to think that because we are not in fact the underdog we can act the top dog. Our nuclear power is great. But so too is the nuclear power of the Soviet Union. We have the power to deter. But the Soviet Union has the power to deter us from dictating. We can afford no hot-blooded juvenile notions about the weakness of the Soviet nuclear power or about the invincibility of our own. ¶25

The Power Balance

If I judge correctly, the favorable turn of the global tide has made it far less likely than it was in 1961 that the cold war will turn into a hot war. The acute tension is reduced. Though the balance of power is favorable, it is nevertheless a balance. It is reasonably evident, moreover, that we are not now in sight of being able to negotiate a provisional settlement of the cold war. For the effect of reducing the tension is not to bring about a settlement. It is rather to release inside both coalitions interests and ambitions which have been suppressed while the danger of war was more imminent. ¶26

Mr. Kennedy and Mr. Khrushchev may be able to do little more at the present time, it would seem, than to coexist without war. They can broaden their contacts though they can reach no formal agreements. They can remove some of the distrust which beclouds all communication. Neither of them can dictate to the ¶27 other, and neither of them is paramount in his own world. More and more, in fact, each of them is finding himself immersed in the problems of his own world.

¶28 Khrushchev is challenged by China for the leadership of Communism. This is not only a preoccupation for him, it is also a severe limitation upon his ability to make agreements with the West. For Khrushchev has to watch his step.

¶29 President Kennedy will, I would guess, be increasingly preoccupied with the relations between this country and the New Europe which is emerging. Just ahead of us there lies the question whether the United States can and should continue to carry the financial burden of the foreign commitments which were made when Europe was poor and weak. In this country we are on the eve of a complex and far-reaching reappraisal of the share which Europe and America should play in the defense of Europe, in the promotion of transatlantic trade, and in the assistance they should give to the underdeveloped countries.

¶30 In Europe, on the other hand, there is an increasing unwillingness to accept American world leadership. There is a growing dissatisfaction in Europe with our monopoly of nuclear weapons. Behind all the dissatisfaction there is a feeling that if and when some kind of peace is made with Russia, it should be made not between Washington and Moscow but between a united Western Europe and the Russian state.

¶31 At mid-term President Kennedy is facing a world which is less dangerous than it seemed to be in 1961. But it is also much subtler and more complicated. He holds good cards but they are not all trumps, and the game, which is far from won, could readily be lost by recklessness, bad judgment, failure to master special interests at home, and by too much listening to the chattering of the magpies.

I do not, however, think that the game will be lost. Between Cuba April 1961 and Cuba October 1962, John F. Kennedy acquired an exceptional ability to measure the forces with which a

President must deal. The senator and the candidate had become the President. For John F. Kennedy knows how to learn from experience. There was never any doubt about his courage. But in April 1961, there was grave doubt about his judgment of men and of the imponderables. In October 1962, he showed that he has not only the courage of a warrior, which is to take the risks that are necessary, but also the wisdom of the statesman, which is to use power with restraint.

For Greater Insight

1. Professional writers, knowing that their success depends upon the clarity of their work, are careful to make its major divisions quite obvious. How does Lippmann tell you that he has five major divisions following his introduction? What does he call these divisions?
2. In each of the five divisions, Lippmann repeats, within the first, second, or third sentences, at least some of the words used in the side headings. What is the value of such repetition?
3. Within the five sections, can you find any similarities of organization? Any dissimilarities? Illustrate and explain. What is the value in such similarity or dissimilarity?
4. "Let's see, introduction, body, conclusion," recalls Charles Plotkin from his speech course (p. 4). Student writers too are often told to include a beginning, a middle, and an end in their writing. Identify the beginning, middle, and end of the Lippmann article.
5. In his beginning, or introduction, what does Lippmann tell you? Does he give an indication of the points he intends to make? Explain.
6. Read the second paragraph again, noting carefully the second, third, and fourth sentences. What do you notice about them? You may be very sure that Lippmann wrote these as he did intentionally. Why should he have done so? What, in the first sentence, is explained by the next three?
7. In his essay on Lippmann and Reston, Jessup uses the terms "reporter and pundit," and "mandarin and reporter." Justify his use of the terms by referring to portions of Lippmann's and Reston's essays.
8. In Par. 10 of Jessup's essay, he suggests that Lippmann "likes to

stick his neck out" and that he not only criticizes but suggests alternatives. The statement implies a tendency to political prophecy. In Lippmann's essay, find some prophetic utterances. Can you say whether the prophecies have come true?

9. In Par. 31, Lippmann uses figurative language in the sentence beginning "He holds good cards . . ." Explain the figure of speech, and the real meaning of the sentence.
10. About what aspects of Kennedy's time in office do Reston and Lippmann agree? disagree?

Word Study

benefit of *hindsight*:
economy is *stagnating*:
urbanized population:
altogether *uncongenial* to him:
horrifying and *heretical*:
he felt himself *constrained*:
controlled by a *coalition*:
passive and *diffuse*:
charged with *quackery*:
impugned as unsound:
preponderantly on the side of the Administration:
professed to prove:
in one *cataclysmic salvo*:
broke the *moratorium*:
the great *schism*:

What Was Killed Was Not Only the President But the Promise

James Reston

Appearing in the *New York Times Magazine* on November 15, 1964, almost a year from the assassination of President Kennedy, this essay is not only among the first to stress the loss of what might have been, but it is also one of the most calm, balanced evaluations you will find.

The organization of the essay is worth close study, and as you read you should keep in mind the need for a plan or pattern for writing, and seek to discover Reston's plan. Note how he shows almost bluntly some of Kennedy's less successful moments and then in sharp contrast lets us see both an excellent performance and the potentiality of the former President. It is the contrast which helps make the essay an excellent and effective one.

As you read the whole essay, look, too, for patterns of sentences—patterns not only in length of sentences, but in structure.

Time seems to be trying to make amends to John Fitzgerald Kennedy. Robbed of his years, he is being rewarded and honored in death as he never was in life. Deprived of the place he sought in history, he has been given in compensation a place in legend. What was a monstrous personal and historic crime a year ago is now something even more elemental and enduring: It is a symbol ¶1 of the tragedy and caprice of life, and it is likely to be remembered by the novelists and dramatists long after the historians have gone on to other things.

¶2 Will he seem different to the historians from the way the dramatists will see him? What are they likely to say of his conduct of foreign affairs, domestic affairs, the Presidency itself? Are we already confusing myth with reality, as he was always telling us we should not do?

¶3 Probably we are, but this is only fair and maybe even natural. For there was always something vaguely legendary about him. He was a story-book president, younger and more handsome than mortal politicians, remote even from his friends, graceful, almost elegant, with poetry on his tongue and a radiant young woman at his side.

¶4 He was a sudden and surprising person. He never did things when other men were doing them. He went to Congress and the White House earlier than most. He married much later than his contemporaries. His war record, his political record, and his personal life were marked by flashes of crisis and even by a vague premonition of tragedy. He always seemed to be striding through doors into the center of some startling triumph or disaster. He never reached his meridian: we saw him only as the rising sun.

¶5 Accordingly, it is not easy to make an estimate of his 1,000 days in the White House. He didn't have a fair chance and he didn't even give himself a fair chance. He often made his decisions alone after a series of private talks with several individuals, none of whom shared the whole process of his thought.

¶6 Oddly in one who had such an acute sense of history, he was disorderly about keeping records of what led up to his decisions, and though he had a great gift for conversation, he seems to have spent little time talking to his closest associates about how he had decided things in the past.

¶7 All this complicates the task of placing him in the catalogue of the Presidents. We do not have the record. We do not have the full story of the two Cuban crises, or his meeting with Khrushchev in Vienna, or the communications that led up to the atomic test-ban treaty with the Soviets. We have only our clippings, memories, and impressions, and these can be uncertain guides.

I. *Foreign Policy*

Historians—and here we are in the realm of opinion—will ¶8
probably rate President Kennedy's handling of foreign policy higher than his contemporaries did. It is a spotty record. He dreamed occasionally of an interdependent Atlantic world and this has become part of the legend, but the reality is that the alliance was in poor shape during most of his administration. He courted Latin America like a thoughtful lover, but, again, the Alliance for Progress was more dream than reality.

Even so, he had a feeling for the way the world was going. ¶9
He understood the challenge of change. He was fascinated by the political revolution produced by the liberation of the colonial peoples: sometimes too fascinated with it, and too inclined to give it a higher priority than it deserved. He studied and understood the intricate problems of the atomic revolution and the scientific revolution, probably better than any of his predecessors.

Yet this keen, analytical intelligence was not always a help. ¶10
It enabled him to see the problems, but it often depressed him about finding the answers. I always thought—perhaps wrongly—that his intelligence made him pessimistic. The evidence that science was transforming the world seemed so clear and overwhelming to him that he was irritated by the failure of men and institutions to adapt and keep up.

In his very first State of the Union message, 10 days after he ¶11
had been sworn in, he told the Congress and the nation: "Before my term has ended, we shall have to test anew whether a nation organized and governed such as ours can endure. The outcome is by no means certain. The answers are by no means clear."

¶12 His bungling of his first foreign-policy gamble, when he tried to help the Cuban refugees overthrow the Castro Government, made him all the more conscious, not only of the complexities of political decision, but of the possible consequences of failure.

¶13 The events at the Bay of Pigs contributed to his natural caution, and added to his problems with the Communists for most of the rest of his days in the White House. It is impossible to be sure about this, but I was in Vienna when he met Khrushchev shortly after the fiasco of the Bay of Pigs, and saw him 10 minutes after his meeting with the Soviet leader. He came into a dim room in the American Embassy shaken and angry. He had tried, as always, to be calm and rational with Khrushchev, to get him to define what the Soviet Union could and would not do, and Khrushchev had bullied him and threatened him with war over Berlin.

¶14 We will have to know much more about that confrontation between Kennedy and Khrushchev, one now deprived of life and the other of power, before we can be sure, but Kennedy said just enough, in that room in the embassy, to convince me of the following: Khrushchev had studied the events of the Bay of Pigs; he would have understood if Kennedy had left Castro alone or had destroyed him; but when Kennedy was rash enough to strike at Cuba but not bold enough to finish the job, Khrushchev decided he was dealing with an inexperienced young leader who could be intimidated and blackmailed. The Communist decision to put offensive missiles into Cuba was the final gamble of this assumption.

¶15 The missile crisis brought out what always seemed to me to be Kennedy's finest quality and produced the events on which Kennedy's place in history probably depends. There is a single fact that repeats itself in the Kennedy story like the major theme in a symphony: He was always at his best in the highest moment of crisis.

¶16 He could be ambiguous and even indecisive on secondary

questions. He obviously trifled with the first Cuban crisis. He also temporized with the Vietnamese crisis, partly supporting those who wanted to intervene "to win," partly going along with those who reminded him that the French had suffered 175,000 casualties against the same Communist army, but never really defining his aims or reconciling his power with his objectives.

Yet always in his political life he acted decisively when faced with total defeat. He was supremely confident, almost presumptuous, in going for the Presidency in the first place against the opposition of the most powerful elements in his party. He was bold and effective when first Hubert Humphrey, then Harry Truman and finally Lyndon Johnson challenged him publicly during the campaign for the nomination. He probably won the Presidency in the critical debates with Richard Nixon. And this same quality came out in the missile crisis in Cuba. ¶17

Then he was, as Robert Frost had urged him to be, "more Irish than Harvard" but with a dash of Harvard intelligence, too. If the first Cuban crisis was the worst example of the uses of American power and diplomacy in this generation, the second Cuban crisis was the best. And the significance of this fact can be understood only in relation to the longer perspective of war in this century. ¶18

Twice in this century, the leaders of the free world have been confronted by the menacing power of a totalitarian state. From 1912 until 1914, and again from 1935 until 1939, Germany made a series of moves that clearly threatened the peace and order of the world, and during those critical testing periods, Britain, France and the United States failed either to raise enough military power or to show enough will power to avoid the holocaust. The resulting tragedies of the two great wars transformed the history of the world. ¶19

The Soviet decision to place long-range missiles in Cuba, capable of firing atomic rockets into almost any part of the United States, was a similar and in some ways even more ominous ¶20 test. This lunge into the Western Hemisphere was clearly an effort to change the world balance of power in Moscow's favor, and Kennedy faced it at the risk of war and turned it back.

¶21 It is ironic that he went to his grave with many of his fellow countrymen condemning him for failing to get rid of all the Communists and all the defensive missiles in Cuba as well as all the offensive missiles. Yet this view has not been shared by most of the political leaders and historians of the world.

¶22 I saw Prime Minister Macmillan of Britain just before he resigned and before President Kennedy was murdered. "If Kennedy never did another thing," Macmillan remarked, "he assured his place in history by that single act. He did what we failed to do in the critical years before the two German wars."

¶23 Within a year of Kennedy's death, Khrushchev was removed from power, partly as a result of his humiliating defeat in the Cuban missile crisis, but something important and maybe even historic remained: The Communist world was relieved of the illusion that the United States would not risk atomic war to defend its vital interests. This new awareness greatly reduced the danger of miscalculating American intentions and led almost at once to the first really serious steps to bring atomic weapons under control.

II. *The Home Front*

¶24 Mr. Kennedy was more at ease in the larger world of diplomacy and the struggle between nations than he was in the world of Congressional politics and the struggle between contending national forces. He had more freedom of action in foreign than in domestic policy. He did not seem to mind the small talk of ceremonial meetings with heads of state or foreign students at the White House, and he had a rare combination of informality and dignity that made him very effective in this role. But blarneying with pompous Congressmen bored him and he simply would not take time to do it, as his successor, President Johnson, has with such marked success.

This was odd, in a way. He was a superb politician in plan- ¶25
ning and running a Presidential campaign, but he didn't really know the deck on Capitol Hill and he did not really like to play the political game there. Even though he spent most of his political life in the House and the Senate, he was always sort of a non-resident member of those peculiar clubs, always a backbencher with a high truancy record and an excessive respect for the chairmen of the committees and the other elders of Congress.

The very qualities of appearance, style and cast of mind that ¶26
won him the admiration of the intellectual and diplomatic worlds somehow marked him as an outsider in his dealings with the Congress. He had little patience for the tiresome loquacity and endless details of legislation, and he never cared much for the boisterous bantering and backslapping of the cloakrooms.

He had a kind of gay magic as a political speaker, most of ¶27
it as carefully contrived as it sounded spontaneous. He was good at the arts of Hollywood and Madison Avenue, and this delighted his fellow politicians, but he was a little too polished, ambitious and out of the ordinary to escape the envy and criticism of The Hill.

Congress likes typical Americans and Kennedy was not one. ¶28
In his mature life, he probably crossed the Atlantic more often than he crossed the Allegheny range. He never seemed at home in the West. The America he understood best was bounded by Harvard Yard, the State Department, Park Avenue and Palm Beach. His political style and humor were not based on the exaggerated language and gymnastics of the American hustings but on the gentler models of the House of Commons.

Maybe these things had nothing to do with his troubles in ¶29
getting a legislative program through the Congress; maybe it was just the old stubborn resistance of the Congress to change—"the government of the living by the dead"—but the fact remains

that his domestic program was in deep trouble when he was killed, and some of us despaired that Capitol Hill would ever be his field of triumph.

¶30 Part of the Kennedy legend is connected with his introduction of the most radical legislation on behalf of Negro equality in this century. But again the reality is less romantic. He did not normally like to take on anything more than he had to tackle, no matter how worthy. Oddly for a man who wrote a book celebrating the heroes of lost causes ("Profiles in Courage"), he was always saying: "Why fight if you are not sure to win?" The Negro demonstrations in the summer of 1963, however, forced his hand, and he went along when some Republican leaders and his brother Robert urged that action was necessary.

¶31 Yet, on the home front, as in the foreign field, he did start one major innovation of transcending importance. At the urging of Walter Heller, the Chairman of Economic Advisors, he broke with the traditional economic concepts of Capitol Hill and plunged for a large tax cut and a planned budget deficit. Liberal economists in Europe and in the American universities had been arguing for years that it was no longer necessary to redistribute the wealth of the rich in order to elevate the poor, but that the total production of wealth could be increased to the benefit of everybody if modern technology and fiscal measures were applied.

¶32 Kennedy was not by temper a fiscal reformer. He came to the White House as a rather timid liberal, but the longer he was in office the more he cried out against the restraining economic and fiscal traditions of the past and the more he appealed to the country to deal with the world as it is. He never saw his tax bill go through; he died before it was passed. But he was largely responsible for heading the country into the most prolonged period of peacetime prosperity since the last World War. There was a recession when he took over in 1961, unemployment was up to almost 7 percent of the work force. There was a balance-of-payments deficit of nearly $4 billion. The outflow of gold to other countries in 1960 totaled $1.7 billion. But by the time he died, this trend had been reversed, at least in part as a result of his initiatives.

III. *The Imponderables*

Yet even if he turned the tide of the cold war toward the control of nuclear arms, and started the trend toward the acceptance of the new economics of increased production and general prosperity, this is not the Kennedy story that is likely to be remembered. ¶33

These things were only dramatic symbols of his critical mind. He was a critic of his age. He did not think we could deal with the menace of nuclear weapons unless we searched constantly for means of accommodation with the Communists. He did not think we could employ our people in the midst of a revolution in labor-saving machinery unless we changed our attitude toward Federal budgets and Federal deficits. ¶34

He did not think we could deal with the pressures of Communism, rising population, or galloping automation, or that we could contain the rising expectations of the nonwhite races and the new nations unless we moved faster to integrate the races at home and the nations of the free world abroad. In short, he did not believe we could deal effectively with a transformed world unless we transformed ourselves—our attitudes of mind and our institutions. ¶35

This was a youthful mind asking the big questions. He was not one for big plans and grand designs, though contemporary writers often professed to see such things in some of the speeches of Ted Sorenson. Incidentally, it was always difficult to tell where the soaring rhetoric of Sorenson's bolder and more liberal mind left off and the more cautious Kennedy mind picked up, but Kennedy was not a great planner. ¶36

I once asked him in a long private talk at Hyannis Port what he wanted to have achieved by the time he rode down Pennsylvania Avenue with his successor. He looked at me as if I were a ¶37 dreaming child. I tried again: Did he not feel the need of some goal to help guide his day-to-day decisions and priorities? Again a ghastly pause. It was only when I turned the question to immediate, tangible problems that he seized the point and rolled off a torrent of statistics about the difficulty of organizing nations at different levels of economic development.

¶38 Yet there is a puzzle in all this. For while he wanted to transform the thought and institutions of the nation, and regarded the machinery of the Congress as almost an anachronism, he concentrated on working—not, on the whole, very successfully—with the Congress, and he never really exploited his considerable gifts as a public educator.

¶39 "Give me the right word and the right accent," said Joseph Conrad, "and I will move the world." This was Churchill's way, and nobody admired it more than Kennedy. But while he made a few glorious trial flights, something held him back, some fear of appealing to the people over the heads of the Congress, some fear of too much talk (he hated verbosity), some modesty, maybe—always so apparent in his embarrassment before applauding crowds.

¶40 The essence of the tragedy, however, is perfectly clear. What was killed in Dallas was not only the President but the promise. The death of youth and the hope of youth, of the beauty and grace and the touch of magic.

¶41 The heart of the Kennedy legend is what might have been. His intelligence made people think that the coming generation might make the world more rational. It even made it hard for the intellectuals of Europe to be anti-American. His good looks and eloquence put a brighter shine on politics, and made his world relevant and attractive to young people all over the world.

¶42 All this is apparent in the faces of the people who come to his grave daily on the Arlington hill. In the world of their dreams, Presidents would be young and heroic, with beautiful wives, and the ugly world would be transformed by their examples.

John Finley, the master of Eliot House at Harvard, sent me a letter which sums up this sense of loss better than anything else: ¶43

"No doubt like innumerable people, I feel suddenly old without Mr. and Mrs. Kennedy in the White House. On reflection, ours seems a society of older people; it takes a while to reach the top in science, law, business and most other things. Yet, paradoxically, only the young have the freshness to enjoy and not be wearied by the profusion and vitality of present American life.

"Not only by ability, but by sheer verve and joy, the Kennedys imparted their youth to everyone and put a sheen on our life that made it more youthful than it is. Mr. Johnson now seems Gary Cooper as President—'High Noon,' the poker game, the easy walk and masculine smile. But even Gary Cooper was growing older, and the companions and adversaries around the poker table reflect a less fresh, if no doubt practical and effective, mood. All will be well, I feel sure . . . but it is August, not June . . ."

Always we come back to the same point. The tragedy of John Fitzgerald Kennedy was greater than the accomplishment, but in the end the tragedy enhances the accomplishment and revives the hope. ¶44

Thus the law of compensation operates. "The dice of God are always loaded," wrote Emerson. "For everything you have missed you have gained something else. . . . The world looks like a multiplication table, or a mathematical equation, which, turn it how you will, balances itself. . . . Every secret is told, every crime is punished, every virtue rewarded, every wrong redressed, in silence and certainty." ¶45

For Greater Insight

1. Although Reston's essay has three named and numbered sections, there are really four, since the first seven paragraphs serve as an introduction. In several ways the introduction suggests the outline of what is to follow. For example, in the second sentence in the second paragraph Reston uses three phrases which correspond to

his three section headings. What words has Reston used in the second sentence that are not the title of a section? What has he called that section? What is the effect of this type of organization and planning on the task of reading?

Pars. 5 and 7 both contain phrases which suggest what Reston's purpose is. What is that purpose? What does Reston say makes his task difficult?

2. Examine the titles of sections I and II and read with care the opening paragraph of each section. In each, there is a word or phrase which reinforces the title, or repeats it. Why should Reston do this? Does it help the reader in any way? How? Does the opening paragraph of Section III tell what is meant by "The Imponderables" or merely lead you to look further for them?

3. Much of the effectiveness of Reston's writing lies in his use of comparison and contrast. In the first paragraph, in the second and third sentences, point out what are compared and contrasted. Explain "history" and "legend."

   Read Par. 4. What comparisons and contrasts are found there? In what sentences? What does the last sentence mean? Explain the figure of speech here used. What is the relation between the figure and the title of the whole piece?

4. In Par. 4, count the words in each of the sentences, and list the numbers vertically. Where are the shorter sentences? The longer ones? Those of medium length? Do you think Reston planned this arrangement deliberately? Or more or less intuitively? Is the arrangement effective? Why?

   Count the words in Pars. 7 and 9. Again, where is the longest sentence? The shortest? Medium length?

5. What patterns of sentence structure do you find in the second and third sentences in the first paragraph? In the first four sentences in Par. 4, and in all of Par. 16?

6. Sections I and II have similar patterns of construction. Each begins with a general statement, then points out weaknesses, faults, or mistakes and then each names one highly important and successful accomplishment.

   In each of the two sections, identify the paragraphs which contain the general statement, explain what mistakes were made by Kennedy, and describe the major accomplishment.

   This is an interesting example of a rather complex parallel

structure. Was it a deliberate choice, do you think? Is it emphatic? Is the organization a technique that a beginning writer could strive for? Why? What value would it have?

7. There is a good deal of figurative and vivid language in this essay. Explain the meaning of each of the following, and explain the figure of speech wherever possible: In Par. 3, "story-book president" and "poetry on his tongue"; in Par. 8, "courted Latin America like a thoughtful lover"; in Par. 18, "more Irish than Harvard"; in Par. 24, "blarneying"; in Par. 25, "know the deck"; in Par. 28, "language and gymnastics of the American hustings."

   What other examples of figurative or vivid language can you find?
8. If you were to choose one paragraph that gives the whole meaning of the essay, would you choose Par. 40, 41, 42, 44, or 45? Explain your choice.
9. The word "legend" is used in one form or another quite often. In your consideration of Question 3, what did you decide a legend was? Is Reston correct when he speaks of a "Kennedy legend"? What does he think has happened, is happening, or will happen?
10. What actual or fictional character can you name who might be the subject of an essay such as this? Prepare a rough outline of such an essay, making your major points clear.

Word Study

caprice of life:
premonition of tragdey:
never reached his *meridian*:
better than any of his *predecessors*:
fiasco of the Bay of Pigs:
He also *temporized*:
He was . . . *presumptuous*:
power to avoid the *holocaust*:
blarneying with pompous Congressmen:
always a *backbencher*:
tiresome *loquacity*:
the American *hustings*:
almost an *anachronism*:
he hated *verbosity*:
sheer *verve* and joy:

There Are OO Trees in Russia

The Function of Facts in Newsmagazines

Otto Friedrich

Otto Friedrich has worked on four newspapers, a wire service, and two magazines. He is also the author of two novels. The present essay, which appeared in *Harper's Magazine*, October 1964, is not his only report of the methods and techniques of the press, other such reports having appeared in periodicals and as part of his fiction.

The gullibility of the public has long been known, and the magic assurance of "Yes, it's true; I saw it in print" has helped sell worthless patent medicine and has influenced the selection of heads of state. How fact-news-truth find their way onto the printed page and into our minds, for good or ill, is the subject of Friedrich's essay.

As you read, you should keep one question in mind. It is "What does the essay do to my understanding of what I read? Am I more alert, more aware of the importance of facts and their relation to truth?"

¶1 "Of course I'm sure—I read it in *Newsweek*." For several years, this slogan appeared in large advertisements all over the country. The advertisements usually showed no people, simply some scene of affluence and presumed influence, a board room or a golf club. From some unseen figure of authority came a huge white cartoon-style balloon filled with the crushing rejoinder, "Of course I'm sure—I read it in *Newsweek*."

The theory behind the advertisements was probably sound. ¶2
Since *Newsweek* has fewer reporters, writers, and editors than its omniscient rival, *Time*, since it has a smaller circulation and less influence than *Time*, its chief claim to attention is that it makes a reasonable effort at fairness in summarizing the week's events. By boasting of its congeries of columnists, *Newsweek* manages to imply that everything else it publishes is the simple factual truth. Its recent ads promise a magazine "where you can always distinguish fact from opinion." One of them, portraying Walter Lippmann next to Washington bureau chief Benjamin Bradlee, emphasizes the special qualities of the latter: "The facts he gets are often 'firsts'—are always *facts*."

Time, of course, has never admitted the validity of these ¶3
accusing insinuations from its smaller *Doppelgänger*. *Time* has always opposed the idea of mere objectivity, and it acknowledges a certain bias in favor of democracy, free enterprise, and the enlightened human spirit. But it insists that its experienced staff simply distills the facts of the news into the truth. Earlier this year, one weekly Publisher's "Letter," which normally serves as a medium of self-congratulation, sadly criticized the Soviet Union for expelling *Time*'s Moscow correspondent: "Soviet officials have never been able to understand or accept or even get accustomed to our kind of reporting." What the Soviets couldn't understand, *Time* went on, was that "our stories on the Soviet Union come from a wide array of sources available to our writers and editors in New York and to our correspondents elsewhere around the world." Thus *Time*'s kind of reporting doesn't depend primarily on having a reporter at the scene of the event. "From these many sources . . ." *Time* concluded, "we will continue to report frankly and deeply on the Soviets despite last week's reading-out of our correspondent." (There is still one other smaller and less interesting newsmagazine, but *Time* and *Newsweek* understandably

ignore the Brobdingnagian claims of the *U.S. News & World Report*, which purports to be "America's Class Newsmagazine.")*

¶4 Despite the competing claims of *Time* and *Newsweek*, they have a certain identity of both purpose and technique. Not only is the basic function of the two magazines almost the same, but the editor, national editor, and foreign editor of *Newsweek* are all alumni of *Time*, and there is a kind of all-purpose newsweekly office jargon that involves phrases like "the cosmic stuff" and "give it some global scope."

¶5 To anyone who has ever tried to work with these concepts and techniques, the newsmagazines' easy equation of facts, news, and truth can be rather disturbing. A reporter doesn't have to be a philosopher to know that "the facts" do not necessarily represent the truth, and that neither one of them necessarily represents the news. That men should live at peace with one another might be described as truth, but it is not a fact, nor is it news. That a certain number of children were born yesterday in Chicago is a fact, and the truth, but not news. Journalism involves an effort to discover, select, and assemble certain facts in a way that will be not only reasonably true but reasonably interesting—and therefore reasonably salable. Because of the eagerness with which an anxious and uninformed public buys anything which promises "the real story," it is easy for editors to forget these distinctions and boast about producing the facts and the truth in the name of freedom of the press and "an informed electorate."

The Fetish of the Facts

¶6 Behind this forgetfulness lies an enduring and endearing myth of American journalism, the myth of the police reporter and the city editor. Like all myths, it once had a certain reality. When I first went to work on the Des Moines *Register*, I was the police

* At the end of 1963, the ABC circulation figures were as follows: *Time*—2,958,590; *Newsweek*—1,664,563; *U.S. News & World Report*—1,293,836.

reporter, and I turned in my copy to a dour assistant city editor who spoke with a cutting Missouri accent and didn't believe in anything. No three-paragraph story about a minor burglary was immune to his questions about the number of floors in the burgled house, the denomination of the stolen bills, or the location of the shards of glass from the broken window. Of all possible answers, the least acceptable was "I guess so." "Let's not guess, let's know," he would retort. Sometimes I had to telephone him a half-dozen times from my bare, yellow-walled cubicle in the police station to verify trivial details in trivial stories. The copy that he finally sent to the composing room was, as nearly as possible, the facts.

Quite a few years have passed since then, and I no longer expect reporters to know the answers to questions about their stories. I have grown accustomed to their complaints that the facts in question can't be discovered, and to their further complaints about being questioned at all. They have some justification, for what happens in the U.S. Senate or the French cabinet simply can't be covered like a mugging on Sixth Street in Des Moines. The facts are more elusive, and, in a way, less important, for the physical details of who spoke to whom are relatively meaningless until they are put into perspective by an act of judgment and a point of view. In other words, the legendary police reporter and the legendary city editor no longer exist as criteria; their talents and techniques are irrelevant to most of the major news stories. ¶7

The newspapers and news agencies acknowledge this. Later editions of newspapers correct the factual mistakes and the misjudgments caused by the need for speed in getting out the first edition; a wire service revises a story with the euphemistic confession of error: "First lead and correct." It is among magazine editors, many of whom have never worked for newspapers or wire services, much less seen the inside of a police station, that the myth of "reporting the facts" remains strongest. Since a magazine must go to press several days, or even weeks, before it appears on ¶8 the newsstands, and since it remains on display for at least a week, errors and all, magazine editors have developed a fetish about absolute accuracy on the most inconsequential facts, a fetish that even makes "the facts" a substitute for reality. To be sure that you can be sure because you read it in *Newsweek* (or *Time* or, for that matter, *The New Yorker* and a number of other magazines), there has come into existence an institution unknown to newspapers: the checker.

¶9 The checker, or researcher, is usually a girl in her twenties, usually from some Eastern college, pleasant-looking but not a *femme fatale*. She came from college unqualified for anything, but looking for an "interesting" job. After a few years, she usually feels, bitterly and rightly, that nobody appreciates her work. Her work consists of assembling newspaper clippings and other research material early in the week and then checking the writer's story at the end of the week. The beginning of the week is lackadaisical, and so is the research, but toward the end, when typewriters clack behind closed doors and editors snap at intruders, there are midnight hamburgers and tears in the ladies' room. For the checker gets no credit if the story is right, but she gets the blame if it is wrong. It doesn't matter if the story is slanted or meretricious, if it misinterprets or misses the point of the week's news. That is the responsibility of the editors. What matters—and what seems to attract most of the hostile letters to the editors—is whether a championship poodle stands thirty-six or forty inches high, whether the eyes of Prince Juan Carlos of Spain are blue or brown, whether the population of some city in Kansas is 15,000 or 18,000.

¶10 The first question about this fetish of facts, which no newsmagazine ever questions, is whether these facts, researched and verified at such enormous trouble and expense, really matter. Obviously, there is an important difference between saying that Charles de Gaulle accepts Britain's entry into the Common Market, which a number of prominent reporters used to report, and saying that de Gaulle opposes Britain's entering the Common Market, which mysteriously turned out to be the case. But how much does it really matter whether a newsmagazine reports that de Gaulle is sixty-seven or sixty-eight years old, six feet one or six feet two, that he smokes Gaulloises or Chesterfields, that he eats a brioche or a melon for breakfast, that Madame de Gaulle puts fresh roses or does not put fresh roses on his desk every day? Judging by the legend of the police reporter and the city editor, and judging by the amount of space the newsmagazines devote to such minutiae, it matters very much to provide "the facts" and "provide them straight." Despite the public statements of principle, however, the men who usually care the least about such details are the men who actually write and edit the newsmagazines.

Hawks Wheel over Cyprus

There is an essential difference between a news story, as understood by a newspaperman or a wire-service writer, and the newsmagazine story. The chief purpose of the conventional news story is to tell what happened. It starts with the most important information and continues into increasingly inconsequential details, not only because the reader may not read beyond the first paragraph but because an editor working on galley proofs a few minutes before press time likes to be able to cut freely from the end of the story. A newsmagazine is very different. It is written and edited to be read consecutively from beginning to end, and each of its stories is designed, following the critical theories of Edgar Allan Poe, to create one emotional effect. The news, what happened that week, may be told in the beginning, the middle, or the end; for the purpose is not to throw information at the reader but to seduce him into reading the whole story, and into accepting the dramatic (and often political) point being made. ¶11

In beginning a story, the newsmagazine writer often relies ¶12 on certain traditional procedures of his special craft. They change little from year to year, but, for purposes of examination, we might select the first three issues of *Time* and *Newsweek* last May.

¶13 "Flowers were in bloom on the crumbling towers of St. Hilarion, and hawks turned soundlessly high above Kyrenia." This is *Time*'s beginning for a story on civil strife in Cyprus. The "weather lead" is always a favorite because it creates a dramatic tone; because, by so obviously avoiding the news, it implicitly promises the reader more important things to come.

¶14 Then there is the "moving-vehicle lead," most often a description of a plane landing. In one of these May issues, *Time* began a story this way: "One foggy morning in Berlin, a yellow Mercedes from the Soviet zone drew up at the tollgate at the Heerstrasse crossing point." *Newsweek*'s beginning was almost identical: "Shortly after 5 o'clock in the morning a heavily shrouded black Mercedes bearing license tags issued by the Allied Control Commission in Germany rolled quietly into the no man's land between the Western and Russian sectors of Berlin." (There is no real contradiction between the black Mercedes and the yellow Mercedes, for the magazines were focusing on two different vehicles involved in an exchange of spies.)

¶15 Another favorite is the "narrative" opening involving an unidentified person: "The hooded, gambler eyes tracked the jurors as they filed into the courtroom" (*Newsweek*, on the trial of Roy Cohn); or the provocative quote involving an unidentified object: "'She's in there,' pointed one proud Pinkerton. 'She's the most magnificent thing I've ever seen'" (*Time*, on the appearance of Michelangelo's Pietà at the New York World's Fair). Occasionally, the newsmagazine writer just gets bored with it all: "There was a sense of *déjà vu* about the whole affair—an uncanny paramnesic feeling that all of this had happened before" (*Time*, on the May Day Parade in Moscow).

¶16 The writer had some reason to be bored. Presumably assigned to write a full-page lead story on the week's events in Eastern Europe, he had only two things to say—that nothing much had happened at the May Day Parade, and that the Romanians were playing off the Russians against the Chinese for their own benefit. In elaborating on this, he engaged in some characteristic newsmagazine equivocation: "Dej is playing a double game in the Sino-Soviet conflict, one that could lead to plenty of trouble—or perhaps to a certain amount of freedom." But though the story has nothing much to say, it absolutely bristles with the facts that newsmagazines use as a substitute for reality. It tells us what Khrushchev was wearing (a Homburg) and what he had been eating lately (cabbage rather than meat). It tells us how to pronounce the name of Romania's Galati steel combine (Galatz) and what its rolling mill cost ($42 million). It gives us a figure for Romanian industrial growth (15 per cent) and a translation for the name of the Romanian Communist newspaper *Scînteia* (*Spark*). And to persuade us that the activity in Romania is important, the story reports as alphabetical fact that "every Communist from Auckland to Zanzibar took note of it."

As a rule, facts are not scattered around so indiscriminately, ¶17
like sequins ornamenting some drab material, for their main function in a newsmagazine story is to illustrate a dramatic thesis. When *Newsweek* begins a story on an African "summit conference," for example, it is apt to open with a variation of the moving-vehicle lead, which might be called the crowd-gathering lead: "Some came in sleek Italian suits from the Via Condotti . . ." Did any African premier really wear clothing from the Via Condotti? The problem would never arise on an ordinary newspaper, since it doesn't particularly matter where the African statesmen buy their clothes. But since the newsmagazine writer starts with a dramatic concept—the African leaders are a self-indulgent lot—he needs a dramatic concept to illustrate it.

An even more characteristic opening dramatized *Time*'s cover ¶18
story on Henry Cabot Lodge:

> In the early-morning gloom of Saigon's muggy pre-monsoon season, an alarm clock shrills in the stillness of a second-floor bedroom at 38 Phung Khac Khoan Street. The Brahmin from

Boston arises, breakfasts on mango or papaya, sticks a snub-nosed .38-cal. Smith & Wesson revolver into a shoulder holster, and leaves for the office.

¶19 This is a fine example of the well-trained virtuoso at work, not only disguising the subject of the story but combining a series of insignificant facts into a cadenza of exotic weather, breakfast food, strange street names, and gunplay. The author was so pleased with the results that he went on repeating himself for three paragraphs, which disclosed that the temperature that day was ninety degrees, with 90 per cent humidity, that Lodge's moving vehicle was a Checker Marathon sedan, that the U.S. Embassy building is located at 39 Nam Nghi Boulevard, and that Lodge's office desk contains yet another gun, a .357 Smith & Wesson Magnum. There are two reasons for this inundation of minutiae. The first—based on the theory that knowledge of lesser facts implies knowledge of major facts—is to prove that *Time* knows everything there is to know about Lodge. The second—based on the theory that a man who carries a gun is tough and aggressive—is to dramatize the basic thesis, that Lodge would be a good Republican candidate for President.

In Search of the Zip

¶20 But what does the specific fact itself matter? Does it matter whether Lodge carries a .38-cal. Smith & Wesson or a Luger or a pearl-handled derringer? Does it make any difference whether he lives on the second floor of 38 Phung Khac Khoan Street or the third floor of some other building? The newsmagazines have provided their own answer by evolving a unique system which makes it theoretically possible to write an entire news story without any facts at all. This is the technique of the "zip." It takes various forms: Kuming (a deliberate misspelling of "coming" to warn copy editors, proofreaders, and printers not to use the word itself), or TK, meaning To Kum, or, in the case of statistics, 00 (the number of zeros is purely optional). This technique enables the writer to ignore all facts and concentrate on the drama. If he is describing some backward country, for example, he can safely write that 00 per cent of its people are ravaged by TK diseases. It obviously doesn't matter too much whether the rate of illiteracy is 80 per cent or 90 per cent. Any statistic will sound equally authoritative. It is the checker who is responsible for facts, and she will fill in any gaps.

¶21 Filling in the "zips" is sometimes costly. One former newsmagazine writer, for example, recalls some problems that arose when he was writing a cover story on General Naguib, then the President of Egypt. Naguib, he wrote, was such a modest man that his name did not appear among the 000 people listed in *Who's Who in the Middle East.* Moreover, Naguib disliked luxury and had refused to live in the royal palace, surrounded by an 00-foot-high wall. A cable—as the writer tells the story—duly went to the Cairo stringer. There was no answer. Indignant at the stringer's fecklessness, the editors changed the copy so that neither of the missing facts was needed. A week later, came a cable saying something like this:

> AM IN JAIL AND ALLOWED SEND ONLY ONE CABLE SINCE WAS ARRESTED WHILE MEASURING FIFTEEN FOOT WALL OUTSIDE FAROUKS PALACE AND HAVE JUST FINISHED COUNTING THIRTYEIGHT THOUSAND FIVE HUNDRED TWENTYTWO NAMES WHOS WHO IN MIDEAST

¶22 When both the writer and the researcher accept this as a game, the search for the key fact can become pure fantasy. On one occasion, for example, a newsmagazine editor wrote into a piece of copy: "There are 00 trees in Russia." The researcher took a creative delight in such an impossible problem. From the Soviet government, she ascertained the number of acres officially listed as forests; from some Washington agency she ascertained the average number of trees per acre of forests. The result was a wholly improbable but wholly unchallengeable statistic for the number of trees in Russia.

¶23 In the normal case of the 00, however, someone calls a government agency to get the official answer. The results are sometimes equally strange. One *Newsweek* researcher recalls the story of the Sudanese army, which a writer had described as "the 00-man Sudanese army." No newspaper clippings could fill in the figure, and telephone calls to the Sudanese Embassy in Washington indicated that nobody there could either. The Sudanese may well have been surprised that anybody should want to know such a figure. As the weekly deadline approached, an editor finally instructed the checker to make "an educated guess," and the story appeared with a reference to something like "the 17,000-man Sudanese army." There were no complaints. The *Newsweek* story duly reached Khartoum, where the press complaisantly reprinted it and commented on it. Digests of the Khartoum press returned to Washington, and one day a Sudanese Embassy official happily telephoned the *Newsweek* researcher to report that he finally was able to tell her the exact number of men in the Sudanese army: seventeen thousand.

Documenting the Dream

¶24 Once you go beyond the Des Moines police station, you find yourself dealing more and more with some equivalent of the Sudanese Embassy. The "facts," which are supposed to form the basis of the news, are often simply unknown. Yet in any week's issue of any magazine of journalism, you can find the most impressive statistics—00 per cent of the people of Brazil are illiterate, or the per capita income of the Burmese is $00.00.

¶25 Newsmagazine writers are very skilled in the popular sport of statistics. With the cooperation of various partisan sources, they make comparative projections of the American and Russian gross national product in 1970—when nobody has more than a vague estimate of what these figures will be even in 1965. The birth-control lobby issues horrendous statistics about the number of human beings who will be living on every cubic yard of earth in the year 2000, and yet all such projections are based heavily on the estimated future populations of China and India, estimates that vary even today by hundreds of millions. All over the world, in fact, most estimates of population, illiteracy, illness, industrial growth, or per capita income are little more than wild guesses. "Let's not guess, let's know," the assistant city editor in Des Moines used to say, expressing a characteristically American desire for certainty. At one point during one of the periodic crises in Laos, however, an American correspondent bitterly complained to a Laotian government spokesman that he had spoken to sixteen government officials and got sixteen different versions of the facts. The Laotian was bewildered. It seemed perfectly natural to him, he said, that if you spoke to sixteen different officials you would get sixteen different answers.

The Laotian was wise in acknowledging and answering the ¶26
first fundamental question about the fetish of facts: Does it really matter which "fact" is to be officially certified as "true"? He was equally wise in acknowledging and answering a second question: Does anyone really know which "fact" is "true"? He was equally wise in raising a third question, and implying an answer: Every man sees the "facts" according to his own interests.

Governments and business corporations have long acknowl- ¶27
edged this by employing public-relations men and "information officers" to make sure that any facts make them look virtuous. *Time* once quoted a French spokesman's poetic definition of his job: "*mentir et dementir*" (to lie and to deny). And in the world of newsmagazines, seeking the certainty of unascertainable facts, official government statistics carry a surprising weight. On one occasion, for instance, I was writing a story about the economic problems of Sicily, and I wrote that approximately 30 per cent of the inhabitants were unemployed, which I believed to be

roughly true. When I saw the story in print, I read that something like 8 per cent of the Sicilians were unemployed. In other words, one of Europe's poorest areas was scarcely worse off than the United States—but this was the official statistic that the Italian government had given to the researcher. "After all," as one of the researchers once said, "we have to protect ourselves."

¶28 The basic purpose of the newsmagazines' facts, however, is not to report the unemployment statistics in Sicily, or the shopping habits of African statesmen, but to provide an *appearance* of documentation for what are essentially essays. The *Time* cover story on Lodge, for example, with its fact-choked lead, eventually arrives at the question of whether the Republicans might nominate Goldwater because no Republican can defeat President Johnson anyway. "This defeatist attitude is pretty silly," comments *Time, The Weekly Newsmagazine.* "Sure as his political moves have been, Johnson could still stumble politically. And healthy as the President may seem, there is always that dread possibility of disablement or worse. The Republican nomination is therefore nothing to give away for the mere asking." After that Olympian declaration, the *Time* story goes on to outline the Lodge supporters' hopes for their candidate's triumphant return to the United States. "A foolish fantasy?" *Time* wonders. "Perhaps. But that is one of the most enchanting things about U.S. politics: dreams can and do come true."

¶29 Unfortunately, the perils of prophecy are high. The week after the Lodge story, which assumed that the Ambassador would sweep onward from a victory in the Oregon primary, *Time* had to rush out with a cover story that began, a little hysterically: "Battling Nelson did it! Battered, bloodied, beaten, taunted, hooted, and laughed at during bitter, frustrating months, Republican Nelson Rockefeller never gave up, never stopped swinging." This story, too, concluded with a warning to Republicans not to accept defeat: "Nelson Rockefeller doesn't think like that—and in Oregon he demonstrated that perhaps it is a pretty poor way of thinking." No man waits for *Time*, however, and when Barry Goldwater finally won the Republican nomination, the editors declared that it had been inevitable: "Goldwater won the presidential nomination by arduously cultivating support at the precinct and county levels . . . What helped clinch it for Goldwater was the fact that a strong conservative tide was running in the U.S., fed by a deep disquiet at the grass roots over the role of an ever-expanding Government. Goldwater and the tide came together, and the one could not have succeeded without the other."

On a less exalted plane, the typical newsmagazine story ¶30
almost invariably reaches a point where the writer drops the factual ballast and summarizes his views on the importance of the week's events. And there is nothing wrong about this. In view of the general inadequacy of American newspapers and the ignorance of the American public, an informed evaluation of the week's news is something to be commended. Yet if the reality were candidly admitted, it would antagonize the newsmagazine readers. The English, who read newspapers on a scale that should shame most Americans, appreciate magazines that frankly comment on a body of presumed knowledge, such as *The Economist, The New Statesman,* or *The Spectator*. Most Americans, however, taught to believe that they should assimilate the "facts" for themselves, reject such American counterparts as *The New Republic* and *The Nation*. They accept the newsmagazines not as magazines of commentary or interpretation but as magazines which will tell them yet more facts, "the real story."

News Break or News Leak?

Here is the flaw in the newsmagazines' equation of fact and ¶31
truth. For if you assume that nobody really knows or cares how many men there are in the Sudanese army, as newsmagazine editors do every time they use the term "C•J," you acknowledge the hypocrisy of your claim to be simply reporting the facts; then

you take on the sacerdotal role of providing not the facts but "the truth." (It is worth noting that newsmagazine reporters chronically complain that their "files"—the reports they send in—are ignored when the final story is written.) Apart from the size of the Sudanese army, what is really going on in the Sudan? Apart from the number of trees growing on the steppes, what is really going on in Russia? Or in London and Paris and Washington?

¶32 It is in the major political capitals, where the major news is made, that the myth of the police reporter in pursuit of the facts has become particularly irrelevant. A skillful police reporter turned loose in the Pentagon not only wouldn't be able to get the right answer, he wouldn't even be able to find the person who knew the answer. The officials of the State Department or the Quai d'Orsay speak only to people they know well. And the reporter who persuades himself that he represents the so-called "Fourth Estate" very often becomes an unofficial and perhaps unconscious spokesman for the government he is assigned to cover. At the very least, the capital correspondent thinks he is the intermediary divinely chosen to interpret the activities of politicians to the electorate; quite often, he acquires a vocation to educate and inspire the politicians themselves; rarely does he realize that in representing a "Fourth Estate" he serves the government as an instrument for leaks, propaganda, and outright lies. After all, if you're having a candlelit dinner with a Secretary of State, isn't it the better part of valor to assume that anything he tells you is "the truth"?

¶33 The situation remains much the same from one Administration to another, but one incident that still seems most illustrative occurred a few years ago. At a time when no Berlin crisis was visible in the daily press, the Washington bureau manager of a newsmagazine telephoned his superiors to say that a major Berlin crisis was imminent. Having had access to the President, he reported that "the only thing on the President's desk" was a melodramatic plan to evacuate U.S. dependents from Berlin, to mobilize reserves, and to behave as though war were imminent.

This was a little puzzling since the Russians apparently hadn't done anything about Berlin recently, but the newsmagazine was so impressed by the President's supposed anxiety that it printed a major story about the supposed "emergency plan." When that issue appeared, the President was reported to have telephoned an executive of the magazine and asked how he could jeopardize the national interest with such an article. He even announced publicly that he was calling in the FBI to investigate the Pentagon to see who had leaked such a dangerous story to the magazine. The editors, who had thought they were acting for rather than against the national interest, were very much embarrassed. But the FBI somehow never succeeded in finding or punishing the culprit who had leaked the story.

It remained for the *New York Times*, one of the last redoubts of independent journalism in Washington, to suggest that the ¶34
President had called in the FBI to investigate the leaking of a highly tentative "emergency plan" so that the Russians would think it was a real emergency plan. Not long after this, the President was on the air, urging Americans to build bomb shelters because of the impending Berlin crisis. And the newsmagazine, which spends tens of thousands of dollars every year to verify the per capita income of nonexistent peasants in Thailand, was left wiping the pie off its face. It could only wipe in dignified silence. For unlike the daily newspaper, which can publish a political "leak" one day and the official denial the next, the newsmagazine purports to tell not just the facts but the inside, authoritative, "real" story, and thus it remains peculiarly vulnerable to inside, authoritative, real propaganda. It cannot deny what it has authoritatively told as the truth without denying itself.

My Own de Gaulle

And yet the myth survives—we must report the facts. Every ¶35
statement must be checked and double-checked. One day in March of 1958, when it seemed that France was drifting toward

chaos, a newsmagazine editor assigned me to write a generally sympathetic story about Charles de Gaulle and his views on France's future. Our Paris bureau chief was an ardent Gaullist and sent a long file to explain de Gaulle's policies. And since I had long been an admirer of de Gaulle, I felt no misgivings about writing an article outlining the hopeful prospects for a Gaullist France. But there was nothing in the Paris file and nothing in de Gaulle's own writing that seemed to provide an adequate summary of the Gaullist contempt for the Fourth Republic. And so I ended with a note of typical newsmagazine rhetoric, that France's main problem was to remake itself. This, I concluded, "involves a change in outlook and atmosphere, an end to the meanness, corruption, and squabbling that have darkened the past decade." When I saw the published version, I saw to my surprise that my own rhetoric had somehow become de Gaulle's rhetoric. "This, he adds," it said, referring to de Gaulle, " 'involves a change in outlook and atmosphere . . .' " And so on. When I asked the researcher how my words had become de Gaulle's words, she said that the quotation marks had been added by an editor, who had answered her protests by saying, "Well, that's his idea, isn't it? He *could* have said it."

¶36 So the matter rested, for a few weeks, and then I went on vacation. During my vacation, the army and the mob seized control of Algiers, and France shook, and de Gaulle announced his readiness to return to power, and the researcher sent me a page torn from the New York *Herald Tribune*, quoting de Gaulle on every known issue. And what was his view on the basic condition of France? France must remake itself, he said, and this "involves a change in outlook and atmosphere, an end to the meanness, corruption, and squabbling that have darkened the past decade."

¶37 By now, I can only assume that this statement is a documented "fact," like the "fact" that there are 00 men in the Sudanese army and 00 trees in Russia. Until some Laotian, who never met a Des Moines police reporter, suggests that neither facts nor news is necessarily the truth.

For Greater Insight

1. If you were going to determine an important action of your own, would you rely more on your own personal knowledge of facts, or on the considered opinion of an expert who has based his opinion on the same facts? Would the nature of the decision make a difference? Medicine and health? Purchase of property? Investing money? Choice of a college or university? Choice of a husband or wife? To continue education or not to? Defend your answers.
2. Explain what is meant in Par. 3 by distilling "the facts of the news into the truth." Can you do this yourself, or must you trust others?
3. Using Par. 5 as a start, try to explain the differences between fact, news, and truth. Use different examples. Which of the three do you want when you read? Comment on "Any statistic will sound equally authoritative."
4. In Par. 7, what do "an act of judgment and a point of view" have to do with Friedrich's attitude toward reporters and their stories?
5. What is sad about the type of hostile letter that gets sent to editors?
6. Explain the difference between the news story and the newsmagazine story.
7. What are some possible reasons that newsmagazine writers use so many little facts in their writing? The facts may be just that, but do they necessarily make an important truth? What is the psychological effect on the reader of the mass of facts?
8. ____________ PLANES TURNED TAIL

   ____________ PLANES DISENGAGED

   Put the words "ENEMY" and "OUR" in the above headline-type sentences. Have you changed the fact? The truth? The news? How do you justify your choice? What is the relation between what you did and the last sentence in Par. 26?
9. In Par. 30 Friedrich makes some rather sweeping criticisms, and a comparison between English and American readers of newspapers. Explain the charges. They are in print; do you accept them as fact, as news, or as truth? Should you? Explain.
10. Read Jessup's comments on Reston and Lippmann (pp. 11ff.). Do you get the idea that one of these men is the reporter of facts, and the other the interpreter? If so, which is which? Comment about the value of their services to their reading public.

11. What conclusions can you draw as a result of Friedrich's two stories about the President of the United States (Pars. 33 and 34) and President de Gaulle (Pars. 35–37)? Friedrich has given you facts. Has he interpreted them for you? In other words, has he created a truth? Can you do that for yourself? What is the truth?

Word Study

the crushing *rejoinder*:
its *omniscient* rival:
its *congeries*:
accusing *insinuations*:
its smaller *Doppelgänger*:
mere *objectivity*:
the *Brobdingnagian* claims:
"the *cosmic* stuff":
are more *elusive*:
put into *perspective*:
techniques are *irrelevant*:
euphemistic confession:
developed a *fetish*:
not a *femme fatale*:
beginning . . . is *lackadaisical*:
story . . . is . . . *meretricious*:
to such *minutiae*:
it *implicitly* promises:
sense of *déjà vu*:
paramnesic feeling:
so *indiscriminately*:
well-trained *virtuosos*:
cadenza of *exotic* weather:
inundation of minutiae:
pearl-handled *derringer*:
to the Cairo *stringer*:
stringer's *fecklessness*:
ascertained the number:
complaisantly reprinted it:
various *partisan* sources:
horrendous statistics:

appearance of *documentation*:
arduously cultivating:
hypocrisy of your claim:
sacerdotal role:
so-called "*Fourth Estate*":
a *melodramatic* plan:
jeopardize the national interest:
last *redoubts*:

The World of Sports

Stanley Woodward

Red Smith

If you examine the pages of almost any daily newspaper, and count the pages devoted to sports, you will find that a generous amount of space is given over to reports of games played and races won, to news of player-heroes, to forecasts of things to come and criticism of what has gone. What are the people like who write best about America's national games and contests?

To find out, we turn to material by and about Stanley Woodward, long one of the most respected sportswriters in the country.

This essay appeared in the now defunct New York *Herald Tribune* on November 30, 1965, the day after Woodward's death. As you read, you will discover why Red (W. Wesley) Smith is himself known as one of the best sportswriters in the business. (His syndicated column is now running in the New York *World-Journal-Tribune*.) Smith's piece was his regular column, devoted this time to memories of his friend.

As you read both this essay and the following one, you will notice ample evidence of the depth and sincerity of their feeling. You should notice also the general organization of the two.

The best and kindest man I ever knew died yesterday. His name was Rufus Stanley Woodward. He was my idol, twice my editor, and perhaps my truest friend. He was 71 and his health had been failing. A bronchial condition made breathing difficult. Early yesterday morning it became too difficult. ¶1

¶2 "Kindest" may not be the first word that would pop into the mind of a man who had drawn Stanley's wrath, and there were a lot of them over the years. But it popped into Joe Palmer's mind when Joe was asked to characterize his former boss. "Stanley is frequently disdainful of his superior officers," he said, "he tolerates his equals, and he is unfailingly generous to his subordinates."

¶3 "Make no mistake," Stanley's friend Jack Martin, of Bear Mountain, told a crowd of newspaper men and sports guys gathered to salute Coach Woodward when he retired as sports editor of the *Herald Tribune*, "this man is a giant."

¶4 He was indeed—the finest of craftsmen, a leader who commanded loyalties almost as fierce as the loyalty he gave, a giant of integrity, dedication and honor, a brooder, a worrier, a fighter, and the dearest of friends.

Wrostling Match

¶5 He was also that rarest of phenomena, an honest wrestler. One winter we were scouting football players for the All-Star game he used to run for the *Herald Tribune* Fresh Air Fund. (It was his enthusiasm for football and his eminence as the game's best and most knowledgeable reporter that won him the title of respect, Coach Woodward.)

¶6 Actually, Stanley was doing the scouting. He was just up after a bout with pneumonia and I was along as chauffeur and male nurse. In Pittsburgh we joined Jock Sutherland and his staff for dinner at the home of Frank Souchak, the All-American end who was an assistant to Jock with the Pittsburgh Steelers. As the party was breaking up, Dr. Sutherland casually dropped a gauntlet: "Stonley, would you care to wrostle?"

¶7 They stripped to the waist. The Doctor was about 58 then, the Coach six years younger. Stanley removed his thick glasses, lunged blindly for a headlock and missed. A quarter-ton of beef smashed to the floor. The house trembled. Stanley was pinned. He lay gasping.

"Smith," he said weakly, "help me up." I handed him a scotch and soda where he lay. He knew I went on newspapers because I disliked lifting things. ¶8

The Battler

I realize that's no kind of story for a time like this, but some of us must laugh, lest we cry. Stanley, as all his friends knew, was helpless without his glasses. His sight failed when he was a boy in Worcester, Mass., defeating his father's ambition to bring him up to be a major league catcher. During his blindness he learned to play the fiddle. ¶9

A series of operations partially restored his sight. He had no peripheral vision, which made riding with him as a passenger a memorable adventure, yet with the throttle on the floor the old bird-watcher could identify a Cooper's hawk darting across the highway. ¶10

Instead of a catcher, he became a pitcher, fast and wild, on the college and town team level, and a rough tackle at Amherst. "I once started a beautiful riot on that field," he remarked one day passing a New England pasture that still bore traces of a baseball diamond. "Beautiful." He didn't elaborate and it wasn't necessary. No doubt he had only intended to brush the hitter back. ¶11

As a fighter in print he was immense. For the fun of it, he picked a quarrel in his column with his friend Dan Parker, of the *Mirror*. Friends warned Stanley that Dan at the typewriter was like Juan Marichal with a Louisville Slugger. ¶12

"Oh," he said mildly, "I know Dan's smarter than I am, but I fight dirtier." ¶13

The Right Word

Stanley Woodward could do any job on a newspaper and do it superbly. In spite of an educated and discerning taste, he had a ¶14 blind spot where his own writing was concerned and never regarded it highly. Yet no one could write with more smashing impact. He could deflate the pompous, expose the ridiculous or explode a fallacy with one devastating line.

¶15 His great friend Red Blaik, coaching football at West Point, decided after studying the films of a horrendous defeat by Michigan, that Army's weakness lay in the center's failure to give the ball a quarter-turn on delivering it to the T-formation quarterback.

¶16 "Attributing that catastrophe to such a cause," Stanley wrote, "is like blaming the Johnstown flood on a leaky toilet in Altoona, Pa."

¶17 One winter Jack Kramer, the tennis pro whose checkbook ended more amateur careers than old age, helped coach the United States Davis Cup team through the challenge round with Australia.

¶18 Putting the old pro in such a job, Stanley wrote, was "like electing Jean Lafitte commodore of the New Orleans Yacht Club."

¶19 One clings to the happy memories. The day Stanley's and Rice's younger daughter, Mary, was married, the bridal couple left the reception in a shower of rice and Stanley followed outside to see them drive away. When he returned, the guests fell silent, for Mary was the baby. For a moment they looked at Stanley and he looked at them.

¶20 Then he shrugged. "Oh, well," he said, "easy come, easy go."

To Guide Your Thinking

1. What is a euphemism? Is the last sentence of the first paragraph a euphemism? You already know Woodward died. Why does Smith repeat the fact?
2. One of the constructions used effectively in the first paragraph is also used in Par. 4. What is it? Is this climactic arrangement? Why or why not?
3. Is "a quarter-ton of beef" hyperbole? Explain. In what other way

could this sentence have been written? Is one of your ways more effective? Why?

4. In Par. 9 how does Smith use transition to bridge the gap between a story and a bit of chronological biography?
5. Smith says, "As a fighter in print he was immense." If you have read "One Strike Is Out," you will know whether or not you agree with Smith's evaluation. Do you? Why? Was it dirty fighting, to use Woodward's own term?
6. In the last sentence referred to in Par. 14, you are told that Woodward could do three things. Explain each. If you have read "One Strike Is Out," point out examples of one or more of these abilities.
7. In the quoted comments on the defeat of West Point, and on the coaching of Jack Kramer, Woodward uses a kind of ridiculous simile. Explain the similes and show why they are effective. What is Woodward attempting in these statements?
8. If you have read the other pieces by and about Woodward, you should know him rather well. Would he have liked what Smith said, and the way he said it? Justify your answer.

Word Study

frequently *disdainful*:
rarest of *phenomena*:
eminence as the game's best . . . reporter:
dropped a *gauntlet*:
peripheral vision:
discerning taste:
deflate the *pompous*:
explode a *fallacy*:
one *devastating* line:
a *horrendous* defeat:

Stanley Woodward

John Rogers

This piece was written when Mr. Rogers, now an Associate Editor of *Parade*, was a staff member on the *Herald-Tribune.* It appeared in the paper side-by-side with Red Smith's column on the day after Woodward's death. Rogers' piece is an obituary notice as well as an essay about Woodward. The concluding paragraph of this piece, naming the survivors and stating time of the funeral service, has been omitted here as not relevant to the essay itself.

¶1 Stanley Woodward, 71, former sports editor of the *New York Herald Tribune*, one of the country's foremost authorities on football and the man who coined the phrase Ivy League, died yesterday in White Plains Hospital of a bronchial affliction.

¶2 Mr. Woodward, who lived in retirement in Brookfield Center, Conn., since April 1, 1962, entered the hospital six days ago and was in a coma for some 48 hours before his death.

¶3 Everybody called him The Coach, probably from the days when he selected a squad of college football players to play a benefit game with the New York Giants for the *Herald Tribune* Fresh Air Fund.

¶4 He served twice as *Herald Tribune* sports editor—1937 to 1948, and 1959 to 1962. In his farewell column three years ago,

Mr. Woodward explained what he called his 11-year "exile" from the paper.

"I was given the bum's rush," he wrote, "for addressing the ¶5
former management in tones of insufficient servility."

The explanation was typical of The Coach, a bluntly honest ¶6
man whose nature was to bite straight to the core of any subject, usually with a wry humor and a dash of disrespect. In 1959, when he wrote the first column of his second stretch, he opened:

"As I was saying before I was so rudely interrupted . . ." ¶7

There was one subject for which he had no humor. That was ¶8
sloppy writing. Offenders trembled when he unleashed wrath over a cliché or a poor word. When a young man wrote that so-and-so had "belted a home run." The Coach stripped off his own belt and handed it to the writer and snarled, "Let's see you hit a home run with this."

In World War II The Coach found himself impatient with ¶9
the fun-and-games department and though he was nearing 50, he converted to a very active war correspondent. He was with the 101st Airborne Division for the *Herald Tribune* when it invaded the Netherlands in September 1944 by parachute and glider, and subsequently was made an honorary member of the division.

The next year, in the Pacific with Task Force 58, he rode ¶10
the carriers Hornet and Enterprise during the time when Japanese suicide planes were most active.

Mr. Woodward was born in Worcester, Mass., in 1895 and ¶11
christened Rufus Stanley Woodward. He was a superior student, especially as a Latin scholar, and also a lover of active games. His father planned a future for him as a major league baseball catcher but cataracts in both eyes, which required nine operations in his first 23 years, ruled that out for the young man.

A 220-pounder with a somewhat foreboding exterior and ¶12
thick-lens glasses, Mr. Woodward played four years of football at Amherst College, though he insisted that because of his poor eyesight he at times operated mainly by feel.

¶13 After college, The Coach joined the merchant marine in World War I and when that was over he went back to his home town and became a reporter on the *Worcester Gazette* whose city editor taught him:

¶14 "A man who gets what he is sent for is a reporter. A man who gets what he is sent for and something more is a good reporter. A man who does not get what he is sent for is a goddamned nuisance and will be fired."

¶15 Three years later Mr. Woodward moved on to Boston as both general and sports reporter with the *Herald*. In 1930 the *Herald Tribune* beckoned him and after seven years as a sports writer he took over as editor on the death of George Daley.

¶16 Mr. Woodward soon demonstrated that sports could be covered with class, style, brilliance and humor rather than with the "unholy jargon" that had become somewhat traditional. He demonstrated a controlled cynicism, a balanced attitude about the relative importance of sports. His own writing was crisp and clear and he demanded the same from his staff.

¶17 When he coined the phrase Ivy League, he did it in Latin—Hedera Helix. To poke fun at the folly of picking all-America teams, of presenting 11 men as the best in the nation, he would select his own "all" team each year with such names as Diferderole, Rutgers; and Grantuc, Richmond.

¶18 He had a fine faculty of indignation. When Army coaches held that a slaughter by Michigan could be blamed on the center's failure to give the ball a quarter turn on snapback, the Coach wrote:

¶19 "This is like blaming the Johnstown flood on a leaky toilet in Altoona."

¶20 Mr. Woodward, who won a number of awards for his own writing, was directly responsible for hiring Red Smith, generally regarded as the country's foremost sports columnist.

¶21 A man of almost belligerent independence, The Coach detested interference in his department from the front office and would put up with mighty little. Once in an economic move he was asked to submit the names of two people to be fired. "Stanley Woodward and Red Smith," he replied.

In 1948 Mr. Woodward so forcefully told management to keep its nose out of his sports department that he was discharged. In the next 11 years, he wrote a nationally syndicated column, edited for Dell Publishing Co., a magazine called *Sports Illustrated*, a title later sold to the Luce interests; and was sports editor of *The Miami* (Fla.) *Daily News* and *The Newark* (N. J.) *Star Ledger*. ¶22

In 1959, after control of the *Herald Tribune* had passed to John Hay Whitney, The Coach was invited to return to his old spot. Red Smith wrote in his column, "Stanley Woodward is back . . . all's right with the world." ¶23

By this time, though, Mr. Woodward's health was slipping away. In 1962, as his retirement became imminent, he wrote: "The press boxes are cold and there are too many steps to climb . . . I don't want to do anything regularly any more. Over the years I've attempted to write English and see that others did, too. I've had it now." ¶24

More than 300 persons attended his farewell luncheon at Toots Shor's and dozens sent messages. John Martin, then manager of the Bear Mountain Inn, spoke to and for the profession of newspapermen when he said, "Make no mistake about it, this man is a giant in your company." ¶25

For Greater Insight

1. Much newspaper writing differs physically from other writing. One difference is in the length of paragraphs. Count the sentences in each of the first six paragraphs. What do you find? Why does the newspaper writer use paragraphs like those of Rogers?
2. Young and inexperienced writers sometimes tend to believe that sports stories must use what Rogers calls "unholy jargon." Find in any newspaper a sports story that uses jargon, and identify the

words and expressions that are jargon. What is a danger in the use of such language? Is it accurate or inaccurate language? Explain.

3. Why does Rogers use the expression "fun-and-games department"? Is he doing this disparagingly? Is he revealing a feeling Woodward had? Explain.
4. How would you explain what Rogers meant when he said that Woodward "demonstrated . . . a balanced attitude about the relative importance of sports." Relative to what? Would such an attitude help or hinder Woodward in his work? Why?
5. The term Woodward invented—Ivy League—is now so familiar that its meaning and significance are missed. The two words are an interesting example of figurative writing. Explain the meaning of the term thoroughly. What is the figure of speech?
6. Woodward is said to write with "wry humor and a dash of disrespect." An example of "wry humor" is found in the names of the players on Woodward's "all" team. The humor may need explanation. Can you explain? Is this also slightly disrespectful? Why?
7. Skim through the essay and pick out words and phrases that describe both Woodward and his writing. Do these justify the closing statement, "This man is a giant"? Explain.
8. What is "controlled cynicism"? Can there be an uncontrolled cynic? Which person would you rather know? Why?

Word Study

tones of *insufficient servility*:
wrath over a *cliché*:
subsequently was made:
"unholy *jargon*"
a controlled *cynicism*:
belligerent independence:
retirement became *imminent*:

One Strike Is Out

Stanley Woodward

Irving T. Marsh and Edward Ehre, who edited *Best of the Best Sports Stories* for E. P. Dutton, said in their headnote to this essay:

"Stanley Woodward's two-part 'One Strike Is Out' impressed the jury to such an extent that they unanimously voted it a first place. Sports writing up to this point (1947) had never been too concerned with social problems, but when one was dumped into the laps of the scribes in the person of Jackie Robinson, who was about to be denied the chance of making a living playing baseball, the author took to his column and wrote this devastating blast."

As you read, look for the qualities in Woodward's writing that Smith and Rogers have told you about, and for the qualities that make the essay "this devastating blast."

A National League players' strike, instigated by some of the St. ¶1
Louis Cardinals, against the presence in the league of Jackie Robinson, Brooklyn's Negro first baseman, has been averted temporarily and perhaps permanently quashed. In recent days Ford Frick, president of the National League, and Sam Breadon, president of the St. Louis club, have been conferring with St. Louis players in the Hotel New Yorker. Mr. Breadon flew East when he heard of the projected strike. The story that he came to consult

with Eddie Dyer, manager, about the lowly state of the St. Louis club was fictitious. He came on a much more serious errand.

¶2 The strike plan, formulated by certain St. Louis players, was instigated by a member of the Brooklyn Dodgers who has since recanted. The original plan was for a St. Louis club strike on the occasion of the first game in Brooklyn, May 6, in other words last Tuesday. Subsequently the St. Louis players conceived the idea of a general strike within the National League on a certain date. That is what Frick and Breadon have been combating in the last few days.

¶3 It is understood that Frick addressed the players, in effect, as follows:

> If you do this you will be suspended from the league. You will find that the friends you think you have in the press box will not support you, that you will be outcasts. I do not care if half the league strikes. Those who do will encounter quick retribution. All will be suspended, and I don't care if it wrecks the National League for five years. This is the United States of America and one citizen has as much right to play as another.
>
> The National League will go down the line with Robinson whatever the consequences. You will find if you go through with your intention that you have been guilty of complete madness.

¶4 Several anticipatory protests against the transfer of Robinson to the Brooklyn club were forthcoming during spring training when he was still a member of the Montreal Royals, Brooklyn farm. Prejudice has been subsequently curbed except on one occasion, when Ben Chapman, manager of the Phillies, undertook to ride Robinson from the bench in a particularly vicious manner.

¶5 It is understood that Frick took this matter up with the Philadelphia management and that Chapman has been advised to keep his bench comments above the belt.

¶6 It is understood that the players involved—and the recalcitrants are not all Cardinals—will say, if they decide to carry out their strike, that their object is to gain the right to have a say on who shall be eligible to play in the major leagues. As far as is known the move so far is confined entirely to the National League. Ringleaders apparently have not solicited the cooperation of the American League players.

In view of this fact it is understood that Frick will not call ¶7
the matter to the attention of Harry Chandler, the commissioner. So far, it is believed, Frick has operated with the sole aid of Breadon. Other National League club owners apparently know nothing about it.

The *New York Herald Tribune* prints this story in part as a ¶8
public service. It is factual and thoroughly substantiated. The St. Louis players involved unquestionably will deny it. We doubt, however, that Frick or Breadon will go that far. A return of "No comment" from either or both will serve as confirmation. On our own authority we can say that both of them were present at long conferences with the ringleaders and that both probably now feel that the overt act has been averted.

It is not generally known that other less serious difficulties ¶9
have attended the elevation of Robinson to the major leagues. Through it all, the Brooklyn first baseman, whose intelligence and degree of education are far beyond that of the average ball player, has behaved himself in an exemplary manner.

It is generally believed by baseball men that he has enough ¶10
ability to play on any club in the majors. This ability has asserted itself in spite of the fact that he hasn't had anything resembling a fair chance. He has been so burdened with letters and telegrams from well-wishers and vilifiers and efforts to exploit him that he has had no chance to concentrate.

It is almost impossible to elicit comments about Robinson's ¶11
presence in the National League from anyone connected with baseball. Neither club owners nor players have anything to say for publication. This leads to the conclusion that the caginess of both parties, plus natural cupidity which warns against loss of salaries or a gate attraction, will keep the reactionary element under cover.

¶12 When Robinson joined the Montreal club last year, there was resentment among some Royal players. There was also a fear on the part of league officials that trouble would be forthcoming when the Royals played in Baltimore. Both the resentment and the fear were dissipated in three months. Robinson behaved like a gentleman and was cheered as wholeheartedly in Baltimore as anywhere else. Incidentally, Baltimore had its biggest attendance in 1946 and the incidence of Negroes in the crowd was not out of proportion.

¶13 Since Robinson has played with Brooklyn many difficulties have loomed, sometimes forbiddingly, but all have been circumvented. This was in part due to the sportsmanship of the fans and in part to the intelligence and planning of the Brooklyn management.

¶14 It is understood the St. Louis players recently have been talking about staging the strike on the day that Brooklyn plays its first game in St. Louis. Publicity probably will render the move abortive.

¶15 The blast of publicity which followed the *New York Herald Tribune*'s revelation that the St. Louis Cardinals were promoting a players' strike against the presence of Jackie Robinson, Brooklyn's Negro first baseman, in the National League, probably will serve to quash further strolls down Tobacco Road. In other words, it can now be honestly doubted that the boys from the Hookworm Belt will have the nerve to foist their quaint sectional folklore on the rest of the country.

¶16 The *New York Herald Tribune*'s story was essentially right and factual. The denial by Sam Breadon, St. Louis owner, that a strike was or is threatened is so spurious as to be beneath notice. The admission by Ford C. Frick, National League president, that the strike was contemplated was above and beyond the rabbitry generally adhered to by the tycoons of our national game. Such frankness, when compared with the furtiveness of other baseball barons, makes Frick the Mister Baseball of our time, whoever gets the $50,000.

From behind his iron curtain, Abie Chandler, through his ¶17
front man, Walter Mulbry, denied any knowledge of the projected St. Louis players' strike. This is true. The commissioner was uninformed. Inasmuch as the projected strike did not transcend the boundaries of the National League, Abie was told nothing about it, or at any rate, that was the reason ascribed.

When this department was investigating the story, it was dis- ¶18
covered that almost no one except the St. Louis personnel and the astute Branch Rickey, president, had knowledge of it, though numerous lesser Robinson impasses had badgered the Flatbush mahatma earlier in the season. Rickey declined to talk about the case even though silence had not been imposed on him. The lack of such imposition was due to the fact that the commissioner, knowing nothing about it, had not got around to placing additional gags.

Frick also kept his peace, but due to a leak similar to the one ¶19
seeping from Abie's office to *The Sporting News*, we were able to discover he had knowledge of it. Knowing him to be an honest man, we decided he would not deny the story. Therefore we went ahead and printed it. If Frick had denied it, its truth might still be unestablished. As it is, whatever Mr. Breadon may conjure up, people will laugh at him.

We made no pretense of quoting Frick verbatim in the ulti- ¶20
matum he delivered to St. Louis. We were wrong, apparently, in stating he personally delivered it to the players. It seems he delivered it to Breadon for relay to said operatives. In view of the fact that it obviously is the most noble statement ever made by a baseball man (by proxy or otherwise) we hereby reprint it, giving Ford full credit if he wants it:

> If you do this [strike] you will be suspended from the league. You will find that the friends you think you have in the press

box will not support you, that you will be outcasts. I do not care if half the league strikes. Those who do will encounter quick retribution. All will be suspended and I don't care if it wrecks the National League for five years. This is the United States of America and one citizen has as much right to play as another.

The National League will go down the line with Robinson whatever the consequences. You will find if you go through with your intention that you have been guilty of complete madness.

¶21 Enough of sweetness and light. Just to supplement our story, let us say that Robinson's presence in organized baseball has been attacked by minorities ever since he joined Montreal last year. There was nothing but trouble throughout training this spring. Extravagant measures have been taken to see that untoward incidents do not occur. Most of the trouble has been caused by players from the Hookworm Belt, but at least one major-league owner has openly expressed his dim view of the situation. We hesitate to name him. He is fatherly and venerable.

¶22 It is also known that another tycoon, who has expressed no open disapproval, has filed with the commissioner a secret document in which he is supposed to have stated that the presence of a Negro in baseball jeopardizes the holdings of all the major-league owners.

¶23 Boy, are the clients going to run out to see Robinson when he tours the West!

For Greater Insight

1. An essay may be narrative, descriptive, expository, or any combination of these. What type of essay is this? Was the author's choice of style deliberate, or was it forced on him by the purpose of the essay? What is the purpose of the essay?
2. Why should Woodward use several times the phrase, "It is understood"?
3. Par. 8 has a purpose very different from the purpose of the paragraphs preceding it. What is the purpose? Note the style of the

sentences. Each one, read aloud, falls like the blow of a hammer. What quality of the sentences produces this effect?

4. If you had been one of those involved in the situation Woodward is describing, could you effectively deny the whole business after reading Par. 8? What is the relationship between the possibility of such a denial and Woodward's purpose in the paragraph?
5. At the end of Par. 8 is this: ". . . that the overt act has been averted." Replace "overt" and "averted" with synonyms, using either words or phrases. Is one of your substitutions more effective than Woodward's choices? Give reasons.
6. The last sentence in Par. 14 tells what the purpose of the essay is. Explain that purpose.
7. Why is the reference to Tobacco Road in Par. 15 a devastating criticism of those planning the strike? The sentence beginning "In other words . . ." is an example of Woodward's "smashing impact." Explain why this is so.
8. What observation can you make about Frick's courage in making the statement he directed to the players threatening to strike?
9. This essay illustrates several of the statements made about Woodward and his writing by both Red Smith (pp. 65ff.) and John Rogers (pp. 70ff.). Choose some comment made by either, and show how the comment is illustrated in Woodward's own essay.
10. What feeling do you think was in Woodward's mind as he wrote this essay? Does Woodward lose his temper anywhere? What is the difference between losing one's temper and being angry? If you were displeased with some act you knew was being planned, how could you use Woodward's essay as a guide for something you wanted to write to cause the plan to fail?
11. Reference is made in several places in this text to the "intellectual sauntering," the leisurely style, and pleasant discursiveness and dalliance to be found in essay style. (See Question 2, p. 123; 1, p. 153; 6, p. 215; 3, p. 291; and the headnote on p. 216.) Do you find any of that quality of essay writing in Woodward's essay? Why or why not?

Word Study

instigated by some:
permanently *quashed*:

has since *recanted*:
quick *retribution*:
anticipatory protests:
recalcitrants:
thoroughly *substantiated*:
an *exemplary* manner:
vilifiers:
to *elicit* comments:
the *caginess* of both parties:
natural *cupidity*:
were *dissipated*:
incidence:
have been *circumvented*:
render the move *abortive*:
foist their *quaint* sectional folklore:
is so *spurious*:
above and beyond the *rabbitry*:
compared with the *furtiveness*:
astute Branch Rickey:
lesser Robinson *impasses*:
may *conjure* up:
quoting Frick *verbatim*:
in the *ultimatum*:

Violence and Noninvolvement

The Desensitization of Twentieth-Century Man

Norman Cousins

The problem that Mr. Cousins speaks about has been growing more and more important since he wrote this essay in 1959. Sociologists, police, doctors, nurses, and ordinary citizens are worried about the lack of concern shown by so many people for the welfare and safety of their fellows. The fear of "getting mixed up" in an unpleasant situation overcomes any feeling of duty.

Cousins has been editor of *Saturday Review* for more than twenty-five years, and is a respected observer, critic, and commentator.

This essay is one of the editorials that Cousins turns out for weekly issues of *Saturday Review*. There are subtle differences in style from that found in other essays. Note, for example, the smoothness of the narrative, and the thoughtful development of his idea right up to the final words. Although the matter is a serious one, Cousins' writing remains reserved.

It happened at the Stamford, Connecticut, railroad station. It was Sunday evening, at about ten P.M. Some two dozen persons, among them several young men in uniform, were waiting for the express to New York. ¶1

The door to the waiting room flew open. A woman, shrieking hysterically, burst into the room. She was pursued by a man just a few steps behind her. The woman screamed that the man was ¶2 trying to kill her and cried out for the people to save her. I was standing nearest the door. The woman grabbed me, still shrieking. I tried to protect her behind me. The man tried to sweep me aside to get at her. He rushed at me, caught the woman's wrist with one hand, tore her loose and pulled her through the doorway. The woman fell to the ground and was dragged by the wrist just outside the waiting room. I tried to free her wrist. The man broke off, grabbed the woman's pocketbook, and fled on foot.

¶3 We carried the woman inside the waiting room, sat her down, then telephoned the police. The woman's eye was badly cut; she was moaning. I looked around the room. Except for three or four persons who now came up to her, the people in the room seemed unconcerned. The young men in uniform were still standing in the same place, chatting among themselves as before. I am not sure which was greater, the shock of the attack that had just occurred or the shock caused by the apparent detachment and unconcern of the other people, especially the men in uniform.

¶4 The next morning, I read in the newspaper of another attack. This one was carried out in broad daylight on a young boy by a gang of teen-agers. Here, too, a number of people stood around and watched.

¶5 It would be possible, I suppose, to take the view that these are isolated instances, and that it would be a serious error to read into these cases anything beyond the fact that the bystanders were probably paralyzed by the suddenness of the violence. Yet I am not so sure. I am not sure that these instances may not actually be the product of something far deeper. What is happening, I believe, is that the natural reactions of the individual against violence are being blunted. The individual is being desensitized by living history. He is developing new reflexes and new responses that tend to slow up the moral imagination and relieve him of essential indignation over impersonal hurt. He is becoming casual about brutality. He makes his adjustments to the commonplace, and nothing is more commonplace in our age than the ease with which life can be smashed or shattered. The range of the violence sweeps from the personal to the impersonal, from the amusements of the crowd to the policies of nations. It is in the air, quite literally. It has lost the sting of surprise. We have made our peace with violence.

No idea could be more untrue than that there is no connection between what is happening in the world and the behavior of the individual. Society does not exist apart from the individual. It transfers its apprehensions or its hopes, its fatigue or its vitality, its ennui or its dreams, its sickness or its spirituality to the people who are part of it. Can the individual be expected to retain the purity of his responses, particularly a sensitivity to the fragility of life, when society itself seems to measure its worth in terms of its ability to create and possess instruments of violence that could expunge civilization as easily as . . . destroy a village? Does it have no effect on an individual to live in an age that has already known two world wars; that has seen hundreds of cities ripped apart by dynamite tumbling down from the heavens; that has witnessed whole nations stolen or destroyed; that has seen millions of people exterminated in gas chambers or other mass means; that has seen governments compete with one another to make weapons which, even in the testing, have put death into the air? ¶6

To repeat, the causative range is all the way from petty amusements to the proclamations of nations. We are horrified that teen-age boys should make or steal lethal weapons and then proceed to use them on living creatures; but where is the sense of horror or outrage at the cheapness of human life that is exploited throughout the day or night on television? It is almost impossible to see television for fifteen minutes without seeing people beaten or shot or punched or kicked or jabbed. It is also almost impossible to pick up a newspaper without finding someone in a position of power, here or elsewhere, threatening to use nuclear explosives unless someone else becomes more sensible. ¶7

¶8 The young killers don't read the newspapers, true. They don't have to. If they read at all, they read the picture-story pulps that dispense brutality as casually as a vending machine its peanuts. In any case, the heart of the matter is that the young killers do not live in the world of their own. They belong to the larger world. They may magnify and intensify the imperfections of the larger world but they do not invent them.

¶9 The desensitization of twentieth-century man is more than a danger to the common safety. It represents the loss or impairment of the noblest faculty of human life—the ability to be aware both of suffering and beauty; the ability to share sorrow and create hope; the ability to think and respond beyond one's wants. There are some things we have no right ever to get used to. One of these most certainly is brutality. The other is the irrational. Both brutality and the irrational have now come together and are moving towards a dominant pattern. If the pattern is to be resisted and changed, a special effort must be made. A very special effort.

For Greater Insight

1. The beginning of a piece of writing should catch the attention of the reader and make him want to read more. What is the effect of Cousins' first paragraph? How is the effect accomplished?
2. What comment can you make about the kinds of sentences and their length, in the second paragraph? What is the reason for using such sentences?
3. What two shocks did Cousins have as a result of his experience in the Stamford station? Which was the greater shock? Why should it have been greater? Would it have been greater for you? Why?
4. Explain in your own words what Cousins means in Par. 5 when he says he "believes that the natural reactions of the individual against violence are being blunted." Continue into the next sentence and explain "desensitized by living history." Do you think his theory or belief is acceptable? If so, what other aspects of society could be explained by his theory?

5. Note in Par. 5 the phrase, "commonplace in our age." Note also the date of publication of Cousins' essay. What was happening in the world when the essay was written and published? What gives Cousins his ideas about the ease with which life can be smashed?
6. Explain Cousins' idea in Par. 6 about the connection between the world and the individual. Do you agree with his idea? Will that same relationship exist in other areas, in other times? Explain and illustrate why it will or will not.
7. Do not the actions of individuals make in their total the kind of world they live in? Is this idea right? Is Cousins right? Can both be right? Instead of world and the individual, consider school and the individual. Is what you call school spirit involved? Explain each point you make.
8. The first sentence in Par. 7 mentions "petty amusements," and "proclamations of nations." Then Cousins illustrates both. Identify both illustrations.
9. Explain Cousins' expression "causative range," in Par. 7. What is caused by what? Explain what "they" do not invent. Who are they?
10. What is the "noblest faculty of human life" (Par. 9)?
11. What are the two things Cousins says we have no right ever to get used to? Explain the meaning of the second of the two. What does he mean by "have now come together?"

Word Study

detachment of the other people:
reactions . . . are being *blunted*:
developing new *reflexes*:
transfers its *apprehensions*:
its *ennui*:
fragility of life:
could *expunge* civilization:
impairment of the noblest *faculty*:
The other is the *irrational*:

Who Cares?

Leonard Gross

Barely five years after Mr. Cousins wrote the preceding essay, it was all too apparent that the "very special effort" he spoke of had not been made. When *Look* wanted to preface a series of pictures about Peace Corps activities, they used as a preface this essay by Mr. Gross, a *Look* Senior Editor. The question in the title is answered in two sharply contrasting ways. First, according to the essay, a great many do not care. Second, according to their pictures of the Peace Corps, there are many who do care, and who do something about it. This was effective use of contrast.

In this essay, note the frequent use of short, terse sentences, the condensed illustrative narratives, and the use of transitional devices.

¶1 This country is toying with a dangerous new idea. Twice a world savior, it has begun to wonder if its people will save one another.

¶2 The growth of this suspicion can be cleanly traced. It was born in New York City at 3:25 a.m. last March 13, when a man attacked 28-year-old Catherine Genovese as she was returning to her home from work. He stabbed her. She screamed for help, and he fled. Twice in the next half hour, he returned to stab her. Repeatedly, she called to her neighbors for help. At least 38 of them heard her, but none of them helped her, and she died.

The story stunned the nation. In succeeding weeks, news- ¶3
papers the country over produced local versions of what had all the appearances of an epidemic of apathy. Examples:

In Chicago, 60 persons ignored a uniformed policeman's cries ¶4
for assistance as he battled two youths. In Santa Clara, Calif., several motorists saw a taxicab driver being robbed, but none even summoned police. In San Pedro, Calif., other motorists drove by two policemen struggling to prevent a man from jumping off a 185-foot-high bridge. "We were hanging on for dear life and trying to get someone to stop. But they all drove on like they didn't want to be bothered or get involved," one of the patrolmen reported later. Back in New York City, a Broadway crowd stood by while eight men stomped two; a Bronx crowd would not rescue a naked girl from a rapist's attack, and bystanders fled from a 19-year-old college student who had just been stabbed by one member of a gang of toughs. His statement to the *New York Times* is unforgettable:

"I put my hand down and saw blood. I went over to a car ¶5
that had stopped to watch. 'Please help me to a hospital,' I said. They rolled up their windows and drove away. I went to another car and asked for help, but they did the same thing, drove away. Then I went to a truck and asked the driver for help. He pulled around me and drove away and left me there. Nobody on the street helped me."

Who cares? Seldom in our history has a question so un- ¶6
American seemed so necessary. It strikes at the jugular of our national life—our historic readiness to sacrifice personal safety for the public good.

Who cares? Millions of Americans do, a national survey by ¶7
Look indicates—the swollen ranks of volunteer charity workers, the battlers for civil rights, the numerous civilian heroes and the unnumbered Americans who, seeing danger, summon police. Rochester, Detroit, Atlanta, St. Louis, San Francisco—these and many other cities report excellent citizen cooperation. Even in

New York, where a single telephone call would have saved Catherine Genovese, there were 436,149 cases last year in which one or more persons summoned help.

¶8 *Who cares?* An unknown number of Americans do not—not, at least, enough to act. To the widely publicized incidents above can be added innumerable incidents uncovered by *Look*. Some can be excused because those who failed to act may not have understood what was happening, or did not know what to do. But most such incidents cannot be excused at all. "The fact that they do happen is a danger signal," says Dr. Arnold Abrams, a Chicago Medical School clinical psychologist. That there is an epidemic of noninvolvement is unlikely; that there is a problem is irrefutable. It must be explained.

¶9 Many explanations are being offered. All of them make some sense. None is very pleasant. One is that Americans are becoming too dollar-minded to risk the costs of involvement. Getting involved means being a witness. You lose time, pay, even popularity. A man in a building close to the one in which the young girl from the Bronx was raped railed at reporters for calling attention to the story. It was bad for business, he said. Now women wouldn't come to his office anymore. In New Orleans, Mabel Simmons, book-page editor of the *Times-Picayune,* saw a woman lying, apparently unconscious, on a sidewalk in the city's business district. No one seemed too concerned. Mrs. Simmons went into a nearby store, where she received permission to call the police. When they asked for the address, she, in turn, asked the store owner. He refused to give it to her. He didn't want the store connected with a police incident. In disgust, she set down the phone and checked the address herself.

¶10 Fear of involvement is widespread and pronounced. Sometimes, it is the fear of hurting someone. More often, it is the fear of getting hurt. One veteran social worker reports, "If a boy is stabbed in the hallway of a project, he can die, and no one will help him. They're all afraid of retaliation." Many Americans are loath to testify at trials, and serve on juries with reluctance. Judge Nathan M. Cohen of Chicago's Criminal Court excused more than 200 persons before he could complete a jury to hear a recent case involving organized crime. Male prospects asking to be released spoke in low voices, fidgeted with their clothing and refused to look the judge in the eye. The case was finally heard by an all-women jury.

¶11 In a New Orleans suburb two years ago, a young girl was leaning over her hi-fi set when a bullet shot past her head. Outside, residents found two drunken constables shooting off their guns. But no one—not even the girl's parents—reported the incident to authorities. "We didn't know when we might need them," someone said lamely.

¶12 Enforcement authorities blame cumbersome legal processes and a tendency to "understand" rather than punish criminals as causes of citizen reluctance. Despairing of getting satisfaction, people do not press charges. But at least one veteran police chief, Edward J. Allen of Santa Ana, Calif., cites the police themselves as one source of the problem. "They don't integrate. They develop a feeling that they have been set aside by society," he contends. Whatever the causes, there is a decisive feeling of estrangement between the public and law-enforcement agencies that accounts, in part, for the phenomenon of noninvolvement.

¶13 Another suggestion offered by authorities is that because we are now provided for in so many ways, the principle of individual responsibility is vanishing from American life.

¶14 Aaron M. Kohn, managing director of the New Orleans Metropolitan Crime Commission, Inc., speaks with dismay about the "metropolitan complex," which enables the citizen to rationalize away his obligations to society. Dr. Joel Elkes, psychiatrist-in-chief of The Johns Hopkins Hospital in Baltimore, decries the synthetic quality of contemporary experience, "when staring at the TV replaces good talk with a neighbor; or the phonograph, community singing in the church hall; or the latest what-to-do-next book on child-rearing, a real involvement with one's children." So much do we simulate, says Dr. Elkes, that when a real, live situation impels action, we are out of the acting habit. In Las Vegas, Nev., some time ago, a Federal narcotics undercover agent was shot while sitting in his car in a residential neighborhood. Many people ran to their doors and peered into the darkness, but none of them ventured outside to investigate. When police asked later why they hadn't, several explained they had been watching *The Untouchables* on television and wanted to see the end of the program.

¶15 A frequently mentioned source of noninvolvement is what the technicians call "a breakdown in primary groups"—groups united by culture, language, religion or common purpose. One American in four moves every year, the small-town resident to the city in search of opportunity, the city dweller to the suburbs in search of peace. In his new environment, he feels no identity, sinks no roots, has no stake. Strangeness frightens him; feeling threatened, he seeks to eliminate risks. He stays in line; he conforms. His world is now so complex that "the only way to survive is to cut a lot of it out," says Dr. Alfred J. Kahn, professor of social-welfare planning at Columbia University. Adds Alvin L. Schorr, a research chief of the Social Security Administration, "The man doesn't want to do too much. He adjusts by shutting things out. It may not work for society. But it works for him."

¶16 The problem appears to be greatest in cities where a sense of community is lowest. California's Bay Area offers a striking example. San Francisco is noted for the community pride of its residents. Police Chief Thomas J. Cahill speaks glowingly about the cooperation he receives from the public. If an assault of the Catherine Genovese type occurred in San Francisco? "We'd get fifty calls in five minutes." Oakland, across the Bay, is an unobtrusive city with many migrants and little civic verve. Its police chief, E. M. Toothman, lists 10 recent cases of public refusal to become involved—including one in which at least six persons failed to help a 63-year-old man who was being fatally stomped—and offers some dejected views about the moral breakdown of society.

When an individual leaves the neighborhood that knows him, he loses his first line of defense. The New York college student who was stabbed is probably alive today because he managed to make his way to his own block, where neighbors summoned aid. ¶17

The relationship of an aroused, unified neighborhood to individual safety shows clearly in the recent history of Hyde Park on Chicago's South Side. Once a secure, middle-class area dominated by the beautiful University of Chicago campus, Hyde Park by 1953 had become a lair of muggers. So unsafe were the streets that the existence of the university itself was threatened. Then one crime—the abduction and disrobing of a woman—aroused the neighborhood. Hyde Park's residents, including some of the best minds in the country, mapped a cleanup. The community was organized. Slums were razed, and new row houses built. A gospel of cooperation was preached. Today, Hyde Park is the envy of neighborhoods around it. Such is the sense of community that a cry for help brings instant action. Responding to a scream one evening this spring, sociologist Philip Hauser rushed from his house to find a number of his neighbors, all brandishing baseball bats, fire pokers and other makeshift weapons, chasing a would-be purse snatcher down the street. "I doubt that he tried Hyde Park again," says Hauser. Such community response has helped cut the crime rate nearly 50 percent since 1953. ¶18

"Success can be found only where there exists citizen zeal," states *Mental Health in the Metropolis*, the work of several prominent scholars. "What is needed is community feeling—when inhabitants have a *central* feeling of belonging." ¶19

But the problem is that tendencies in our society are leading ¶20 us away from the kind of life in which community feelings can flourish. As we move further from old ways, we must rely more and more on the individual's will to act.

¶21 *Who cares?* The question applies as urgently to me, the writer, as it does to you, the reader. There are no exemptions. I know, through recent personal experience, that an acceptable answer does not come easily. One morning a few weeks ago, I was walking my dog at 6 o'clock when I saw a man enter a car next to Riverside Park on Manhattan's West Side. I thought nothing of it. When I next looked, the same man was entering a different car—and suddenly I had a great deal to think about. Should I get involved? I didn't want to. But then I knew that I had to. Nervously, I asked myself, how? Attack him? And if he was armed? Who would help me? I found a telephone and called the police. Should I give my name? I decided I would. But the policeman didn't ask for it. I ran outside, only to see my quarry, two blocks away, leaving the area. Should I trail him? Again, the struggle. I trailed him. On West End Avenue, he got into another car.

¶22 Then a police cruiser came into view. I waved. The car pulled over. I gave directions. The police pulled in front of the car the thief was working. Hands on guns, they stepped out.

¶23 As they frisked the thief, I watched. Then I walked away, relieved. I had done my duty, and I was away clean. No involvement, no lost time in court, no fear of retaliation. Fifty feet away, I stopped, swore at myself and turned back to give my witness.

¶24 One by one, I had tasted the temptations of noninvolvement. Why I did not succumb goes back to an incident of 16 years ago that I have thought about a lot lately. I had just moved into a new building in Beverly Hills, Calif.; the only other tenant in my wing was a woman on the floor below. I was studying late one night when I heard her scream. I rushed downstairs. Another man was there. Together, we broke in. The woman was on the phone, calling the police. She had red marks on her throat. Near the door was her estranged husband, assuring us that everything was all right. Moments before, he had climbed in through a window and tried to strangle her. Our shouts had stopped him.

I have never considered myself a particularly brave man. I know that I reacted without thought. I know also that by the time I got to the woman's door, I was very frightened. But something, I now realize, frightened me more than the possibility of physical harm, and that was the possible loss of my self-respect. ¶25

I have, in other words, a vision of the way I would like to be. Most people do. "The self-image is what propels one—if one has it," says psychiatrist Elkes of Johns Hopkins. One gets it from the expected sources—father and mother, primarily, teacher and preacher as well. If that self-image is strong enough, it makes you confront events you would rather avoid. You call the police. You stop and give aid. At times, you even take risks. ¶26

To a man, the authorities counseling *Look* agree that the question of willingness to take risks, of individual responsibility, goes back to some pretty old-fashioned fundamentals in human relationships. ¶27

If you don't pick up a telephone, it's pretty certain that your son won't either. "He doesn't receive the cues, if you don't give them to him," says Dr. Elkes. If you counsel him to conform, get by, keep his nose clean, you'll find he sticks pretty closely to such advice. In Chicago last summer, 5′4″ Royace Prather smashed a chair over the head of an armed 6-foot robber who was holding up a restaurant cashier. Analyzing his motives recently, he recalled his father, a farmer "who tried to treat people nicely. He got mad at me one time, I remember, when I forgot to say thanks on the telephone to someone when I was in high school. He always returned borrowed things in better shape than he got them. He always believed in helping people." ¶28

In the end, the man who responds is the man who feels something for others. If a child is loved, he can take the risk of loving—or helping—others in turn. "You've got to be able to ¶29 believe that you can get involved in the lives of others without getting hurt," says a Washington, D.C., psychologist.

¶30 The man on the sidelines may well be one who was never given a sense of his own worth. Such a man cannot appreciate the worth of others. When others are in trouble, he will not respond.

¶31 Clearly, the emerging problem of noninvolvement in the United States is not simply a matter of human indifference. "Apathy is not the right word," says Dan Carpenter, executive director of the Hudson Guild Settlement House in New York City. "Apparent indifference can be a form of protection, a defense mechanism." Because a man on shore does not rush into the water to save another man from drowning does not necessarily mean that he is apathetic. It may simply mean that he can't swim.

¶32 But if he *can* swim, and does not, then he sentences himself to the self-punishment endured by the haunted narrator in Albert Camus's *The Fall.* An established, impeccable French lawyer, he has his world totally under control until he hears a drowning woman's cry one night, and turns away. Years later, ruined, he winds up talking to himself in an Amsterdam bar: ". . . please tell me what happened to you one night on the quays of the Seine and how you managed never to risk your life. You yourself utter the words that for years have never ceased echoing through my nights and that I shall at last say through your mouth: 'O young woman, throw yourself into the water again so that I may a second time have the chance of saving both of us!' "

¶33 The events of recent months are not an indictment. But they *are* a warning. They have exposed a dangerous incapacity in our society of which we have largely been unaware. We are living in a new world, and we are being tested everywhere—in Vietnam, New York, Mississippi—in ways we have never been before. The rediscovery that we need one another, that we are involved in all mankind, that we have got to care, could atone in part for the murder of Catherine Genovese.

For Greater Insight

1. There can be little doubt that the murder of Catherine Genovese called attention to a phenomenon of society. Gross says "It was born . . ." Exactly what was born? The phenomenon, or reaction to it? (See "The Desensitization of Modern Man," p. 90.)
2. In Par. 4, note the beginnings of the first three sentences. Why does Gross use this construction? If you had done this, would you expect to be criticized for repetition, or praised for good parallel construction?
3. Explain the metaphorical meaning of "jugular" in Par. 6. What is the characteristic of our national life which is being threatened?
4. Gross says that "innumerable incidents [were] uncovered by *Look*." Since he wrote this, innumerable other incidents of non-involvement have been reported. What have you heard or read about lately? In each case you report, what should have been done? Why wasn't it done?
5. What is the basic fear behind all the noninvolvement related in Par. 9? In the instances set forth in the next two paragraphs, what are people afraid of?
6. In Par. 14, how does the quoted passage following the words "synthetic quality of contemporary experience" explain these words? What other illustrations of "synthetic quality" can you name?
7. Explain the difference between San Francisco and Oakland, and the reactions of their citizens. What reason is given for the difference? Can you judge what kind of community you live in? What are the forces that make your community what it is? Is the answer in Par. 15? Or do you have some other answer?
8. The story of a community that did care is told in Par. 18. What are the differences between that community and its action and a community such as the one in which Catherine Genovese was killed?
9. In Pars. 21–25 Gross tells of personal experiences. Can you tell of a personal experience (or one of which you know) in an incident related to involvement?
10. Imagine that you are in a car and see a group of children mistreating a dog in such a way as to endanger its life. What would you do? Would the situation be changed if the incident occurred

in your own neighborhood, and you knew the children? If the dog were your own pet? Do these last two questions change the morality of the situation for the children? Do they change your responsibility?

11. Can you think of any situation in your school life about which you might pose a hypothetical question like the one in Question 10? Be sure it relates to involvement or noninvolvement, and to a choice of action.
12. The phrase "we are involved in all mankind" comes from *Devotions XVII*, by John Donne. Find it, and read the first paragraph or so. What are some of the implications? If a man used Donne's idea as a guide how would he behave in a crisis such as those mentioned in Gross's essay, and in Questions 10 and 11?

Word Study

in *succeeding* weeks:
an *epidemic* of *apathy*:
strikes at the *jugular*:
is *irrefutable*:
railed at reporters:
someone said *lamely*:
cumbersome legal processes:
feeling of *estrangement*:
phenomenon of *noninvolvement*:
rationalize away his *obligations*:
synthetic quality of *contemporary* experience:
so much do we *simulate*:
an *unobtrusive* city:
many *migrants*:
little civic *verve*:
a *lair* of *muggers*:
I did not *succumb*:
are not an *indictment*:
could *atone* in part:

Youth, Education, and Educators

American Youth Goes Monogamous

Charles W. Cole

Charles W. Cole has spent most of his life in academic activities and in government service. For six years he served as president of Amherst College, following that with work in the Rockefeller Foundation. In 1960 and 1961 he was United States Ambassador to Chile.

Essayists have an infinite variety of purposes behind what they write. Their purposes may be to prove, to disprove, to convince, to analyze, to amuse, to share both facts and emotions, and hundred of others. As you read Cole's essay, which appeared in *Harper's Magazine*, March 1957, try to find out what his purpose was.

Young people are often defensive and angry when one of an older generation writes about them and their habits. (This is an aspect of the gulf or chasm Cole says exists.) Does Cole attack the custom he describes? Does he find good in it? Has he been fair? How would you describe the purpose and style of this essay?

It was an autumn Saturday in 1935 when I was eight years out of college that I first realized I belonged to the older generation. But I did not understand that I was witnessing the first stages of a revolution which has dramatically altered the folkways of American youth and created a new and strange chasm between my generation and the next. Across the gulf which divides the adults who reached maturity in the early 1930s and the youngsters ¶1 growing up today, communication on some subjects is difficult if not impossible.

¶2 The occasion was a dance at a fraternity house. My wife and I were chaperons. It was the first such dance we had attended since 1927. We noticed that the stag line was very small in comparison to our day, but thought that perhaps it was harder to get stags to come in depression times. One of my students was a tall dark basketball player named Fred. We saw him dancing with a vivacious girl in a bright yellow dress. Twenty minutes later he was still dancing with the same girl. We commented to each other on the fact that he was stuck with the girl and felt sorry for him. Another twenty minutes passed. He was still dancing with the same girl over in a corner by the fireplace. At this point I felt so perturbed about his plight that I went up to one of his fraternity brothers and said:

¶3 "Fred is stuck with that girl in the yellow dress; can't one of you do something about it?"

¶4 The young man looked at me wide-eyed and replied, "Oh, no! That's Fred's girl."

¶5 It was another five years before "going steady" was fully established as the standard and persuasive pattern for the social life of the young. But today it is so completely dominant that the debutante parties in some large cities where, through a kind of stubborn conservatism, stags are still used and the girl brings two or three young men with her are regarded as oddities by the young people.

¶6 Youth at present is almost completely monogamous in a thoroughly established fashion, and it is aggressively sure that its customs and ways are right.

¶7 Not long ago, I was talking with three college seniors. They had been questioning me about the social customs of the 'twenties, which to them are as quaint (and as remote) as the 'nineties were to my generation, but appealing because of the good music like "Tea for Two" or "St. Louis Blues" and dances likes the

Charleston. I had been telling about stag lines and cutting in and getting stuck and the old story of the five-dollar bill held behind the girl's back. One of the seniors asked:

"But why did you cut in on a girl?" ¶8

I replied, "Well, maybe you knew her and she was a good ¶9
dancer, or fun to talk to or had what we called a 'good line.' Or perhaps you didn't know her and got introduced and cut in. Then if the two of you got on together you asked her for a date."

There was a hushed pause. Then another of the seniors ques- ¶10
tioned me a little timidly. "Do you mean that when another man brought the girl, you felt you could ask her for a date right at the dance?"

"Certainly," I answered; "in fact, that was the way you met ¶11
new girls."

A pall of disapproving silence settled over us, as the young ¶12
men contemplated the immorality, the stark and blatant indecency of their parents' generation. Then one of them with visible tact changed the subject.

A boy today who seeks to make friends with a girl somebody ¶13
else brings to a dance is known as a "bird-dog" and what he does is called "bird-dogging." The origin of the phrase is neither known nor obvious. But the activity is frowned on in the most thoroughgoing fashion. There was the case of Weston Brewer. He was a member of the Alpha Beta Gamma fraternity. At one of the house dances to which he had brought his own girl, he met a girl named Maureen, from Boston, who had been brought by one of the other brothers, Tim Morton. With Weston and Maureen it was love at first sight in the best romantic tradition. Weston went to Boston to see her. He went every weekend. When this fact became known, the matter was brought up at the next chapter meeting and it was proposed that Weston be expelled from the fraternity for bird-dogging a brother's girl. But Weston's friends—though in no way condoning his actions—pointed out that Maureen was not really Tim's girl, since he had only one date with her before

the dance. It was concluded, therefore, that, while Weston was guilty of the worst taste, expulsion from the chapter would not be justified.

Timing and Liking

¶14 One of the delicate questions in going steady is when the relationship may be said to have been established. Here, there is some difference of opinion. But in general three dates in fairly rapid succession are not enough and six dates are plenty. So the fourth or the fifth date may be considered crucial. I once saw a girl from the Middle West in tears. She had had three dates with a boy and had got on well with him. But she felt she did not like him enough to go with him on a steady basis and therefore was compelled to refuse the fourth date. "Like" is now, by the way, a word of art. In "Bill likes Sue," it implies the first stages of what, if all goes well, may result in love.

¶15 Going steady is a rather stylized relationship. (The phrase "going steady" is used in high schools though not much in college circles. But the institution is as strong in the latter as the former.) When it is fully established, it means that the boy will not go out with any other girl or the girl with any other boy. It means further that each can count on the other for any date, dance, or other social event. There are certain exceptions—concessions as it were to the weakness of the flesh. Let us say that Jack comes from Missoula, Montana, and is attending an Eastern college. In Missoula, he is going steady with Mary. But to be denied female companionship for months at a time is more than he can be expected to endure. It is not, then, wholly improper for Jack, under these conditions, to go out with Nancy from Vassar while he is in the East. Ideally Jack should tell Nancy about Mary and Mary about Nancy. And Nancy (or perhaps Mary) should be aware that she is secondary, the under-steady so to speak.

¶16 But it would be even better and Jack would be more admired by his fellows—granted that Mary is really his girl—if he lived a completely celibate and monastic life while at college. This would be regarded as a great sacrifice, but it would bring him respect and sympathy.

This sympathy might even take concrete form. There was ¶17
the case of Donald, a junior in the Gamma Beta Alpha house. He was a scholarship boy with means so limited that he could not go home to Beaver Falls, Minnesota, for Christmas vacation. At home he had a girl named Grace, whom he dearly liked and to whom he was completely faithful. The time came for the spring house dance and all the chapter members were urged to bring dates. Don sadly refused and thought mournfully of Grace. The brothers were so deeply impressed by his constancy that they raised a pool to buy Grace an airplane ticket East and to pay all her expenses. The big scene took place before the dance when his friends said to Don, "We've got a blind date for you," led him protesting to the library, threw open the doors, and there was Grace beaming over a corsage of orchids. This romantic denouement made the weekend a happy and thrilling one for the whole chapter.

Going steady is a progressive not a static relationship. At the ¶18
start, it means merely a monogamous social arrangement, but it is likely to move on to a point where the couple gets "pinned." (The typical symbol is the fraternity pin, but if the college has no fraternities, a Phi Bete key, a club emblem, or military insignia may be used.) Overtly "pinning" merely means that the girl can and does wear the boy's fraternity pin. Inwardly it means more than that, though there are various degrees. Merely "pinned" implies that the boy and girl plan to go steady in the future, like each other a good deal, and expect the relationship to develop further. To be seriously pinned means "engaged to be engaged" or perhaps even "engaged" preparatory to getting a ring, securing parental approval, and clearing up other details.

Since pinning is in many ways the equivalent of the be- ¶19

trothal of earlier times, it is frequently quite ceremonious. Friends of the pinned couple may give a little party, at which the girl appears with the pin on for the first time, and toasts may be drunk in champagne. There was the case of a returning alumnus of elder vintage who started to go into the music room in his fraternity house, but was stopped with the admonition, "Don't go in there, Joe is pinning his girl." The alumnus completely misunderstood the situation until the young couple emerged wreathed in smiles, the girl with the pin on her bosom, to receive congratulations.

¶20 The relationship of going steady, even of a pinned couple, may be ended with somewhat more ease than an engagement can be broken. It may be terminated by either party or by mutual agreement. If either the boy or the girl ends it firmly, he or she is said to have "axed" the other.

¶21 The duration of the "steady" arrangement is most variable. It may last from a few days to many years. There are instances where a couple started going steady in junior high school, continued through high school and college, and got married after eight or more years of going together. A boy or girl on the other hand may have several "steadies" in the course of a single year. But it is considered frivolous and light-minded to change too often. So monogamous (pro tem) is the younger generation that after losing a steady, it is thought proper to wait a decent interval before seeking another.

¶22 The philanderer of the 'twenties who dated a different girl every night and went out with dozens in the course of a year has disappeared. So has the prom trotter of earlier times. A clever girl today might conceivably have a male friend in four or five different colleges, but she would not be much admired if she had two at the same college. If she collected an array of fraternity pins from several boys—I knew of girls in the 'twenties who had as many as seven—she would be condemned by her acquaintances.

The dances have perhaps changed most visibly of all the social institutions. While the system of going steady has become more formalized, dances have tended to become more informal. (Why dress up for someone you see so often and know so well?) They have tended to become shorter. (When you dance with only one partner, two hours or so is enough.) There is a good deal of sitting around and listening to music or entertainment instead of dancing. In fact, an effort is made to secure bands worth listening to rather than those whose music is especially suitable for dancing. The dances are a little heavy and somber because the excitement and shifting around of cutting in has disappeared and because neither the boys nor the girls feel under any special obligation to be gay or entertaining. The big dance of the prom type is fading slowly away. Since a couple is going to dance together anyhow they may as well do it in an informal fashion to phonograph records, or at a night spot, without going to the trouble and expense of attending a big formal affair. ¶23

Getting Married

The revolution in the courtship and dating procedures of our youth has had profound effects on our society and even on our economy. ¶24

The average age of marriage has dropped very rapidly. A college girl of the 1920s *said*, at least, that she was looking forward to a career. Most of them did not expect to get married until two or three years after graduation. The college girl today declares quite frankly that she wants to get married and she frequently does so while still in college. A girl who gets as far as junior year in college without having acquired a man is thought to be in grave danger of becoming an old maid. A manless senior is considered to be more or less on the shelf. ¶25

Matrimony at an early age is facilitated by the disappearance of the idea that a man should be able to support a wife before ¶26 he gets married. The GI Bill of Rights with its higher allowances for married veterans seems to have destroyed the older notions, and to have made the idea of married undergraduate students acceptable. Nowadays, one or both sets of parents are expected to "help." If the parents cannot be of assistance it is perfectly normal for the girl to take a job and help to support her husband through medical school or law school.

¶27 And then there is the birth rate. Thirty years ago a young couple usually planned to have two children and usually did. Today the ideal seems to be four or five children. The effect of this shift in attitude on the birth rate has been spectacular. Among college graduates of both sexes the classes ten years out already have substantially as many children as the classes twenty-five years out. It is known also of course that all by itself an earlier average age of marriage will raise the birth rate.

¶28 Why young people want more children is by no means clear. Partly the new attitude may arise from the fact that there is no servant problem. Since there are no servants, there is no question of waiting till it is possible to afford a maid to look after the baby. Housekeeping has, moreover, been much simplified by washing machines, frozen foods, diaper services, and a score of other developments. Baby-sitting has become a national and fairly well organized institution. Partly the trend to large families may arise from the fact that many of the young people marrying today were only children or had a single sibling. They seem to envy the children who come from large families and had a more varied and exciting family circle. Partly, too, young people seem to be seeking in their own families the security that is outwardly denied by the unsettled state of the world.

¶29 In the 'twenties and early 'thirties, when the social pattern was one of multiple or polygamous dating—on the part of both boys and girls—young people did not think nearly so much about marriage as they do today. Thirty years ago a boy and a girl could have dates over a long period without seriously considering that they might some day get married. They dated each other for the fun of it, because they enjoyed each other's company, because they liked the same things, or merely because in the competitive social life of their time it was a good thing to have dates—the more, the better. Today young people often play with the idea of marriage as early as the second or third date, and they certainly think about it by the fifth or sixth. By the time they have been going steady for a while they are quite apt to be discussing the number and names of their future children. The fact that the steady may well be a future spouse gives a different color to the social life of the youth. It makes it more serious, less frivolous. The boys and girls spend a lot of time discussing their relationship and whether it is solidly founded on bases of long-run compatibility.

The oddest thing about the revolution in the social life of ¶30
youth in the last twenty years is that it constitutes the triumph of rural nineteenth-century American mores in the urban and suburban society of the mid-twentieth century. Anybody over seventy who was brought up in a country village or town finds the social customs of young people today strangely familiar. In the 1880s or 1890s it was normal to have boys and girls pair off in a more or less stable fashion, and such pairing often ended eventually in marriage. The very phrase "going steady" has the ring of rural America under President Cleveland.

The Passing of the Wall Flower

Why have our young people reverted so sharply to the ways ¶31
of an earlier era and a simpler society? There seems to be no clear-cut answer. The change has often been ascribed to the second world war, when the sudden shortage of men made each girl eager to hold on to any available male. But it was well under way before 1939. The new folkways may be related to the Great Depression when a boy putting out money for a girl on dances, movies, or

the like wanted to be sure of some return on his investment. It is also true that the fiercely competitive social life of the 'twenties with the stag lines and the cutting in and the multiple dates meant that a popular girl had a very good time indeed. But the majority of girls were not popular. They dreaded being wall flowers. They were the ones with whom boys sometimes got stuck. It may be that the less popular majority of girls slowly created the present democratic system, under which any girl with a steady is just as well off as any other girl with a steady. Since each boy wants a steady too and since the numbers of boys and girls are about equal everybody seems better off at present, though it is possible that some polygamous male instincts are thwarted. On the other hand, girls would insist that the new system was created by the boys who are aggressive, possessive, and jealous of all rivals.

¶32 The new ways may also be related to the search for security. The boy or girl who has a steady is secure. Each partner knows that the other can be counted on for the coming high-school dance or the next football game. In a day when the population moves from home to home with such freedom and when so many homes are broken by divorce or otherwise, this kind of security is very precious to young people. Perhaps, too, the general decline of competition under the welfare state has led to less competitive social customs. Just as the retail stores have tried to shelter themselves from all price competition behind the so-called Fair Trade laws, so our young people have divided into noncompeting twosomes.

¶33 Whatever the origin of the present pre-marital monogamy of youth, it is one of the most important phenomena of recent times. Already it is responsible for the new birth rate that has exploded the predictions that our population would become stable in numbers in the 1970s. It looks as if the United States would grow in population rapidly and indefinitely. Already it has produced the tidal wave of babies that will overwhelm the high schools in 1961 and the colleges in 1964. Already it has created a situation where parents and children find it hard to communicate on social matters. The mother who says to a daughter, "Why do you always have dates with Jimmy? Aren't there other nice boys?" seems to the daughter to be lacking in elementary understanding of the facts of social life.

It is too early to determine what the new system will do for the stability of marriage. On *a priori* grounds the oldsters would predict that a boy who had dated only one girl or at the most half-a-dozen would be less likely to find a permanently compatible mate than one who had gone out with fifty or a hundred. It would seem even that there might be anti-eugenic consequences, since the intelligent girl would have less chance of finding an intelligent boy to marry. ¶34

But it is also possible that a marriage relationship based on an elaborate system of premarital companionship progressing through recognized stages (dating, going steady, getting pinned, becoming engaged) may be built in a solid and enduring fashion. It is conceivable too that the fiercely monogamous premarital folkways may carry over into married life and erect strong buttresses to the institutions of marriage and the family. ¶35

For Greater Insight

1. Is there anything in the first paragraph that makes you think Cole believes that the chasm or gulf he speaks of is a new phenomenon, or one which has always existed? What is your opinion about the gulf?
2. What was the older custom about dances, explained in Par. 5? Who benefited from the custom?
3. In what paragraph does Cole express the idea that history repeats itself? Be sure you can explain rural, urban, and suburban. In which area did the custom originate? Where did it move to?
4. In Pars. 30–31 Cole gives some possible reasons for the reappearance of the practice of going steady. With which of his reasons do you agree? Can you suggest other reasons?
5. What are some of the results Cole attributes to the custom of

youthful monogamy? Note that the essay was published in 1957. Was Cole a good prophet? Why should youthful monogamy make communication difficult between parents and children? Whose fault —if any—is the difficulty?

6. In the last two paragraphs Cole suggests possible consequences, some unfortunate, others desirable. Which of these do you think have occurred or are likely to occur? Why?
7. Is the custom of going steady as much a part of youthful society today as it was when Cole's essay was published? If so, what good aspects have lead to its retention? If not, why?

Word Study

perturbed about his *plight*:
persuasive pattern:
completely *monogamous*:
pall of disapproving silence:
stark and *blatant* indecency:
condoning his actions:
considered *crucial*:
stylized relationship:
celibate and *monastic* life:
romantic *denouement*:
static relationship:
equivalent of *betrothal*:
elder vintage:
monogamous (*pro tem*)
philanderer of the 'twenties:
is *facilitated* by:
a single *sibling*:
polygamous dating:
long-run *compatibility*:
American *mores*:
on *a priori* grounds:
anti-eugenic consequences:

Teaching Not Facts, But How to Think

Gilbert Highet

What does the teacher of a class think of the students in front of him? Is he aware of them as individuals? As he speaks to them of sines, acceleration, transition, Freud, structure, tenses, concepts, reactions, what is he really hoping for?

Dr. Highet answers many of these questions, and many others, from his long experience as a professor of Latin and Greek at Columbia University, where he began teaching in 1937. (This essay appeared in *The New York Times Magazine*, February 25, 1951.) In addition to his work at Columbia, Dr. Highet has written books of criticism, essays, and translations, served in the British Army during World War II, and has conducted a series of programs about books, programs described as "flavorsome, scholarly, and charming talks."

You have probably noticed that nowadays, when you talk to young men and women of college age, they do not hear you very well. Their thoughts are elsewhere. They say, "Sure" and they say, "So do I" and often they ask, "What was that?" But their eyes do not quite focus. Nor do their minds. ¶1

We cannot blame them. All that we can do is to sympathize, to keep them calm, and to remember what it was like for ourselves to be very young and to be faced with war (I), unemployment (1921—), inflation (1924), unemployment (1929—), war (II), or the other crises which have been a recurrent feature of ¶2 the twentieth century. But it makes it much more difficult to teach the young, in schools and in colleges.

¶3 Have you ever tried to make a long-distance call in the middle of a party? The host says, "This is for you. Cleveland calling," and hands you the receiver. Faint and distant, a little voice speaks in your ear, explaining something you have forgotten and asking questions you cannot answer. From time to time it is interrupted by roars and crackles of electricity, and occasionally a total stranger's voice, like a ghost, floats along the wire uttering disembodied fragments of an unintelligible speech. But your caller in Cleveland goes on earnestly explaining and eagerly inquiring.

¶4 Meanwhile, your host has gone back to the other guests, and is engaged in a loud argument about the hydrogen bomb that comes into your other ear with much more force and stridency than the Cleveland talker. Two late-comers are taking off their coats and chatting just beside you in the hall. Music is coming from the middle distance, where Jeff and Mary have been persuaded to do their own special version of "Baby, It's Cold Outside," and there are regular shouts of laughter at the end of each verse. And over and under the various utterances, all demanding your attention, there flows a steady stream of miscellaneous noise, random conversation and isolated words and competitive dialogue and hum and clink and clatter, topped off by the furious trumpeting of taxis threading their way through the double-parked cars outside the door.

¶5 At last Cleveland says "Now, you're sure you've got all that? Nine o'clock on Monday without fail and bring *both* zigms, they're sending Presncjx as well. 'Bye now." And you go back to the party wondering what on earth it was all about, and trying desperately hard to make a connected story out of the message. Sometimes you ring back next morning for confirmation. Sometimes you put the bits together into the wrong pattern and blame the other fellow. Sometimes you get it right, and it is at least partly luck.

Anyone who teaches young men and young women is in the ¶6
position of the man calling from Cleveland. He has a consistent and carefully prepared message to deliver. They know something of what he is trying to tell them, and they have one ear open for the message. They are not uncooperative. They will listen. But their attention is distracted, not occasionally, but continuously, by a torrent of other voices and excitements against which the message can hardly make its way.

To begin with, they are young. And youth, with health and ¶7
energy, is (for all the dangers that beset it) rather like being at a perpetual party. We oldsters lead a dull life, they think. Certainly we have far fewer pleasures. We could scarcely endure them, even if we tried. Recently I reread some of the diaries I kept when I was at college, and they made me dizzy. Into one day I tried to cram as much excitement as would keep me going for a month now: a debate at the union at which I spoke, a boxing lesson in which I became speechless, a meeting of the musical society to fix next month's program, an angry session of the magazine board, plus a dance in the evening, not to mention three hours' lectures. . . . And the point is that all these things were apparently occupying my mind at the same time.

Exciting, yes, and the essence of growth, but distracting. To ¶8
sit and listen to a reasoned exposition of vector analysis or the policy of the Habsburg Empire, difficult enough for an adult, is almost impossible for a young man or woman. I sometimes look at them in the classroom with real astonishment, and wonder what keeps them in their seats when every one of them is a mass of explosive force.

The biggest excitement of all, the one which corresponds to ¶9
the cocktails at the party, is, of course, love. Usually their minds are at least half occupied by love—for at least half of the time. Either they are in love—and are puzzled by its power, or saddened by its cruelties, or terrified by its dangers, or exultant at its delights—or else they are lonely, and would like to be loved,

but cannot find anyone lovable or loving. It is strange for a teacher to look at all those young faces and reflect that although their owners are mentally immature, physically they are adults who could very well have children of their own.

¶10 The quiet little fellow in the front seat with the big glasses looks as though he were concentrating hard on the tax structure of South America, but he is also trying to decide whether, since he thinks he is too unattractive ever to catch a real beauty, he ought to abandon the idea of love altogether, and become a recluse, a hermit of the intellect. Farther back, the calm girl with the sleek hair and the neat, quick handwriting is taking down the figures apparently with interest and efficiency. She is also wondering whether she is going to have a baby, for she married another graduate student last summer, and they agreed to postpone the family till they get their degrees, and yet . . .

¶11 Older people—I almost wrote "grown ups," but these youngsters are grown up, too—older people have usually had enough experience and have thought enough about love to know what it can do to them and how they should live with it. For the young it is all new. Sometimes I think there are only four great experiences in life: the baby's discovery of the world, the youth's and girl's discovery of love, and the adult's discovery of art and of religion. All of these are overwhelming in their excitement and their power. The difficulty about the discovery of love is that it competes with almost irresistible power against the training of the intellect; and still both must go on at the same time.

¶12 Then there are all the other excitements, which, like the noise coming out of the party, keep the message from being fully heard, or even fully attended to. Instead of listening to the man in Cleveland, you would rather be inside listening to Jeff and Mary singing. In the same way, young men and women can scarcely ever concentrate 100 or even 80 per cent on the intellectual messages which their teachers send them; because their will power is not yet fully trained.

Very few students ever go through a course without wondering at least half a dozen times whether they ought to drop it. Very few students ever complete their education, at school or at college, without having several periods of distraction or discouragement or despair, when they almost decide it would be better to throw up the whole thing and take a job. If there is a job handy, it is all the more difficult to resist the temptation. ¶13

One of my friends who is now a successful surgeon played with me in the college dance band. He was offered the equivalent of $300 a week to turn professional. And although he had entered college in order to become a doctor, although he had made his way by scholarships and had been getting excellent grades, although he really liked the profession and was looking forward to curing the sick, he still had a long period of doubt when that $300 a week, so close and easy, looked far more attractive than the long years of training and interneship before a distant and doubtful career. He used to talk to me about it by the hour, when he should have been studying the anatomy of the thorax; and I used to discuss it with him by the hour, when I should have been reading Lucan on the civil wars of Rome. ¶14

War is a violent teacher, said the Greek historian Thucydides. And it is extremely hard for any human teacher to compete with war for the attention of his students. It is not that they are afraid of that violence—American youngsters are good in combat, and very few of them permit themselves to be "chicken." No, it is that they can scarcely concentrate on long preparation and careful thinking (which are the essence of a sound education) if a violent interruption may alter their whole lives. Young men nearly always prefer a quick and complete decision to vagueness and hesitation, and postponement; and you can see them now, struggling against the temptation to throw up years of work and solve the whole problem by joining the Marines. ¶15

But perhaps we have all talked too much about the fate of the nation hanging on military preparedness alone; perhaps they ¶16 feel that this is a powerful imperative, too powerful to resist or reason out; and probably we should tell them—what is undoubtedly true—that the fate of the nation depends also upon the education and the wisdom of the young people who, after every war and every crisis, have to guide it and to rebuild it. Just as we have a duty to educate them, so they have a duty, subordinate only to immediate military necessity, to be educated.

¶17 When we tell them that, we are telling them the truth. We are also training their will power. But it is not only their will power which is not fully trained. Their minds are not fully trained, either. It is the teacher's chief duty to train them. That is even more important than filling them with the right facts. What the young learn in high school and in college is not primarily sets of facts, or special skills, or theories, or explanations. They learn how to think.

¶18 This is the most important of all, for it changes them into human beings. Some of them never learn it. Uneducated people all over the world seldom learn it. That is why there is such a terrifying gulf between those who can think generally and logically and those who cannot. Those who can think for themselves see the world as a complex of events and forces which can be explained by fitting them into a number of intellectual patterns: history, for example, is such a pattern, and so is physics.

¶19 Those who have never learned logical thought can seldom see these patterns. Usually they refuse to believe that the patterns exist. They substitute vague and sullen emotional burps for logic. Or else they believe—when one tries to explain the pattern to them—that the explanation is only "a lot of talk," words, words, words, intended to deceive and not to communicate. Most of the authors who have written about the peasants of Russia agree in saying that, though often shrewd in solving particular problems, the peasants would not accept logical explanations because they did not believe in the possibility of logical argument.

¶20 Winston Churchill, in the last volume of the magnificent history of the war, quotes Stalin himself as feeling and expressing this difficulty. "You explain a plan carefully to the peasant," said Stalin, "and he scratches his head and says he must talk it over with his wife or his herdsman. Then he comes back and rejects the whole thing." It was not, apparently, that the peasant understood the plan and opposed it on carefully reasoned grounds. It was simply that he distrusted it because it was an intellectual structure and he could not cope with intellectual structures any more than he could fly without wings. Stalin could have educated the peasants. But he chose to liquidate four or five million of them instead.

We see the same kind of thing whenever we travel into ¶21
remote parts of the world. Talking to illiterate farmers, or to isolated villagers in the back-country of Mexico or Spain or India (even after the language difficulty has been partly solved), we feel another difficulty, this one insoluble. It is that they do not think as we do. They are primitives. They will not make a general statement. Instead, they will tell a story. (That is why all the great religions of the world begin not with philosophical systems, but with wonderful stories.) They will not argue, and reach a general conclusion by to-and-fro discussions. They simply make counterstatements, and stop. And all the time they look at us with the same puzzled but intense gaze that we see in the eyes of an animal trying to decide between attack, or investigation, or escape.

Long afterward, when we have left their village and gone ¶22
back to our homes, they will still remember us, with photographic vividness though without the power to generalize—because we had a *machine that clicked*, or smoked a pipe with a *silver band*. In their own land they are cleverer and wiser than we. They would survive where we would die. But outside their own land they would be miserable, for they could not assimilate their new experiences. Without the general processes that we call logical thought they cannot think.

¶23 So when we teach the young we must remember that, for a good deal of the time, they are trying—not always with success—to think as we think. Our minds are trained to put two and two together. Their minds are not trained to put anything together except emotional experiences. Our minds can detect remote similarities and build up large patterns of thought. Their minds cannot make those jumps and fill in those connections.

¶24 Almost automatically, after our training, we single out cause and effect, principle and example, ground and variation, rule and exception, pro and con, general and particular. These very concepts are strange to the young. I remember puzzling for years over the meaning of "cause." What is a "cause"? How can we say that the murder of an archduke "caused" a war? What "caused" the murder? Was it the bullet, or the powder, or the impulse of the murderer, or the coincidence of his meeting the archduke, or his accurate aim, or what? It was really a revelation to me when I was given a logical analysis of the idea of causation, and learned that there were several different types of cause (Aristotle said four types) and that the whole concept of cause and effect was merely a human convenience in selecting from the process of events a few separate aspects which were important for our own purposes.

¶25 And so it is with all the young. Again and again, in talking to them, we use words which seem perfectly clear and easy. We say "There is an analogy . . ." or "Suppose we look for a precedent . . ." The young look dutifully at us, but they are not quite sure what an analogy is or what function a precedent performs. Therefore the good teacher will always remember that it is not only the subject-matter of his teaching which is strange to the class; it is the actual method of his thinking. The young have to learn it. Without learning the principles of general reasoning, they will never be able to understand the laws of their country or grasp its history; they will never be fit to plan a factory or organize a business, to criticize a book or detect a fallacy, to arrange their own lives or to educate their children.

But it is difficult to learn thinking, and we must be patient with them while they learn it. When they do or say silly things, it is not unnatural. It is the upsurge of disorganized emotion, the random gesture of the animal or savage out of which they are evolving. ¶26

That is why teaching is such a wonderful profession. Doctors make sick people well again. Lawyers reconcile people's differences. Clergymen make people better in spirit. But teachers make children and youngsters, half-animal and half-savage, into human beings. Even that would not be possible unless they wanted to become human. Every child, every boy, every youth, in his heart wants to learn and to grow in mind, to the fullest powers of which he feels himself capable. The best teacher in the world cannot force him to do so. All that he can ever do is to help and encourage. His best reward is to see, not a "product," but a free and independent human being who can think. ¶27

For Greater Insight

1. Highet says "It makes it much more difficult to teach the young . . ." What does the first "It" refer to? Why do their "eyes . . . not quite focus"?
2. The style of some essays is leisurely and slow, sometimes narrative, sometimes reminiscent. Highet's analogy of the call from Cleveland is an example of such an essay style. In what paragraph is the analogy explained? Does the analogy help make the point clear?
3. At the end of Par. 6 Highet mentions "a torrent of voices and excitements." Is he speaking of things he has already referred to, or is he developing new thoughts? Do the first three words of Par. 7 help you decide the answer? What do you call such an expression as these three words?
4. What are some of the distractions Highet brings up? Could you add any ideas to Highet's?
5. In Par. 9 the sentence beginning "Either they are in love—" is forceful and effective. Why?
6. Carrying on educational activities at a time when young people

are so concerned about themselves and their relations with the world and with other people is a very serious problem. Do you think this has always been so? It was so when Highet was writing. Is it so now? Why? Does Highet suggest any remedy? What suggestion can you make?

7. In Par. 16, Highet says ". . . probably we should tell them . . ." Who is going to tell what to whom? Have you ever been told this? Do you believe it? Why do you think it is either true or false? What are the duties imposed upon parents, teachers, and students?
8. In what sentence in what paragraph does Highet first refer to the title of his essay? What rather startling change in young people comes about? What does Highet feel they were before the change occurred?
9. Explain your idea of the meaning of logical thought. What are the dangers of not being able to think logically, and what are the benefits of logical thought?
10. What does Highet say the good teacher will always remember? And what will teachers accomplish? What is your reaction to Highet's explanation of what happens to young people in school?
11. In Par. 27 Highet begins a sentence "Every child, every boy, every youth . . ." Is Highet correct? Explain. What are the implications and the problems?
12. Do the same distractions that Highet mentions trouble young people today? Are there other distractions that are a part of the different world in which you live? Do they help arouse an interest in studies, or do they diminish such interest? Explain.

Word Study

disembodied fragments:
force and *stridency*:
a *perpetual* party:
exultant at its delights:
become a *recluse*:
periods of *distraction*:
essence of a sound education:
terrifying *gulf* between:
sullen and emotional *burps*:
illiterate farmers:

this one *insoluble*:
assimilate their new experiences:
is an *analogy*:
look for a *precedent*:
detect a *fallacy*:
reconcile people's differences:

Public Schools Are Better Than You Think

Sloan Wilson

Sloan Wilson is the author of best-selling novels, including *The Man in the Gray Flannel Suit*, and served as Assistant Director of the White House Conference on Education. He has long been, as this essay demonstrates, much concerned with the public schools. The essay appeared in the September 1955 issue of *Harper's Magazine*.

John Kenneth Galbraith in Chapter 17 of *The Affluent Society* says that there is a well-recognized unwillingness on the part of citizens and the government to support financially the public services our society requires. Wilson's point, while different in detail, does include his observation of a marked degree of reluctance to support public education as he feels it should be supported. As you read, try to note the evidence he provides that while public schools do a good job, they need to do still better, and could, if properly supported.

¶1 Ever since the war, I've put up with about as much debate concerning the public schools as I can stand quietly, and I'm going to get into the act. Of course, I'm no great expert on the technical aspects of the thing, but I need only to inspect the torrent of recent books and articles attacking or defending the schools to realize that this is a subject which offers marvelous opportunities to a writer tired of research. Here is a field in which uninformed opinions are at a premium. A truly ignorant man can easily work himself up into a feverish fury about the public schools, and in a brief article or book can unburden himself of enough righteous indignation to heat a summer hotel in January.

On the other hand, a person who has really learned some- ¶2
thing about the schools is almost hopelessly crippled when it comes to writing genuinely dramatic books and articles. He finds he has to qualify his generalities, and all kinds of awkward facts keep getting in the way of rich, rolling prose and sweeping accusations. For a man who seeks to say something startling about the public schools, a little knowledge is a dangerous thing, and a lot of it is almost an insuperable handicap. It's impossible for an informed person to give easy answers to the hard questions besetting the public schools, yet how can hard answers compete in the literary market place with easy ones? One reason why true educational savants are such notably dull writers is simply that they know too much.

The verbal splendor resulting from recent charges that the ¶3
schools are not teaching reading right, and older charges that they aren't teaching *anything* right, is undeniably exhilarating. Abraham Lincoln is supposed to have said that a man should preach as though he were fighting bees, and I can't help admiring the way critics of the schools have transferred his advice to their line of endeavor. We haven't heard much lately about the evils of Progressive Education—in fact, the very phrase has acquired a nostalgic ring—but there are still a few people around who seem convinced that the public schools are promoting socialism of some kind, or worse. The schools have been called Godless, and their administrators have been widely described as just plain cotton-headed. A good argument can be started almost anywhere over the question of whether there should be federal aid to education. Businessmen voice pathetic complaints that the high-school graduates they hire as secretaries just can't spell, and college professors snort about the qualifications of entering freshmen. The phrase "crisis in education" has become a cliché, used by some to

mean that the schools are incredibly inept, and by others to mean that they are woefully short of money. A visitor to this country would almost inevitably deduce from the headlines that things have never been so tough. As a rather bewildered friend of mine said recently at a PTA meeting, what's going on around here, anyway?

Something for Nothing

¶4 I have an uneasy answer. In the last fifty years, and especially in the last ten years, our nation has gone humanitarian to a great and wonderful degree, but it doesn't yet want to pay for it. The schools have never been anywhere near as good as they are today, but the gap between what they are and what the people want is greater than ever before. Nobody really wants to provide the money, time, and thought necessary for closing that gap—the hope is that it can just be argued away. Most of the controversy over public education stems from a strong desire to get something for nothing.

¶5 To understand the truth of this, it is necessary to have a clear, unsentimental picture of the way the schools were in the past. The idea that we once had marvelous public schools in this nation, and that modern philosophies of education have ruined them, is the most obvious kind of nonsense. As a matter of fact, no nation through all history has ever had good public schools for all its people, or seriously tried to. Really good education for every child is a startling new concept, one of which the United States can be justifiably proud.

¶6 Anyone who doesn't believe this should go to the trouble of consulting records to find just what kind of public schools existed in his own town fifty years ago. What most people would discover is that fifty years ago, city schools were dull and dingy buildings, with classes of forty or more pupils common. Country schools were usually one-room affairs, with children of widely varying age and ability taught at the same time. Few of the teachers fifty years ago had anywhere near as much education of any kind as most teachers today. The elementary school curriculum was pretty much limited to the Three Rs, and the high schools confined themselves to a college-preparatory program. As someone has said, the subjects were optional: the pupil could take them or stay home. The vast majority of the students never went to high school.

Admittedly, there was a certain clarity about the school situ- ¶7
ation fifty years ago that is lacking today. Most high-school graduates could spell quite well, because it was usual for only brilliant students to go to high school at all. There were no remedial reading classes, because those who couldn't read were simply dropped. It was also undeniably true that the great majority of all American children got very little education of any kind. Apparently, people didn't care about that much fifty years ago—there was far less talk about an educational crisis then than there is today. Throughout all history most people of the world had got very little education, so why get excited about it? Of course the public schools were threadbare, and the classes crowded, and the teachers little educated, but they were, after all, charity schools, and it was pretty good to have any free schools at all. Most people who could afford it sent their children to private schools as a matter of course, and they supplemented straight classical programs of education with tutors: the dancing master, the music teacher, the tennis instructor, and all the rest of them. The children of working men got their vocational education by dropping out of school early and becoming apprentices, and no one brooded about their lack of general education. There was no crisis—most people saw nothing whatsoever to worry about.

The Quiet Revolution

The extraordinary thing is that the revolution against this age- ¶8
old concept has been so quiet, and so invisible that many people today aren't aware that it took place. It all happened very simply.

Every year more and more pupils sought admittance to the high schools. A high-school education was part of the American dream, and people in those days dreamed hard and fruitfully. High schools which dropped too many pupils began to get a bad reputation. Public schools are, after all, managed by politically selected school boards, and are designedly sensitive to public pressure. The theories of professional educators did not instigate the great change in public education—it was the demand of the public, insistently voiced through every school board in the land. And what the public wanted was perfectly clear: a high-school education for every American child.

¶9 But all children aren't capable of a straight classical program, plenty of educators objected. Well all right, the answer came: most children are capable of acquiring *some* education, aren't they? Give each child as much as you can. Don't kick them out of school. It's a disgrace to be kicked out of school, and schools shouldn't be in the business of disgracing children. Just keep all the children, and give them as much as possible.

¶10 No one voice, no one proclamation, gave this answer. It was worked out gradually by thousands of day-to-day decisions at countless school-board meetings throughout the country. Professional educators tried to find a way to obey the command. They devised new programs for those who were unable or unwilling to take the college-preparatory work. The sound of the hammer was heard in the land as courses in manual training and mechanics proliferated. For the girls there were "domestic arts," a new phrase for cooking, sewing, and other housewifely chores. And of course, the traditional subjects were still taught—they were taught to more people than ever before. The educators did their best to provide something useful for the slow without handicapping the gifted.

¶11 As school enrollments increased, the demand of the public proved insatiable. At school-board meetings, wistful parents kept showing up to ask for something new. Why not courses in dancing and music and tennis—it didn't seem fair that the children of the poor should be entirely cut off from such things. Shrewd managers of factories appeared to ask that vocational education be tailored to meet their immediate employment needs. People worried about safety asked why courses in driving automobiles couldn't be instituted to help cut down the terrible death toll on highways. Others requested courses in family life to help reduce the divorce rate, and instruction about alcoholic beverages to help reduce alcoholism. The schools were asked to encourage good citizenship, patriotism, and international understanding. And how about moral and spiritual values? Sure, the schools can't teach sectarian religion, but moral and spiritual values can't be entirely left out, can they?

Everybody wanted to add something, and nobody wanted to cut anything out. Certainly no one has ever suggested that the Three Rs are less important than they ever were—in fact, shrill proofs have been offered that in this highly technical age, they are *more* important, and the schools should emphasize them more. More of everything has been the cry—more and yet more! ¶12

Well, we'll try, the educators said. Educators I've met are a remarkably cheerful and resilient crowd. They had to say they'd try, for school administrators are paid to carry out the educational programs voted for by school-board members. They didn't, of course, always succeed. All kinds of new problems loomed before them. ¶13

Say that a town which fifty years ago had a hundred high-school pupils now has a thousand—that's a conservative amount of growth in this nation. How do you find which of those thousand pupils are capable of college-preparatory work, and how do you give it to them without splitting them off from all the others and creating a socially dangerous kind of elite group within each school system? How do you teach a hundred subjects as efficiently as you once taught a dozen? ¶14

¶15 The answers usually involved requests for more money. The public was demanding more of the schools, and inevitably, the schools had to demand more of the public. Here, of course, the controversy began, for the people who asked new courses were under the impression that public education is free. What do you mean, it costs money? What's getting into the schools, anyway? They're spending more and more every year, they're going hog wild! Taxes are going up. Somebody must be getting something out of this. It's socialism, that's what it is. The two great American ideals of good universal education and low taxation collided with a bang—or more accurately, with a long series of bangs which continues to deafen our ears today.

¶16 The people also found that the addition of millions of new high-school students and hundreds of new courses had somehow changed things. Bewildered complaints about the schools mounted. A high-school diploma didn't mean what it used to—it meant simply that the schools had done all they could for the recipient during the prescribed number of years. That, after all, was what the public had asked, wasn't it?

¶17 Yes, but the able children are getting as good an education as they ever did, and millions more of them are getting an opportunity for it, the educators said soothingly. But was it true? Sometimes not. The intent of neither the public nor the educators had changed, but immediate realities sometimes forced the dilution of college-preparatory courses. It takes a lot of money to run a topnotch college-preparatory program in the midst of all the other duties the schools have been called upon to perform. In some schools—indeed, in many schools—children who wish to prepare for college are a real minority group. All kinds of unpredictable things happen. Recently a great many Negroes moved to a large Midwestern city from a rural part of the South where the Negro children had had woefully inadequate schools. The schools in the Midwestern city had to help the Negro children to make up for years of poor preparation, and there was no special appropriation to meet the emergency. No one should be much surprised to find that for a while, the general level of education offered by those schools sank.

Ninety Times More Pupils

What's the matter with public education, people want to know. And at the same time they say, too many American children have bad teeth. Can't the schools provide free dental inspection, and free dental care for those who can't afford treatment? Sure, that's public health, not public education, but few towns have public-health agencies capable of providing free dental inspection or care for so many children. It would be cheaper to do it through the schools than to create special agencies. After all, we can't let the children's teeth rot, can we? Look at the great number of young men rejected by the draft boards during the last war because they had poor teeth. ¶18

What it all amounts to is that the American people rather suddenly subscribed to the ideal of public schools which will do all they possibly can to help each child become as healthy, wealthy, and wise as native endowments permit. It's perhaps a logical ideal for this country—it tends to set a sort of one-generation limit on class barriers, and it certainly glorifies the holiness of the individual, be he poor or rich. I rather doubt that the public thought of such fancy theories. Somehow it just didn't seem fair to allow a child to go to hell in a basket because his parents wouldn't or couldn't get his teeth examined, or because he couldn't learn French. There must be some good in every child, the feeling was—let's do what we can to develop it. So the decision was made, without any real recognition of the fact that something new was being conceived. Having set the goal, the people have apparently forgotten that enormous effort and expense are needed to reach it. They seem to expect the great change in the schools to take place smoothly, without any bother or confusion at all, and certainly without more expense. ¶19

In spite of that, an extraordinary amount of progress has ¶20 been made. In the past seventy-five years or so, high-school enrollments have been multiplied by about ninety. More education is being passed on to more children than ever before in history, as well as more health care, entertainment, and all the rest of it. The advance is perfectly measurable: the average scholastic attainments of soldiers in World War II were tested and found to be much higher than those of the soldiers in World War I. Most suburban schools in America are incredibly good, compared to any sort of school in the past. Many centralized rural schools give the children of farmers an education as good as anyone in the nation can get. The people seem to vacillate between complacency at these gains and exaggerated horror at weaknesses which have not yet been overcome.

¶21 There are still plenty of one-room schools where the wood stoves glow with no sign of progress. What is worse, from the point of view of the number of children involved, big city schools have shown perhaps the least improvement of all. In the big cities, those who can afford it still send their children to private schools, and the middle-class people are rushing to the suburbs. The result is that many big-city schools exist almost exclusively for the children of the very poor. Those are the children who need the best schools, and all too often, they get the worst. Not much is being done about their plight.

Some Children Can Read

¶22 The natural vacillation of the public between complacency and outrage is encouraged by books, news stories, and magazine articles. Books like *The Blackboard Jungle* give a picture of the worst big-city schools, and everybody gets into a tizzy. Articles about Utopian suburban schools, protected by the suburb's own brand of economic segregation, calm things down. Then a book charging that the schools are using the wrong method to teach reading whips things up again. Halfway measures are apparently no good in books of this kind—the one I'm thinking of gives the impression of assuming that *no* children are learning to read properly these days. To parents like myself, whose children learned to read beautifully in the public schools, this sort of thing can be confusing, but there is a wonderful authority in the printed word—I sometimes catch myself wondering if my daughters really can read, even while they're contentedly curled up with books which I at their age found incomprehensible. Critics of this kind have one thing in common: they lead the reader to believe that if one relatively inexpensive step were taken, like the use of more phonics to teach reading, everything would be just dandy in the schools.

This is a perfect example of what I mean by an easy answer to a hard question. Here we have slum schools, with miserable buildings, swollen classes, and disturbed children in need of special care. Here we have an increasing birth rate which demands more and more facilities just to keep the quality of education where it is. Here we have a shortage of teachers resulting from the fact that the birth rate was lowest twenty-five years ago when young teachers were born, and from increasing industrial competition for capable young adults. Here we have more and more demands placed upon the schools every day, and a constantly proliferating list of school duties, with no clear system of priorities governing either the expenditure of money or the pupil's time. And here also we have a book which attracts more public attention than any other book on education recently published, and it appears to give a very simple answer: teach more phonics, and everything will be all right. ¶23

Maybe there is an easy answer, after all—easy to say, if not easy to do. Maybe everything would be all right if the public just realized the nobility of the goal it has set for the schools, and also realized the enormous amount of money, time, and thought needed to achieve it. Maybe everything would be all right if ¶24 everyone realized that the goal of schools capable of wasting no human talent is eminently worth pursuing, and that a nation with the economic power of this one could for the first time in history achieve it.

¶25 The common realization of those things would be the first step. The second step would be for thoughtful people in every state and community to sit down and examine the facts about their schools, hear all relevant opinions, and chart their own course. Programs like that of the National Citizens Commission for the Public Schools and the White House Conference on Education have been designed to encourage that process. The business of getting together to look at facts isn't very dramatic, and often it's downright dull, but it probably is the only way the bright dream of good schools for everyone can be made a reality.

¶26 The job of figuring out how righteous indignation about weaknesses of the schools can be converted into constructive action will not be done by people who wave their arms while criticizing the schools as though they were fighting bees. It will be done by serious-minded people calmly appraising the schools in their own community. It will be done by people who have learned to be patient of differing points of view, and who know how to enlarge areas of agreement, rather than capitalizing on controversy. Somehow an ancient fallacy will have to be righted. *The schools are no good,* many people are saying nowadays, and they imply, *therefore, do not support them.* I certainly agree that many schools are pretty poor now, as they have been always, and I believe that they therefore should be supported doubly. The job of creating schools capable of developing all the abilities of all American children will never be easy, but without any doubt the American people are in their own curious way plodding toward it. There is certainly hope in the fact that for the past fifty years, they have plodded with the speed of hares.

For Greater Insight

1. When Wilson says that the subject (schools) offers marvelous opportunities to a writer tired of research, and that here is a field in which uninformed opinions are still at a premium, is he attacking the writers of other articles, or apologizing for himself? What is the reason for your answer?
2. What is Wilson suggesting when he says that critics of the schools are following Lincoln's advice? Is he being complimentary? Explain your answer.
3. Par. 4 begins with the sentence "I have an uneasy answer." An answer to what? Is the word "uneasy" well chosen? What is Wilson telling us about what he is going to say?
4. What does Wilson mean by "gone humanitarian"? What is the "startling new concept" he refers to?
5. Explain the "certain clarity" that existed fifty years ago, remembering that this means fifty years from the time the author was writing. Were the conditions that created the clarity desirable? Explain.
6. Who was responsible for the quiet revolution? What was remarkable about it? Is it still continuing? Explain. What did the revolution demand?
7. There are critics of schools and educational policies who complain that the schools are taking on more and more of the responsibilities which should be borne by the home. Does Wilson agree? Explain.
8. Par. 23 begins with the sentence, "This is a perfect example of what I mean by an easy answer to a hard question." Explain what the hard question is, and what the easy answer is. Later Wilson says there may be an easy answer. Is it the same answer? What answer is a false answer? Explain.
9. Apply Question 10 on p. 81 to Wilson's essay, substituting Wilson's name for Woodward's. You may want to make some comparisons in your answer.
10. After reading Wilson's essay, do you think you would (1) like to be a teacher, (2) want to be an administrator of a public school system, or (3) try to serve on a school board or school committee? If you say no, explain why. If you say yes, tell what you think you would like to accomplish.

Word Study

at a premium:
righteous indignation:
qualify his *generalities*:
besetting the public schools:
educational *savants*:
incredibly inept:
deduce from the headlines:
has gone *humanitarian*:
subjects were *optional*:
schools were *threadbare*:
instigate the great change:
insistently voiced:
courses . . . *proliferated*:
demand . . . proved *insatiable*:
resilient crowd:
for the *recipient*:
vacillate between *complacency*:
gets into a *tizzy*:
found *incomprehensible*:
system of *priorities*:
hear all *relevant* opinions:
speed of *hares*:

Here Lies Miss Groby

James Thurber

James Thurber was acknowledged for many years to be one of the outstanding humorists in the United States. As a newspaper writer, he began sending contributions to the *New Yorker*, and finally left the newspaper to spend his time writing—and illustrating—his short, keenly observant pieces.

Although his work seems light and almost casual, he was known to have rewritten pieces ten times, and he spent two years on one small book. He collaborated with Elliott Nugent on the play *The Male Animal*, a movie was made from *The Private Life of Walter Mitty*, and several of his sketches were put together on the stage as the *Thurber Carnival.*

This Thurber essay and the one that follows it are both about teachers, although they are written for different purposes and in different styles. As you read these, you should try to discover whether each author is trying to amuse you, to enlighten you, to present a caricature, to pay a sincere tribute, or simply to reminisce.

Miss Groby taught me English composition thirty years ago. It wasn't what prose said that interested Miss Groby; it was the way prose said it. The shape of a sentence crucified on a blackboard (parsed, she called it) brought a light to her eye. She hunted for Topic Sentences and Transitional Sentences the way little girls hunt for white violets in springtime. What she loved ¶1 most of all were Figures of Speech. You remember her. You must have had her, too. Her influence will never die out of the land. A small schoolgirl asked me the other day if I could give her an example of metonymy. (There are several kinds of metonymies, you may recall, but the one that will come to mind most easily, I think, is Container for the Thing Contained.) The vision of Miss Groby came clearly before me when the little girl mentioned the old, familiar word. I saw her sitting at her desk, taking the rubber band off the roll-call cards, running it back upon the fingers of her right hand, and surveying us all separately with quick little henlike turns of her head.

¶2 Here lies Miss Groby, not dead, I think, but put away on a shelf with the other T squares and rulers whose edges had lost their certainty. The fierce light that Miss Groby brought to English literature was the light of Identification. Perhaps, at the end, she could no longer retain the dates of the birth and death of one of the Lake poets. That would have sent her to the principal of the school with her resignation. Or perhaps she could not remember, finally, exactly how many Cornishmen there were who had sworn that Trelawny should not die, or precisely how many springs were left to Housman's lad in which to go about the woodlands to see the cherry hung with snow.

¶3 Verse was one of Miss Groby's delights because there was so much in both its form and content that could be counted. I believe she would have got an enormous thrill out of Wordsworth's famous lines about Lucy if they had been written this way:

A violet by a mossy stone
Half hidden from the eye,
Fair as a star when ninety-eight
Are shining in the sky.

¶4 It is hard for me to believe that Miss Groby ever saw any famous work of literature from far enough away to know what it meant. She was forever climbing up the margins of books and crawling between their lines, hunting for the little gold of phrase, making marks with a pencil. As Palamides hunted the Questing Beast, she hunted the Figure of Speech. She hunted it through the clangorous halls of Shakespeare and through the green forests of Scott.

Night after night, for homework, Miss Groby set us to search- ¶5
ing in "Ivanhoe" and "Julius Caesar" for metaphors, similes, metonymies, apostrophes, personifications, and all the rest. It got so that figures of speech jumped out of the pages at you, obscuring the sense and pattern of the novel or play you were trying to read. "Friends, Romans, countrymen, lend me your ears." Take that, for instance. There is an unusual but perfect example of Container for the Thing Contained. If you read the funeral oration unwarily—that is to say, for its meaning—you might easily miss the C.F.T.T.C. Antony is, of course, not asking for their ears in the sense that he wants them cut off and handed over; he is asking for the function of those ears, for their power to hear, for, in a word, the thing they contain.

At first I began to fear that all the characters in Shakespeare ¶6
and Scott were crazy. They confused cause with effect, the sign for the thing signified, the thing held for the thing holding it. But after a while I began to suspect that it was I myself who was crazy. I would find myself lying awake at night saying over and over, "The thinger for the thing contained." In a great but probably misguided attempt to keep my mind on its hinges, I would stare at the ceiling and try to think of an example of the Thing Contained for the Container. It struck me as odd that Miss Groby had never thought of that inversion. I finally hit on one, which I still remember. If a woman were to grab up a bottle of Grade A and say to her husband, "Get away from me or I'll hit you with the milk," that would be a Thing Contained for the Container. The next day in class I raised my hand and brought my curious discovery straight out before Miss Groby and my astonished schoolmates. I was eager and serious about it and it never occurred

to me that the other children would laugh. They laughed loudly and long. When Miss Groby had quieted them she said to me rather coldly, "That was not really amusing, James." That's the mixed-up kind of thing that happened to me in my teens.

¶7 In later years I came across another excellent example of this figure of speech in a joke long since familiar to people who know vaudeville or burlesque (or radio, for that matter). It goes something like this:

A: What's your head all bandaged up for?
B: I got hit with some tomatoes.
A: How could that bruise you up so bad?
B: These tomatoes were in a can.

¶8 I wonder what Miss Groby would have thought of that one.

¶9 I dream of my old English teacher occasionally. It seems that we are always in Sherwood Forest and that from far away I can hear Robin Hood winding his silver horn.

¶10 "Drat that man for making such a racket on his cornet!" cries Miss Groby. "He scared away a perfectly darling Container for the Thing Contained, a great, big, beautiful one. It leaped right back into its context when that man blew that cornet. It was the most wonderful Container for the Thing Contained I ever saw here in the Forest of Arden."

¶11 "This is Sherwood Forest," I say to her.

¶12 "That doesn't make any difference at all that I can see," she says to me.

¶13 Then I wake up, tossing and moaning.

For Greater Insight

1. It is a little difficult for a teacher to read an essay like this one of Thurber's and then make up questions to ask you about it. Why do you suppose this is so?
2. When Thurber writes "You remember her. You must have had her, too," what does he mean? Is he being literal?

3. Read the two sentences beginning "The vision of Miss Groby . . ." Is this the way our memories really work? Does the phrase "photographic vividness" apply here? Do you have memories of places or people with such vividness? Can you tell of one?
4. In the second paragraph Thurber writes ". . . put away on a shelf with the other T squares and rulers . . ." What does Thurber mean by "other T squares and rulers"? And by "whose edges had lost their certainty"? Is Thurber using figurative language himself?
5. How can you link the adage ". . . couldn't see the forest for the trees" to Thurber's comments about Miss Groby?
6. If you know the story of Palamides and the Questing Beast or of King Pellinore and the Questing Beast in T. H. White's *The Once and Future King*, you will be able to explain Thurber's simile in Par. 4. What is Thurber telling us about Miss Groby?
7. How should you read Antony's funeral oration? Unwarily, as Thurber suggests? Why?
8. Does Thurber's essay point to a possible overemphasis in the study of composition and literature? Explain.
9. To what extent is Thurber "pulling our legs"? And to what extent is he using hyperbole?

Word Study

example of *metonymy*:
the *clangorous* halls:
read . . . *unwarily*:

Will Strunk

E. B. White

When Marchette Chute presented E. B. White the Gold Medal for Essays and Criticism at the Annual Ceremonial of the National Institute of Arts and Letters on May 20, 1960, she said, in part:

"His best gift is himself. He has permitted us to meet a man who is both cheerful and wise, the owner of an uncommon sense that is lit by laughter. When he writes of large subjects he does not make them larger and windier than they are, and when he writes of small things they are never insignificant. He is, in fact, a civilized human being—an order of man that has always been distinguished for its rarity.

"Equally civilized is his use of English, for he has made a difficult art seem easy. One of the reasons he is so helplessly admired by his fellow writers is that he has Chaucer's gift of making his sentences sound like a man talking, that easy conversational tone which is in fact the product of a strong and steady art.

"We are told that the essay is in decline. Quite obviously it is not, and to its most expert and endearing practitioner, E. B. White, the Institute is proud to present its gold medal."

You will enjoy looking for the qualities in White's writing that Miss Chute has so well described.

Turtle Bay, July 15, 1957

¶1 Mosquitoes have arrived with the warm nights, and our bedchamber is their theater under the stars. I have been up and down all night, swinging at them with a face towel dampened at one end to give it authority. This morning I suffer from the light-headedness that comes from no sleep—a sort of drunkenness, very good for writing because all sense of responsibility for what the words say is gone. Yesterday evening my wife showed up with a few yards of netting, and together we knelt and covered the fireplace with an illusion veil. It looks like a bride. (One of our many theories is that mosquitoes come down chimneys.) I bought a couple of adjustable screens at the hardware store on Third Avenue and they are in place in the windows; but the window sashes in this building are so old and irregular that any mosquito except one suffering from elephantiasis has no difficulty walking into the room through the space between sash and screen. (And then there is the even larger opening between upper sash and lower sash when the lower sash is raised to receive the screen—a space that hardly ever occurs to an apartment dweller but must occur to all mosquitoes.) I also bought a very old air-conditioning machine for twenty-five dollars, a great bargain, and I like this machine. It has almost no effect on the atmosphere of the room, merely chipping the edge off the heat, and it makes a loud grinding noise reminiscent of the subway, so that I can snap off the lights, close my eyes, holding the damp towel at the ready, and imagine, with the first stab, that I am riding in the underground and being pricked by pins wielded by angry girls.

Another theory of mine about the Turtle Bay mosquito is that ¶2
he is swept into one's bedroom through the air conditioner, riding the cool indraft as an eagle rides a warm updraft. It is a feeble theory, but a man has to entertain theories if he is to while away the hours of sleeplessness. I wanted to buy some old-fashioned bug spray, and went to the store for that purpose, but when I asked the clerk for a Flit gun and some Flit, he gave me a queer look, as though wondering where I had been keeping myself all these years. "We got something a lot stronger than that," he said, producing a can of stuff that contained chlordane and several

other unmentionable chemicals. I told him I couldn't use it because I was hypersensitive to chlordane. "Gets me right in the liver," I said, throwing a wild glance at him.

¶3 The mornings are the pleasantest times in the apartment, exhaustion having set in, the sated mosquitoes at rest on ceiling and walls, sleeping it off, the room a swirl of tortured bedclothes and abandoned garments, the vines in their full leafiness filtering the hard light of day, the air conditioner silent at last, like the mosquitoes. From Third Avenue comes the sound of the mad builders—American cicadas, out in the noonday sun. In the garden the sparrow chants—a desultory second courtship, a subdued passion, in keeping with the great heat, love in summertime, relaxed and languorous. I shall miss this apartment when it is gone; we are quitting it come fall, to turn ourselves out to pasture. Every so often I make an attempt to simplify my life, burning my books behind me, selling the occasional chair, discarding the accumulated miscellany. I have noticed, though, that these purifications of mine—to which my wife submits with cautious grace—have usually led to even greater complexity in the long pull, and I have no doubt this one will, too, for I don't trust myself in a situation of this sort and suspect that my first act as an old horse will be to set to work improving the pasture. I may even join a pasture-improvement society. The last time I tried to purify myself by fire, I managed to acquire a zoo in the process and am still supporting it and carrying heavy pails of water to the animals, a task that is sometimes beyond my strength.

¶4 A book I have decided not to get rid of is a small one that arrived in the mail not long ago, a gift from a friend in Ithaca. It is *The Elements of Style,* by the late William Strunk, Jr., and it was known on the Cornell campus in my day as "the little book," with the stress on the word "little." I must have once owned a copy, for I took English 8 under Professor Strunk in 1919 and the book was required reading, but my copy presumably failed to survive an early purge. I'd not laid eyes on it in thirtyeight years. Am now delighted to study it again and rediscover its rich deposits of gold.

The Elements of Style was Will Strunk's *parvum opus*, his ¶5
attempt to cut the vast tangle of English rhetoric down to size and write its rules and principles on the head of a pin. Will himself hung the title "little" on the book: he referred to it sardonically and with secret pride as "the *little* book," always giving the word "little" a special twist, as though he were putting a spin on a ball. The title page reveals that the book was privately printed (Ithaca, N.Y.) and that it was copyrighted in 1918 by the author. It is a forty-three-page summation of the case for cleanliness, accuracy, and brevity in the use of English. Its vigor is unimpaired, and for sheer pith I think it probably sets a record that is not likely to be broken. The Cornell University Library has one copy. It had two, but my friend pried one loose and mailed it to me.

The book consists of a short introduction, eight rules of ¶6
usage, ten principles of composition, a few matters of form, a list of words and expressions commonly misused, a list of words commonly misspelled. That's all there is. The rules and principles are in the form of direct commands, Sergeant Strunk snapping orders to his platoon. "Do not join independent clauses with a comma." (Rule 5.) "Do not break sentences in two." (Rule 6.) "Use the active voice." (Rule 11.) "Omit needless words." (Rule 13.) "Avoid a succession of loose sentences." (Rule 14.) "In summaries, keep to one tense." (Rule 17.) Each rule or principle is followed by a short hortatory essay, and the exhortation is followed by, or interlarded with, examples in parallel columns—the true vs. the false, the right vs. the wrong, the timid vs. the bold, the ragged vs. the trim. From every line there peers out at me the puckish face of my professor, his short hair parted neatly in the middle and combed down over his forehead, his eyes blinking incessantly behind steel-rimmed spectacles as though he had just emerged into strong light, his lips nibbling each other like nervous

horses, his smile shuttling to and fro in a carefully edged mustache.

¶7 "Omit needless words!" cries the author on page 21, and into that imperative Will Strunk really put his heart and soul. In the days when I was sitting in his class, he omitted so many needless words, and omitted them so forcibly and with such eagerness and obvious relish, that he often seemed in the position of having short-changed himself, a man left with nothing more to say yet with time to fill, a radio prophet who had outdistanced the clock. Will Strunk got out of this predicament by a simple trick: he uttered every sentence three times. When he delivered his oration on brevity to the class, he leaned forward over his desk, grasped his coat lapels in his hands, and in a husky, conspiratorial voice said, "Rule Thirteen. Omit needless words! Omit needless words! Omit needless words!"

¶8 He was a memorable man, friendly and funny. Under the remembered sting of his kindly lash, I have been trying to omit needless words since 1919, and although there are still many words that cry for omission and the huge task will never be accomplished, it is exciting to me to reread the masterly Strunkian elaboration of this noble theme. It goes:

> Vigorous writing is concise. A sentence should contain no unnecessary words, a paragraph no unnecessary sentences, for the same reason that a drawing should have no unnecessary lines and a machine no unnecessary parts. This requires not that the writer make all his sentences short, or that he avoid all detail and treat his subjects only in outline, but that every world tell.

¶9 There you have a short, valuable essay on the nature and beauty of brevity—sixty-three words that could change the world. Having recovered from his adventure in prolixity (sixty-three words were a lot of words in the tight world of William Strunk, Jr.), the Professor proceeds to give a few quick lessons in pruning. The student learns to cut the deadwood from "This is a subject which . . . ," reducing it to "This subject . . . ," a gain of three words. He learns to trim ". . . used for fuel purposes" down to "used for fuel." He learns that he is being a chatterbox when he says "The question as to whether" and that he should just say "Whether"—a gain of four words out of a possible five.

The Professor devotes a special paragraph to the vile ex- ¶10
pression "the fact that," a phrase that causes him to quiver with revulsion. The expression, he says, should be "revised out of every sentence in which it occurs." But a shadow of gloom seems to hang over the page, and you feel that he knows how hopeless his cause is. I suppose I have written "the fact that" a thousand times in the heat of composition, revised it out maybe five hundred times in the cool aftermath. To be batting only .500 this late in the season, to fail half the time to connect with this fat pitch, saddens me, for it seems a betrayal of the man who showed me how to swing at it and made the swinging seem worth while.

I treasure *The Elements of Style* for its sharp advice, but I ¶11
treasure it even more for the audacity and self-confidence of its author. Will knew where he stood. He was so sure of where he stood, and made his position so clear and so plausible, that his peculiar stance has continued to invigorate me—and, I am sure, thousands of other ex-students—during the years that have intervened since our first encounter. He had a number of likes and dislikes that were almost as whimsical as the choice of a necktie, yet he made them seem utterly convincing. He disliked the word "forceful" and advised us to use "forcible" instead. He felt that the word "clever" was greatly overused; "it is best restricted to ingenuity displayed in small matters." He despised the expression "student body," which he termed gruesome, and made a special trip downtown to the *Alumni News* office one day to protest the expression and suggest that "studentry" be substituted, a coinage of his own which he felt was similar to "citizenry." I am told that the *News* editor was so charmed by the visit, if not by the word, that he ordered the student body buried, never to rise again. "Studentry" has taken its place. It's not much of an im-

provement, but it does sound less cadaverous, and it made Will Strunk quite happy.

¶12 A few weeks ago I noticed a headline in the *Times* about Bonnie Prince Charlie: "CHARLES' TONSILS OUT." Immediately Rule 1 leapt to mind.

> 1. Form the possessive singular of nouns with 's. Follow this rule whatever the final consonant. Thus write,
>
> Charles's friend
> Burns's poems
> the witch's malice.

Clearly Will Strunk had foreseen, as far back as 1918, the dangerous tonsillectomy of a Prince, in which the surgeon removes the tonsils and the *Times* copy desk removes the final "s." He started his book with it. I commend Rule 1 to the *Times* and I trust that Charles's throat, not Charles' throat, is mended.

¶13 Style rules of this sort are, of course, somewhat a matter of individual preference, and even the established rules of grammar are open to challenge. Professor Strunk, although one of the most inflexible and choosy of men, was quick to acknowledge the fallacy of inflexibility and the danger of doctrine.

¶14 "It is an old observation," he wrote, "that the best writers sometimes disregard the rules of rhetoric. When they do so, however, the reader will usually find in the sentence some compensating merit, attained at the cost of the violation. Unless he is certain of doing as well, he will probably do best to follow the rules."

¶15 It is encouraging to see how perfectly a book, even a dusty rulebook, perpetuates and extends the spirit of a man. Will Strunk loved the clear, the brief, the bold, and his book is clear, brief, bold. Boldness is perhaps its chief distinguishing mark. On page 24, explaining one of his parallels, he says, "The left-hand version gives the impression that the writer is undecided or timid; he seems unable or afraid to choose one form of expression and hold to it." And his Rule 12 is "Make definite assertions." That was

Will all over. He scorned the vague, the tame, the colorless, the irresolute. He felt it was worse to be irresolute than to be wrong. I remember a day in class when he leaned far forward in his characteristic pose—the pose of a man about to impart a secret—and croaked, "If you don't know how to pronounce a word, say it loud! If you don't know how to pronounce a word, say it loud!" This comical piece of advice struck me as sound at the time, and I still respect it. Why compound ignorance with inaudibility? Why run and hide?

All through *The Elements of Style* one finds evidences of ¶16
the author's deep sympathy for the reader. Will felt that the reader was in serious trouble most of the time, a man floundering in a swamp, and that it was the duty of anyone attempting to write English to drain this swamp quickly and get his man up on dry ground, or at least throw him a rope.

"The little book" has long since passed into disuse. Will died ¶17
in 1946, and he had retired from teaching several years before that. Longer, lower textbooks are in use in English classes nowadays, I daresay—books with upswept tail fins and automatic verbs. I hope some of them manage to compress as much wisdom into as small a space, manage to come to the point as quickly and illuminate it as amusingly. I think, though, that if I suddenly found myself in the, to me, unthinkable position of facing a class in English usage and style, I would simply lean far out over the desk, clutch my lapels, blink my eyes, and say, "Get the *little* book! Get the *little* book! Get the *little* book!"

P.S. (April 1962). Soon after this piece about Professor Strunk ¶18
appeared in *The New Yorker*, a publisher asked me to revise and amplify *The Elements of Style* in order that it might be reissued. I agreed to do this, and did it; but the job, which should have taken about a month's time, took me a year. I discovered that for all my fine talk I was no match for the parts of speech—

was, in fact, over my depth and in trouble. Not only that, I felt uneasy at posing as an expert on rhetoric, when the truth is I write by ear, always with difficulty and seldom with any exact notion of what is taking place under the hood. Some of the material in the Strunk book proved too much for me, and two or three times during my strange period of confinement I was forced to turn for help to a friend who is a grammarian and could set me straight.

¶19 When the book came out, it managed to get on the best-seller list, where it stayed for a while. The appearance of a style book on hallowed ground was considered a freak of publishing, and a couple of newspapers ran editorials about it, asking what was happening to the world, that people should show interest in English usage. I was as surprised as the next man, but I think I now understand what happened. The Strunk book, which is a "right and wrong" book, arrived on the scene at a time when a wave of reaction was setting in against the permissive school of rhetoric, the Anything Goes school where right and wrong do not exist and there is no foundation all down the line. The little book climbed on this handy wave and rode it in.

¶20 It was during the permissive years that the third edition of Webster's *New International Dictionary* was being put together, along new lines of lexicography, and it was Dr. Gove, the head man, who perhaps expressed the whole thing most succinctly when he remarked that a dictionary "should have no traffic with . . . artificial notions of correctness or superiority. It must be descriptive and not prescriptive." This approach struck many people as chaotic and degenerative, and that's the way it strikes me. Strunk was a fundamentalist; he believed in right and wrong, and so, in the main, do I. Unless someone is willing to entertain notions of superiority, the English language disintegrates, just as a home disintegrates unless someone in the family sets standards of good taste, good conduct, and simple justice.

¶21 One parting note: readers of the first edition of the book were overjoyed to discover that the phrase "the fact that" had slid by me again, landing solidly in the middle of one of my learned dissertations. It has since disappeared, but it had its little day.

For Greater Insight

1. Question 2 on p. 123 refers to the style of Highet's essay. What comment can you make about the style of the first four paragraphs of White's essay?
2. In the third paragraph White describes his "attempt to simplify my life." What is his problem? Have you ever tried to simplify your life? What were the results?
3. The latter part of Par. 6 has a description of Professor Strunk. What is the relation of this to Thurber's description of Miss Groby in the first paragraph of that essay (p. 139)?
4. White says that Strunk "had a number of likes and dislikes . . ." What was White's opinion of these likes and dislikes? Why did he admire Strunk's position?
5. Do Pars. 13 and 14 mean that young writers can forget the rules? What is your interpretation of these two paragraphs?
6. Do you agree or disagree with Strunk's advice about pronunciation? Defend your feeling. Is White making a mild joke, or is he serious?
7. The edition of Strunk's book that White edited uses a portion of the present essay as the introduction. What part do you think White leaves out?
8. What is White's objection to *Webster's Third New International Dictionary*? Why and in what way does White agree with Strunk?

Word Study

suffering from *elephantiasis*:
hypersensitive to chlordane:
sated mosquitoes:
American *cicadas*:
desultory second courtship:
relaxed and *languorous*:
referred to it *sardonically*:
vigor is *unimpaired*:

for sheer *pith*:
short *hortatory* essay:
interlarded with:
the *puckish* face:
adventure in *prolixity*:
quiver with *revulsion*:
for the *audacity*:
continued to *invigorate* me:
almost as *whimsical*:
sound less *cadaverous*:
fallacy of *inflexibility*:
to be *irresolute*:
expressed . . . *succinctly*:
descriptive and not *prescriptive*:
chaotic and *degenerative*:

Stage and Screen

In His Talent, Shakespeare Summoned Up

Kenneth Tynan

This essay and the one which follows it appeared in *Life* in 1964 as part of the magazine's celebration of the four hundredth anniversary of Shakespeare's birth. Its author, Kenneth Tynan, is one of England's foremost drama critics. After a distinguished career as a writer about the theater, he became literary manager of the British National Theatre.

Many writers are able to write vigorously about a subject they are attacking. The writer—drama critic, political observer, social commentator, or what have you—who can write with almost violent force about something he approves of is rather rare. However, Tynan writes an appreciative essay about Sir Laurence Olivier which does have an unusual degree of strength and enthusiasm. Look for this quality as you read, and try to find words and expressions and techniques that Tynan has used to achieve the result.

The title of the essay is unusual, too, and worth puzzling over to make sure you understand it.

Laurence Olivier at his best is what everyone has ever meant by the phrase "a great actor." He has all the big resources: complete physical relaxation; powerful physical magnetism; commanding eyes that are visible from the back of the gallery; superb timing, which means the capacity to make verse swing, and finally the ability to communicate a sense of danger. ¶1

¶2 These are all vital attributes, and you can list them in many orders of importance (Olivier himself regards his eyes as his ace of trumps), but the last attribute is surely the rarest. Watching Olivier, you feel that at any moment he may do something utterly unpredictable—something explosive, unnerving in its emotional nakedness. There is nothing bland in this man. He is complex, moody and turbulent. Deep in his temperament there is a vein of rage that his affable public mask cannot wholly conceal. I once asked Ralph Richardson how he differed, as an actor, from Olivier. He replied: "I haven't got Laurence's splendid fury."

¶3 Fame, which isolates men from all but their colleagues, has enabled Olivier to preserve into his mid-50s the hair-triggered emotional reactions of adolescence. He has never developed the thick protective social skin beneath which most of us hide our more violent or embarrassing emotions. Within him the volcano remains active, the eruption imminent. This is an actor ruled by instinct, not a rational being or a patient arguer or even a competent chairman. And when you ally this intuitive fire with superb technical machinery and a vast knowledge of audience responses, you have something like the theatrical counterpart of the internal combustion engine.

¶4 Out of a sense of duty, Olivier has occasionally tried to play what is insultingly known as "the common man"—the seedy schoolteacher, for instance, in the film *Term of Trial.* He seldom succeeds. That outsize emotional candor cannot help breaking through. The actor bursts the seams of the role and the common man becomes exceptional. That is why Olivier has spent the greater part of his professional life with his trousers off—playing bare-legged or in tights the exceptional characters around whom the playwrights of the past built their tallest tragedies and highest comedies.

¶5 He has acted in many good movies, but seldom at the height of his talent, partly because the reticence of movie acting is awkward for him, but mostly because his performances need to be seen as flowing, consecutive entities, not chopped up into close-ups and long-shots and spread over months of shooting. You cannot make love by instalments, and Olivier's relationship with his audience is that of a skilled but dominating lover. He is one of that select group of performers (the greatest athletes, bullfighters, singers, politicians, ballerinas and vaudeville comedians are some of the others) whose special gift is to be able to exercise fingertip control over the emotions of a large number of people gathered in one place to witness one unique event. He can do other things, of course, but this is what he can do peerlessly and irreplaceably.

The best English actors often come in pairs. A century and ¶6
a half ago we had John Philip Kemble, all dignity and word-music, and the galvanic newcomer Edmund Kean, all earth and fire. People accused Kean of mangling Shakespearean verse, but Coleridge said that when he acted it was like reading Shakespeare by flashes of lightning; and William Hazlitt described Kean's death scene in *Richard III* in a piece of unforgettably dramatic criticism: "He fought like one drunk with wounds: and the attitude in which he stands with his hands stretched out, after his sword is taken from him, had a preternatural and terrific grandeur, as if his will would not be disarmed, and the very phantoms of his despair had a withering power."

In modern terms John Gielgud is Kemble to Olivier's Kean ¶7
—the esthete, as opposed to the animal. "John is claret," as a wine-loving English critic once put it. "And Larry is Burgundy." But the difference between them reminds me more of Edmund Burke's famous essay on the Sublime and Beautiful. According to Burke's definition, the Beautiful (*i.e.*, Gielgud) is that which is shapely, harmonious and pleasing; while the Sublime (*i.e.*, Olivier) is irregular and awe-inspiring, like thunderstorms and mountain peaks. [A dozen years ago it looked as if a similar

conflict might be brewing between Paul Scofield, the poet, and Richard Burton, the peasant; but Burton went filmwards, and battle was never joined.] Incidentally, one of Olivier's most cherished possessions is the sword that Kean used in *Richard III*. It was a gift from Gielgud, inscribed with characteristic generosity "To the greatest Richard III since Kean."

¶8 Young actors trust and venerate Gielgud—but the man they mostly copy is Olivier. What could be more seductive than his Richard, his Macbeth, his Henry V, his Oedipus, his Coriolanus —acting explosions that opened up such new horizons for each of these parts that we felt we had never truly seen them before. His mimics are countless, but they always miss his essence.

¶9 One half of Olivier loves ceremony, hierarchy and ritual, and I suspect that he would not mind being the first theatrical peer. The other half loves eccentricity—he relishes the abnormal, the antisocial, the offbeat, the bizarre. You could see this split last October in his direction of *Hamlet*, the inaugural production of the National Theatre. It combined—not always too happily —an atmosphere of fanfare and glamor with sharp, unglamorous insights into quirks of character. Ophelia, for instance, behaved in her mad scenes like a suicidal nymphomaniac.

¶10 The two sides of Olivier's own nature met and married most memorably 20 years ago in one supreme coalition: he played a raging psychotic who adored pomp and circumstance—Richard III, multiple murderer and anointed king.

¶11 It wasn't easy to persuade him to play Othello. He was well aware, when we first discussed it, that no English actor in this century had succeeded in the part. The play, he said, belonged to Iago, who could always make the Moor look a credulous idiot —and he spoke with authority, since he had played Iago to Ralph Richardson's Othello in 1938. "If I take it on," he said, "I don't want a witty, Machiavellian Iago. I want a solid, honest-to-god NCO." The director, John Dexter, agreed with this approach, and Olivier thereupon accepted the part.

Soon afterwards I told the news to Orson Welles, himself a former Othello, who expressed an instant doubt. "Larry's a natural tenor," he rumbled, "and Othello's a natural baritone." I passed this opinion on to Olivier. There followed weeks of daily voice lessons that throbbed through the plywood walls of the National Theatre offices. When the cast assembled for the first rehearsal of *Othello*, Olivier's voice was an octave deeper than any of us had ever heard it. ¶12

That first read-through was a shattering experience. Normally on these occasions the actors do not exert themselves. They sit in a circle and mumble, more concerned with getting to know one another than with giving a performance. Into this polite gathering Olivier tossed a hand grenade. He delivered a fantastic, full-volume display that scorched one's ears, serving final notice on everyone present that the hero, storm center and focal point of the play, was the man named in the title. ¶13

Seated, bespectacled and lounge-suited, he fell on the text like a tiger. This was not a noble "civilized" Othello but a proud black despot, aflame with self-regard. So far from letting Iago manipulate him, he manipulated Iago, treating him almost as a kind of court jester. Such arrogance cried out for deflation. ¶14

There are moral flaws in every other Shakespearean hero, but Othello is traditionally held to be exempt. Olivier's reading made us realize that tradition might be wrong, that Othello was flawed with the sin of narcissistic pride. At the power of his voice, the windows shook and my scalp tingled. A natural force had entered the room, stark and harsh, with vowel sounds as subtly alien as Kwame Nkrumah's. And the cast listened, poleaxed. ¶15

To put it baldly, they were learning what it meant to be faced with a great classical actor in full spate, one whose vocal resources were so immense that by every new inflection he could point the way to a whole new interpretation. Every speech, for ¶16

Olivier, is like a mass of marble at which the sculptor chips until its essential form and meaning are revealed.

¶17 In the last 15 years Olivier has played 20 stage parts, ancient and modern. During the same period Marlon Brando, once, potentially, an American Olivier, has not appeared on stage at all. Brando had the quality; but quantity is the practice that makes quality perfect.

¶18 And practice which means discipline, devotion and the relentless nourishing of one's natural gifts is what keeps Olivier secure on his pedestal as the greatest actor on the stages of the western world.

For Greater Insight

1. How would each of the "big resources" help a person be a successful actor?
2. What does Tynan mean by "to make verse swing"? Substitute another word for "swing"; can you find one which does as much for the sentence?
3. Note, in the third paragraph, that Tynan says Olivier has "never developed the thick protective skin . . ." What does he mean by this sentence? Keep the point in mind when you read Olivier's own words in the next essay. Should adolescents be insulted or complimented by the preceding sentence? Why?
4. Is Tynan's simile of the internal combustion engine effective? Would *explosive shell* have been as good? *Bomb*? *Dynamite*? Why?
5. Explain why Olivier's acting in movies has been "seldom at the height of his talent" (Par. 5). As this text is being prepared, the United States is experiencing a resurgence of interest in the live stage. Does anything in this same paragraph suggest to you one reason for the return of enthusiasm for the legitimate theater as contrasted with movies?
6. In Pars. 6 and 7 Tynan uses comparison and contrast to clarify and strengthen a point. What—or whom—is he comparing and contrasting? Does he weaken one while strengthening the other? How many pairs of people are there? What are the qualities of each person?

7. What is an NCO? You may have to talk with a person with military experience, but you should find out the status and function of the NCO in the hierarchy of the military. What sort of person would a "solid, honest-to-god NCO" be?
8. According to Tynan, what is necessary for an actor so that he may attain and keep a dominant position in the theater?
9. Tynan's writing is stimulating and exciting to read because, like Olivier, he is unpredictable. Without warning, he introduces a thought which is provocative, and he likes to shock. One such provocative fragment is ". . . but quantity is the practice which makes quality perfect." Can you find others?
10. If you have never seen Olivier on the stage or in a movie, try to listen to the recording of his *Henry V*, especially the speech beginning "Once more unto the breach, dear friends, once more!" As you listen, try to say the words at the same speed and with the same volume.

Word Study

vital *attribute*:
moody and *turbulent*:
affable public mask:
this *intuitive* fire:
theatrical *counterpart*:
emotional candor:
reticence of movie acting:
consecutive entities:
do *peerlessly* and *irreplaceably*:
galvanic newcomer:
preternatural and terrific *grandeur*:
venerate Gielgud:
more *seductive*:
loves ceremony, *hierarchy*, and *ritual*:
relishes . . . the *bizarre*:
one supreme *coalition*:
a raging *psychotic*:
proud black *despot*:
sin of *narcissistic* pride:
cast listened, *poleaxed*:
in full *spate*:

The Great Sir Laurence

Richard Meryman

This essay is attributed to Richard Meryman, an editor of *Life*, but the words are Sir Laurence's. Mr. Meryman recorded on tape a series of interviews with Sir Laurence, had the material typed, and then edited it, so that what you will read will be Sir Laurence's statements, in a kind of oral essay edited and shaped by Mr. Meryman.

If you had not known of the technique used in preparing the essay, you would probably have guessed something of the sort. While you read, try to locate language that is conversational in tone. How is it different from the language of other essays? How would you have guessed the facts of its preparation?

¶1 God Almighty, I don't know why I chose to do Othello. It is, of course, a challenge, but I don't know who's challenging me. I was saying the other day, I think that Shakespeare and Richard Burbage (probably the original Hamlet, Lear, Othello) got drunk one night and Burbage said, "I can play *anything* you write, *anything* at all." And Shakespeare said, "*Right,* I'll *fix* you, boy!" and I think he then wrote *Othello* for him.

¶2 For one thing, it is a very badly designed role. There are too many climaxes. In the middle act there is the "like to the Pontic Sea" and the "farewell the plumed troops" speeches and all that—that's wonderful, that's very top. Then soon you've got to have a fit—roar and rant, say all sorts of things, like I will tear her into pieces, I will chop her up into messes—all beckoning you on to scream your utmost. In the last scene, you kill Desdemona and that's a big top—followed by two, or three, tremendous outbursts in a very short space of time. If you have too many outbursts, the audience begins to scratch behind the ears.

I'm working on the assumption that Othello's first reaction ¶3
to Iago is, "Come on, I know you're after Cassio's lieutenancy and I'll get the truth out of you." This starts Othello on a step above Iago and means he isn't pulled by the nose from the first word on. But in getting the truth Othello trips himself up, becomes jealous without knowing how it began, and goes over the edge.

There are roughly two types of Iago. One is the cunning, ¶4
Renaissance villain and the other is the noncommissioned officer type. We believe in the NCO type. He's a stolid sort you would not suspect of such guile, so Othello does not look so absurdly gullible and unbelievable and untragic to the modern audience.

Though I played Iago many years ago, I didn't understand ¶5
the part till I'd been in the service during the war. I think when somebody gets a half stripe more than you, your soul can get bitten right into with bitterness and envy. And I felt it myself. I was serving on a Royal Navy air station near Winchester. There was an officer who got this half stripe over me and decided to give me a ride. And he would say, "And how is our film star today?" You know. It began to get me so that I couldn't sleep at night.

Sometimes, in his moods of affluence, he would ask me to ¶6
his farm so I might meet his wife. I'd always refuse the offer. One day I was walking across the aerodrome and I was beginning to say, "How can I get this bastard? How can I *get* this bastard? How can I get him? How can I really kill him?" And I stopped right dead and said to myself, "Of course! He's mar-

ried!" I saw the whole thing: that I could easily have gone to this fellow's farm, met his wife. Then one day I would go without being asked, and he would come upon me with his wife. I would get up rather hastily or something like that, you see, and start him being terribly unhappy. And I suddenly said, "Wow, wow, watch out! Iago!"

¶7 Othello has pretty much always been played as a truly noble man who was overjealous, overgullible. But the director, John Dexter, and I have come together on the idea that he was only a goodish fellow who had merely fixed the earmark of nobility upon himself. And the tragic fissure which destroys him is self-delusion. In the scene with the Senate, when he tells the story of the way he wooed Desdemona, he is obviously absolutely in love with himself, and thinks he is impervious to pride, or impatience, or ill-temper—to all ordinary passions.

¶8 Of course, it is this self-image which makes him so vulnerable to Iago's cunning—plus that he is a savage man—not on account of his color; I don't mean that. He is an erstwhile pagan who abandons Christianity in one of the tirade scenes with Iago. He explores all sorts of hellish caverns of jealousy with Iago. And Othello has that animal wish to find guilty the thing he loves—really one of the temptations. And murder is a temptation in everybody.

¶9 As in all my parts, I won't feel the green light for Othello until I know exactly how to look and sound. I think I'm beginning to sound all right with the slightly careful way of speaking of a Moor who didn't speak Venetian naturally. I'm sure he must have a deeper voice than I'm afraid I can get—a bass part, a sound that should be dark violet, velvet stuff.

¶10 He's always got to look very strong—stand like a strong man stands, with that sort of ease, probably straight-backed, straight-necked. I'm sure that Othello's very graceful. I don't know why I'm so sure, but I am. . . . I haven't found the fellow's walk yet. Of course he should walk like a soft, black leopard.

Creating a Role

In Shakespeare I always try to reassure the audience initially that they are not going to see some grotesque, outsized dimension of something which they can't understand or sympathize with. If you have succeeded in the initial moments, either by a very strong stamp of characterization so they recognize you as a real guy, or by a quiet approach—then I think there's no end to where you can lead them in size of acting a little later in the evening. God knows, you have to be enormously big as *Othello.* It has to be big stuff. ¶11

On the other hand, self-indulgence—getting carried away—is such a very great, common pitfall for an actor. . . . I don't care how big the acting is, how loud you're roaring, how stridently you're screaming—it must never be absolutely quite at the top of your voice. If you hit the ceiling, then the audience can suddenly see the measure of you. Suddenly you look weak instead of strong—and they think, "Oh my, he is straining himself, isn't he?" ¶12

During rehearsals I try things out very extravagantly—ways of using my hands, my eyes, my body. It's a kind of self-flagellation that I've given myself practically all my life—early grasping this nettle of making a fool of myself. The company learns right away how embarrassing it's going to be and I save a hell of a lot of time. If you're frightened of making a fool of yourself, if you start so subtly and so cozily, just giving little impressions—you have to leap a frightful icy hurdle before you really plunge out and do a scene in a big fashion. ¶13

So you skate about, just letting things happen. You listen to yourself, look at yourself—not too savagely at first, otherwise you get tied up into a knot—feeling so god awful you can't go on. Often an accident happens, often a turn of pose and a gesture and a stance and a position, an attitude—suddenly you say "Well, that's the man: I feel it is. That's him." ¶14

¶15 Sometimes you see somebody on a bus or on a train and think, "I'd like to get him into the performance, the way he does his hair, the way he keeps stroking his beard in that funny way or he keeps dusting his lap, or something." And you read things into the reasons for such mannerisms and without knowing it, if you're an actor, you absorb all these things all the time.

¶16 So, my way of creating a character isn't the one so much in vogue these days. I'm a very external actor. External characteristics to me are a shelter—a refuge from having nothing to feel, from finding yourself standing on the stage with just lines to say, without a helpful indication of how to treat them or how to move. I construct my portrait from the outside with little techniques, ideas, images—and once the portrait becomes real, it starts traveling inwards

¶17 Acting is illusion, as much illusion as magic is—and not so much a matter of *being* real. I mean, I would probably shock Lee Strasberg. I remember going to see the Actors Studio and it seemed to me that the Method actors are entirely preoccupied with feeling real to *themselves* instead of creating the *illusion* of reality. They want the absolute kernel of a character before starting to express anything. I decided, perhaps rather hurriedly, that this was wonderful training for film acting, where the camera and microphone can come right in and get your reality —the tiniest shade of your tone of voice, every little twitch of expression. But our problem on stage is to convey an illusion 50 or more yards away. That's where the big stretch comes—that's where imagination, where know-how above and beyond inner reality comes in. But I don't see that it matters where you start, inside or out, as long as the illusion ends up the same.

¶18 I think there is a difference between me and any new school of actors. Look, it stands to reason. I'm 56. If the new generation was required to do what I do, they would have extreme difficulty, because it takes a lot of time to arrive at.

If the new school were to try to teach me their job, I think they would find they could do it quite quickly because I'm extremely versed in my job. The material that is done by these new schools is something which admittedly I don't often do. But, I mean, I don't despair of being as natural as anybody in the world.

I've never felt old fashioned. Like everybody, to myself, inside, I am 17 with red lips. "Old fashioned" is a term of abuse, let's face it. But a lot of drama—attitudes toward the theater, techniques, methods—are not old fashioned so much as out of fashion. ¶19

You see, in an age such as this, in which nostalgia is about the least popular of one's prerogatives, you'd better not be old fashioned—because they don't come and see the old darling to listen to him out of sentiment. I've made great efforts to keep changing, come up with a surprise every so often. Whether I'm changing with the times or not, I wouldn't quite know—being part of them. ¶20

One of the most unnerving things that can happen to an actor on stage is something we call "drying up." It happens when you know a thing too well. When I played Richard III on and off for about four years, toward the end, lines would suddenly mean nothing to me—I'd never heard them in my life, and I'd sort of tail off. I used to rather pride myself on making up lines that would still sound like Shakespeare to cover up. ¶21

I have a horror of a performance becoming mechanical, automatic, and I watch like a hawk for signs of it. Then we try to find fresh lines, fresh ideas and emotions—new deliveries to make them spontaneous again. When you play your role just a little differently, it surprises your fellow actors and keeps them alive. There is a time, in *Uncle Vanya* when Joanie [his wife, Joan Plowright], playing Sonya, is distraught that I am drinking vodka all through this scene. She watches me keep pouring it down and at a certain time I pick my glass up and go to the ¶22 cupboard to get more. At that moment she offers me some cheese to try and stop me drinking. Now I vary the timing of my move so that she has to watch very carefully. It keeps her in the reality of the situation. This gets our juices going.

Acting as a Career

¶23 Acting is an almost childish wish, isn't it? Pretend to be somebody else. . . . I suppose that's the original impulse of acting. That's perhaps why it does become more difficult as you get on in years. I think acting is a young enthusiasm. The childish excitement of it, the glamor disappears very early. And then comes the effort to improve yourself, to carve yourself into different shapes, to be successful—to be famous.

¶24 Once you get to the top, the load of staying there is almost superhuman. And you feel so tired sometimes of the responsibility—the various efforts that have to be made not to let yourself down, not to let other people down, not to let the theater in general down. And there are periods in actors' lives when they fall completely out of tune with their art. Acting seems behind a brick wall and you can't resist going on battering your head against it. I've felt it myself and seen it happen to my friends. It's a sort of lurking nightmare.

¶25 But, you know, an artist—I know that's a bad word to use—is not supposed to find satisfaction in his work. There's too much tears and bloody sweat in it. . . . Intense pumping up of the feelings—it's very hard work. If you're not in the mood, you have to employ all the technique you've ever learnt in order to achieve a certain voltage very quickly.

¶26 But I'm sure if I didn't act for a year, I would be utterly miserable. I'm sure I would. It's hard to describe the workings of work within you. It's like a yoke one is used to, a harness one is used to. But enjoying? I ask the race horse if he enjoys it. I don't know.

When I played Antony in *Antony and Cleopatra* I had a very rare experience at one matinee, and I wrote down in my diary—I came upon it the other day—"enjoyed the performance this afternoon." It was such a rarity. All I ever write in my diary is—well—things like "daughter born today." ¶27

Hollywood

There certainly has been more satisfaction for me in my life than if I had remained a Hollywood actor and become as eminent even as Cary Grant. I don't think that I would have found so much to interest me in dear beloved Cary's life as I have found in my own. But that's merely my particular taste. The film, you see, is not the actor's medium, it's the director's. He is the great man of mystery, the witch doctor. He needn't answer any questions, just says, "Wait and see." I've only directed four films, and it's the nearest I have ever felt to being creative. ¶28

But it was a long time before I got to adore the film world. I hated it, and snobbishly did movie acting for the money. ¶29

When I came to grips with William Wyler, who directed *Wuthering Heights*, I was highfalutin, obstinate—fresh out of the Old Vic with all sorts of thoughts of high dimensions of acting, which Willy Wyler, with his rough method—I may say, his cruelly critical method—had no patience with at all—and quite rightly. ¶30

But Wyler really, through all our quarrels, gave me food for thought. When I told him you couldn't do Shakespeare on the screen, that it's too anemic a medium—you know, the shot is too great for the cannon—of course Willy got slightly wild at having his beautiful medium called anemic. He said, "Look, you can do anything in this medium, anything at all. You've just got to be clever enough to find out how, that's all." And that stuck. And so when, about five years later, the opportunity came to direct and produce and act in *Henry V*, I thought of that; ¶31

I thought of it a lot. I sort of became fired with the challenge of that. Sure enough, there *is* a way of doing Shakespeare on film.

Doing Shakespeare

¶32 When first I played Shakespeare, I was told by the critics that I would never be able to do it, that I wasn't a Shakespearean actor. I was told I couldn't speak verse. That worried me terribly, because ever since I was a boy I felt I spoke Shakespeare like a native. But the lyrical verse-speaking of that time was against the nature of my central feeling about acting, which is reality. I spent a great deal of my early life fighting the lyrical tendencies of my colleagues. The music is only the top half of Shakespeare. There's a bottom half to be observed—animalism, earth, actualities and all that. And I felt so strongly about it that I never learned the lyrical verse-speaking myself.

¶33 There's no such thing as Shakespeare training anymore. I mean, people don't play their little Henry V's until they're considered to be ready to do it. Whereas all of my generation, we came to the Old Vic in London and could have a jolly bash at Macbeth when we were about 27 years old, or younger.

¶34 Today the young actors don't play Shakespeare at all very much, do they? I mean, perhaps they could. Albert Finney understudied me in *Coriolanus* and he went on for me, and he was very good. But they shouldn't have to wait until they're film stars, like dear Marlon, before they play Antony, you know. It's not right that you should risk your neck in the stuff when you've achieved such a height of fame.

¶35 There's such a critical criterion of prejudice loaded up against anybody taking on a huge Shakespearean part. They've teed themselves up into a clay-pigeonlike position. The critics —everybody who sees Hamlet or any great classical role—says, "All right, let us see what he can do with *this*."

¶36 Shakespeare has been, I suppose, the criterion for hundreds of years. It's been the reputation of big acting. Shakespeare is hard to understand. It's hard to do. The characters are usually supermen or kings, great tragic queens. To make them real requires a certain pitch, a level of artistry due to training or an extraordinarily rare instinct.

In these terribly realistic times of drama, that's the actors' great complaint about such roles—that they can't feel real. As I've said, the art of acting isn't always to do with that, which is very hard for people to understand. ¶37

The Public

Oh, I think that there's an awful lot the public doesn't understand about acting. I mean, I think they understand baseball much better than they understand acting. Naturally their sympathies follow the role. I mean, if a man is playing a nasty fellow, no audience in the world likes him so much as they like the man playing the nice fellow—and even more the funny fellow. This is nourished by the trend for type casting. My life's ambition has been to lead the public toward an appreciation of acting, so that they will come not only to see the play but to watch acting for acting's sake. In the 18th and 19th centuries, audiences knew the plays in their sleep. But they came in to see Mr. Kean or Mr. Macready or Mr. Garrick or somebody like that, or Mr. Booth, or Mr. Forest. ¶38

To engage the audience's attention more to acting, I went into theater-in-the-round—tried that picture frame. I asked Chris Plummer what it was like, and I remember I made him laugh. He said, "You can't lie." And I said, "My God, what are we going to do?" ¶39

I love the masses like every good fellow should. But a character in Arnold Wesker's play *Roots* said what I fear about the public's taste—"You are third rate because you want to be third rate, and that's the truth of it." So much of the entertainment, ¶40 so many of the newspapers, so much of what you see on the idiot box—all prove this. It's deliberately cheap because the public gobbles it up, but I still have faith that the public will like better things if they're provided.

¶41 These are reasons why I've made the British National Theatre my whole life—and why I certainly think there should be a United States national theater. I think it should develop and grow and have children. It should sprout state theaters in Detroit and Los Angeles, Cincinnati and Indianapolis, everywhere. Every state should have its theater that it's proud of and takes a great interest in. Texas should be wildly jealous of the Missouri state theater! Then we shall get schools of acting and all of your acting in TV, in films, everywhere, will be of a higher standard.

¶42 For God's sake, is acting not as important as football? The theater is the initial glamorizer of thought. It sugarcoats the pill of thought more than any form of teaching.

¶43 I daresay that artistry in acting lies somewhere in the relationship with the audience. Between an actor and a spectator wanting to be entertained, there can be a kind of invisible ray. It's like a string of a bow or a harp or a violin, upon which you can play if you're clever enough. That is the moment of artistry to an actor. . . . This all has something to do with love, I think. . . .

¶44 I finally discovered this for myself soon after the Admiralty —with almost shaming lack of reluctance—released Ralph Richardson and myself in 1944 to start up the new Old Vic. The first opening we had was in Manchester in *Arms and the Man.* Ralphie was playing the principal part of Bluntschli. I was playing what was considered the secondary and extremely difficult and rather lousy part of Sergius. I knew I wasn't good in it. I was in my habitual relationship with the critics. I'd always hated them. And for the most part I'd felt antagonistic toward audiences;

I felt I was a good actor and I was in a stupid, wretched state of frustration.

The day after we opened, I went down to the theater with Ralph to collect letters. On the way back he bought a newspaper and I took a look over his shoulder and it said, "Mr. Ralph Richardson was brilliant as Bluntschli. Mr. Laurence Olivier, on the other hand—" And I thought, "I'm going back to the Navy. I just won't take this any more. I can't stick it." ¶45

That evening Tyrone Guthrie—who was our chief administrator for some years—and I walked back to the hotel and he looked down at me from his great height and said, "Liked your performance very much." And I said, "Oh, thanks." And he said, "Do you enjoy it?" And I said, "Are you out of your mind? How can anybody enjoy that idiotic, pantomimic, absurd character?" He looked down at me, as I say, from his great height, and he said, "Well, of course, if you don't *love* Sergius, you'll never be any good in the role, will you?" ¶46

Well, stretch that around a bit, that idea, and you get a young man who had never thought of loving an audience. . . . This may sound sentimental. All right. Everybody can sneer if they want, but it actually made the entire difference to my whole life. I'm very sorry but it is absolutely true. The key word is "love." ¶47

Only a couple of weeks later I finally felt the proper rapport between myself, the work, the critics, and the audience—all as a single entity. And that was 19 years after I first went on stage Jan. 1, 1925. It happened after this rather lucky throw of the dice, apparently on the first night of *Richard III*. I had gone at it in the old way, bashing along and hoping for the best, not knowing if I'd get good criticisms or not. ¶48

But the very next afternoon, when I came on the stage I knew that it had happened. I entered downstage left, through a door which had an iron release catch on it. I used to like to make the noise of "clack" with the latch. And as I turned round ¶49 to start the opening soliloquy, this thing I simply felt. I felt it and for the first time I was buoyed up on the top of a wave provided by the audience—a different feeling than I'd ever had before. And it went to my head to such an extent, I was in the flash of a second so utterly, completely, differently confident from what I had ever felt before, so *conceited* suddenly—that I didn't even bother to do my limp very well as I went across the stage.

¶50 Once you have felt that way, you are sort of inoculated with something. It would take a lot of failure to dishearten you completely and utterly to the same creature that you were before.

¶51 I do want to belie an impression I may have been giving. The most vital factor in acting is humility towards the work—that's one of the bloody awful problems. An equally vital factor is confidence. I'm sure that's why acting goes wrong so often—this is such a very difficult equation to make.

¶52 And there are things about any art—anything intuitive or instinctive—which you probably can't explain to anybody correctly. I remember sympathizing very much with—I think it was Margot Fonteyn. Somebody said to her, "Oh, please explain what it is you are doing in that ballet." She answered, "I explained while I was doing it. At least if I didn't, I'm sorry."

¶53 It is the same for me. Frankly I'm terrified of being taken for an oracle for fear I might change my mind. When I'm asked about acting, ultimately I would have to answer exactly as Margot did.

For Greater Insight

1. The conversational tone and style make this a very different sort of essay, and create some problems as Olivier's mind leaps from idea to idea. For example, what is the relationship between the ideas of the second paragraph and those of the twelfth? Why is *Othello* difficult, and what must an actor avoid? Can he avoid it in *Othello*? Explain.

2. In a number of paragraphs Olivier tells how he approaches or develops a characterization. Try to pick out details and put them together into an explanation of his method.
3. In Par. 13 of Olivier's essay and in Pars. 13 and 14 of Tynan's the subject is the same. How did Olivier behave, and why?
4. What does Olivier mean by ". . . inside, I am 17 with red lips." Has this feeling been a factor in his success? Why?
5. In Pars. 21 and 22 Olivier speaks of two experiences he dreads. Explain both, and what he does to avoid them. Are you surprised by his feeling about either of the situations he describes? Why or why not?
6. Is there any relation between Tynan's comment about Marlon Brando (Par. 17, p. 162) and Olivier's Pars. 23–27? Explain your answer.
7. What does Olivier mean by "lyrical verse-speaking"? Can you see any possible relationship between the feeling of distaste some people have for Shakespeare and what Olivier says in Par. 32? What are "the top and bottom half of Shakespeare"? Which would have the greater appeal for most people?
8. What reasons does Olivier give for thinking that the public's taste is third-rate?
9. The British National Theatre is government-financed. Why does Olivier think the United States should have such an organization? What might some of the results be?
10. What are the meaning and significance of "It [the theater] sugar-coats the pill of thought more than any form of teaching?"
11. Follow the advice Olivier gives in Par. 47—that is, "stretch that around a bit"—and see if, stretched, the idea doesn't apply to fields other than acting. What is your comment? How would you explain ". . . *love* Sergius . . ."?
12. Explain the passage that tells what Margot Fonteyn, the internationally known ballerina, said. Had she failed, or had the "somebody" who requested the explanation? What does Olivier try to do in his acting?

Word Study

roar and *rant*:
suspect of such *guile*:
so absurdly *gullible*:

tragic *fissure*:
impervious to pride:
makes him so *vulnerable*:
an *erstwhile pagan*:
the *tirade* scene:
grotesque, outsized dimension:
how *stridently* you're screaming:
a kind of *self-flagellation*:
grasping this *nettle*:
acting is *illusion*:
kernel of a character:
nostalgia:
prerogatives:
Joanie . . . is *distraught*:
I was *highfalutin*:
too *anemic* a medium:
lyrical verse-speaking:
a *jolly bash* at Macbeth:
critical *criterion* of prejudice:
clay-pigeon-like position:
the initial *glamorizer*:
to *belie* an impression:

Comedy's Greatest Era

James Agee

James Agee (1909–1955) was a reviewer, a novelist, a poet, an essayist, and a scriptwriter. He wrote film reviews for *Time* and *The Nation*, the Pulitzer-Prize-winning novel *A Death in the Family*, the novella *Morning Watch*, a book of poems, *Permit Me Voyage*, and several movie scripts, including *The African Queen*.

"Comedy's Greatest Era" appeared in *Life* on September 5, 1949, and drew one of the heaviest reader responses in the magazine's history. *Life* itself refers to the essay as "one of the most famous of *Life*'s articles."

The consensus was that Agee's early death deprived America of a sensitive, forceful, and highly effective writer whose future had looked even brighter than his past.

In the language of screen comedians four of the main grades of laugh are the titter, the yowl, the bellylaugh and the boffo. The titter is just a titter. The yowl is a runaway titter. Anyone who has ever had the pleasure knows all about a bellylaugh. The boffo is the laugh that kills. An ideally good gag, perfectly constructed and played, would bring the victim up this ladder of laughs by cruelly controlled degrees to the top rung, and would then proceed to wobble, shake, wave and brandish the ladder until he groaned for mercy. Then, after the shortest possible time ¶1 out for recuperation, he would feel the first wicked tickling of the comedian's whip once more and start up a new ladder.

¶2 The reader can get a fair enough idea of the current state of screen comedy by asking himself how long it has been since he has had that treatment. The best of comedies these days hand out plenty of titters and once in a while it is possible to achieve a yowl without overstraining. Even those who have never seen anything better must occasionally have the feeling, as they watch the current run or, rather, trickle of screen comedy, that they are having to make a little cause for laughter go an awfully long way. And anyone who has watched screen comedy over the past ten or fifteen years is bound to realize that it has quietly but steadily deteriorated. As for those happy atavists who remember silent comedy in its heyday and the bellylaughs and boffos that went with it, they have something close to an absolute standard by which to measure the deterioration.

¶3 When a modern comedian gets hit on the head, for example, the most he is apt to do is look sleepy. When a silent comedian got hit on the head he seldom let it go so flatly. He realized a broad license, and a ruthless discipline within that license. It was his business to be as funny as possible physically, without the help or hindrance of words. So he gave us a figure of speech, or rather of vision, for loss of consciousness. In other words he gave us a poem, a kind of poem, moreover, that everybody understands. The least he might do was to straighten up stiff as a plank and fall over backward with such skill that his whole length seemed to slap the floor at the same instant. Or he might make a cadenza of it—look vague, smile like an angel, roll up his eyes, lace his fingers, thrust his hands palms downward as far as they would go, hunch his shoulders, rise on tiptoe, prance ecstatically in narrowing circles until, with tallow knees, he sank down the vortex of his dizziness to the floor, and there signified nirvana by kicking his heels twice, like a swimming frog.

¶4 Startled by a cop, this same comedian might grab his hatbrim with both hands and yank it down over his ears, jump high in the air, come to earth in a split violent enough to telescope his spine, spring thence into a coattail-flattening sprint and dwindle at rocket speed to the size of a gnat along the grand, forlorn perspective of some lazy back boulevard.

Those are fine clichés from the language of silent comedy in its infancy. The man who could handle them properly combined several of the more difficult accomplishments of the acrobat, the dancer, the clown and the mime. Some very gifted comedians, unforgettably Ben Turpin, had an immense vocabulary of these clichés and were in part so lovable because they were deep conservative classicists and never tried to break away from them. The still more gifted men, of course, simplified and invented, finding out new and much deeper uses for the idiom. They learned to show emotion through it, and comic psychology, more eloquently than most language has ever managed to, and they discovered beauties of comic motion which are hopelessly beyond reach of words. ¶5

It is hard to find a theater these days where a comedy is playing; in the days of the silents it was equally hard to find a theater which was not showing one. The laughs today are pitifully few, far between, shallow, quiet and short. They almost never build, as they used to, into something combining the jabbering frequency of a machine gun with the delirious momentum of a roller coaster. Saddest of all, there are few comedians now below middle age and there are none who seem to learn much from picture to picture, or to try anything new. ¶6

To put it unkindly, the only thing wrong with screen comedy today is that it takes place on a screen which talks. Because it talks, the only comedians who ever mastered the screen cannot work, for they cannot combine their comic style with talk. Because there is a screen, talking comedians are trapped into a continual exhibition of their inadequacy as screen comedians on a surface as big as the side of a barn. ¶7

¶8 At the moment, as for many years past, the chances to see silent comedy are rare. There is a smattering of it on television —too often treated as something quaintly archaic, to be laughed at, not with. Some two hundred comedies—long and short—can be rented for home projection. And a lucky minority has access to the comedies in the collection of New York's Museum of Modern Art, which is still incomplete but which is probably the best in the world. In the near future, however, something of this lost art will return to regular theaters. A thick straw in the wind is the big business now being done by a series of revivals of W. C. Fields's memorable movies, a kind of comedy more akin to the old silent variety than anything which is being made today. Mack Sennett now is preparing a sort of pot-pourri variety show called *Down Memory Lane* made up out of his old movies, featuring people like Fields and Bing Crosby when they were movie beginners, but including also interludes from silents. Harold Lloyd has re-released *Movie Crazy*, a talkie, and plans to revive four of his best silent comedies (*Grandma's Boy, Safety Last, Speedy* and *The Freshman*). Buster Keaton hopes to remake at feature length, with a minimum of dialogue, two of the funniest short comedies ever made, one about a porous homemade boat and one about a prefabricated house.

¶9 Awaiting these happy events we will discuss here what has gone wrong with screen comedy and what, if anything, can be done about it. But mainly we will try to suggest what it was like in its glory in the years from 1912 to 1930, as practiced by the employees of Mack Sennett, the father of American screen comedy, and by the four most eminent masters: Charlie Chaplin, Harold Lloyd, the late Harry Langdon and Buster Keaton.

¶10 Mack Sennett made two kinds of comedy: parody laced with slapstick, and plain slapstick. The parodies were the unceremonious burial of a century of hamming, including the new hamming in serious movies, and nobody who has missed Ben Turpin in *A Small Town Idol*, or kidding Erich von Stroheim in

Three Foolish Weeks or as *The Shriek of Araby*, can imagine how rough parody can get and still remain subtle and roaringly funny. The plain slapstick, at its best, was even better: a profusion of hearty young women in disconcerting bathing suits, frisking around with a gaggle of insanely incompetent policemen and of equally certifiable male civilians sporting museum-piece mustaches. All these people zipped and caromed about the pristine world of the screen as jazzily as a convention of water bugs. Words can hardly suggest how energetically they collided and bounced apart, meeting in full gallop around the corner of a house; how hard and how often they fell on their backsides; or with what fantastically adroit clumsiness they got themselves fouled up in folding ladders, garden hoses, tethered animals and each other's headlong cross-purposes. The gestures were ferociously emphatic; not a line or motion of the body was wasted or inarticulate. The reader may remember how splendidly upright wandlike old Ben Turpin could stand for a Renunciation Scene, with his lampshade mustache twittering and his sparrowy chest stuck out and his head flung back like Paderewski assaulting a climax and the long babyish back hair trying to look lionlike, while his Adam's apple, an orange in a Christmas stocking, pumped with noble emotion. Or huge Mack Swain, who looked like a hairy mushroom, rolling his eyes in a manner patented by French Romantics and gasping in some dubious ecstasy. Or Louise Fazenda, the perennial farmer's daughter and the perfect low-comedy housemaid, primping her spit curl; and how her hair tightened a good-looking face into the incarnation of rampant gullibility. Or snouty James Finlayson, gleefully foreclosing a mortgage, with his look of eternally tasting a spoiled pickle. Or Chester Conklin, a myopic and inebriated little walrus stumbling around in outsize pants. Or Fatty Arbuckle, with his cold eye and his loose, serene smile, his silky manipulation of his bulk and his satanic marksmanship with pies (he was ambidextrous and could simultaneously blind two people in opposite directions).

¶11 The intimate tastes and secret hopes of these poor ineligible dunces were ruthlessly exposed whenever a hot stove, an electric fan or a bulldog took a dislike to their outer garments: agonizingly elaborate drawers, worked up on some lonely evening out of some Godforsaken lace curtain; or men's underpants with big round black spots on them. The Sennett sets—delirious wallpaper, megalomaniacally scrolled iron beds, Grand Rapids *in extremis*—outdid even the underwear. It was their business, after all, to kid the squalid braggadocio which infested the domestic interiors of the period, and that was almost beyond parody. These comedies told their stories to the unaided eye, and by every means possible they screamed to it. That is one reason for the India-ink silhouettes of the cops, and for convicts and prison bars and their shadows in hard sunlight, and for barefooted husbands, in tigerish pajamas, reacting like dervishes to stepped-on tacks.

¶12 The early silent comedians never strove for or consciously thought of anything which could be called artistic "form," but they achieved it. For Sennett's rival, Hal Roach, Leo McCarey once devoted almost the whole of a Laurel and Hardy two-reeler to pie-throwing. The first pies were thrown thoughtfully, almost philosophically. Then innocent bystanders began to get caught into the vortex. At full pitch it was Armageddon. But everything was calculated so nicely that until late in the picture, when havoc took over, every pie made its special kind of point and piled on its special kind of laugh.

¶13 Sennett's comedies were just a shade faster and fizzier than life. According to legend (and according to Sennett) he discovered the sped tempo proper to screen comedy when a green cameraman, trying to save money, cranked too slow.* Realizing the tremendous drumlike power of mere motion to exhilarate,

* Silent comedy was shot at 12 to 16 frames per second and was speeded up by being shown at 16 frames per second, the usual rate of theater projectors at that time. Theater projectors today run at 24, which makes modern film taken at the same speed seem smooth and natural. But it makes silent movies fast and jerky.

he gave inanimate objects a mischievous life of their own, broke every law of nature the tricked camera would serve him for and made the screen dance like a witches' Sabbath. The thing one is surest of all to remember is how toward the end of nearly every Sennett comedy, a chase (usually called the "rally") built up such a majestic trajectory of pure anarchic motion that bathing girls, cops, comics, dogs, cats, babies, automobiles, locomotives, innocent bystanders, sometimes what seemed like a whole city, an entire civilization, were hauled along head over heels in the wake of that energy like dry leaves following an express train.

"Nice" people, who shunned all movies in the early days, ¶14
condemned the Sennett comedies as vulgar and naïve. But millions of less pretentious people loved their sincerity and sweetness, their wild-animal innocence and glorious vitality. They could not put these feelings into words, but they flocked to the silents. The reader who gets back deep enough into that world will probably even remember the theater: the barefaced honkytonk and the waltzes by Waldteufel, slammed out on a mechanical piano; the searing redolence of peanuts and demirep perfumery, tobacco and feet and sweat; the laughter of unrespectable people having a hell of a fine time, laughter as violent and steady and deafening as standing under a waterfall.

Sennett wheedled his first financing out of a couple of ex- ¶15
bookies to whom he was already in debt. He took his comics out of music halls, burlesque, vaudeville, circuses and limbo, and through them he tapped in on that great pipeline of horsing and miming which runs back unbroken through the fairs of the Middle Ages at least to ancient Greece. He added all that he himself had learned about the large and spurious gesture, the late decadence of the Grand Manner, as a stage-struck boy in East Berlin, Connecticut and as a frustrated opera singer and actor. The only thing he claims to have invented is the pie in the face, and he insists, "Anyone who tells you he has discovered something new is a fool or a liar or both."

¶16 The silent-comedy studio was about the best training school the movies have ever known, and the Sennett studio was about as free and easy and as fecund of talent as they came. All the major comedians we will mention worked there, at least briefly. So did some of the major stars of the twenties and since—notably Gloria Swanson, Phyllis Haver, Wallace Beery, Marie Dressler and Carole Lombard. Directors Frank Capra, Leo McCarey and George Stevens also got their start in silent comedy; much that remains most flexible, spontaneous and visually alive in sound movies can be traced, through them and others, to this silent apprenticeship. Everybody did pretty much as he pleased on the Sennett lot, and everybody's ideas were welcome. Sennett posted no rules, and the only thing he strictly forbade was liquor. A Sennett story conference was a most informal affair. During the early years, at least, only the most important scenario might be jotted on the back of an envelope. Mainly Sennett's men thrashed out a few primary ideas and carried them in their heads, sure the better stuff would turn up while they were shooting, in the heat of physical action. This put quite a load on the prop man; he had to have the most improbable apparatus on hand—bombs, trick telephones, what not—to implement whatever idea might suddenly turn up. All kinds of things did—and were recklessly used. Once a low-comedy auto got out of control and killed the cameraman, but he was not visible in the shot, which was thrilling and undamaged; the audience never knew the difference.

¶17 Sennett used to hire a "wild man" to sit in on his gag conferences, whose whole job was to think up "wildies." Usually he was an all but brainless, speechless man, scarcely able to communicate his idea; but he had a totally uninhibited imagination. He might say nothing for an hour; then he'd mutter "You take . . ." and all the relatively rational others would shut up and wait. "You take this cloud . . ." he would get out, sketching vague shapes in the air. Often he could get no further; but thanks to some kind of thought-transference, saner men would take this cloud and make something of it. The wild man seems in fact to have functioned as the group's subconscious mind, the source of all creative energy. His ideas were so weird and amorphous that Sennett can no longer remember a one of them, or even how it turned out after rational processing. But a fair equivalent might be one of the best comic sequences in a Laurel and Hardy picture. It is simple enough—simple and real, in fact, as a nightmare. Laurel and Hardy are trying to move a piano across a narrow suspension bridge. The bridge is slung over a sickening chasm, between a couple of Alps. Midway they meet a gorilla.

Had he done nothing else, Sennett would be remembered ¶18
for giving a start to three of the four comedians who now began to apply their sharp individual talents to this newborn language. The one whom he did not train (he was on the lot briefly but Sennett barely remembers seeing him around) wore glasses, smiled a great deal and looked like the sort of eager young man who might have quit divinity school to hustle brushes. That was Harold Lloyd. The others were grotesque and poetic in their screen characters in degrees which appear to be impossible when the magic of silence is broken. One, who never smiled, carried a face as still and sad as a daguerreotype through some of the most preposterously ingenious and visually satisfying physical comedy ever invented. That was Buster Keaton. One looked like an elderly baby and, at times, a baby dope fiend; he could do more with less than any other comedian. That was Harry Langdon. One looked like Charlie Chaplin, and he was the first man to give the silent language a soul.

When Charlie Chaplin started to work for Sennett he had ¶19
chiefly to reckon with Ford Sterling, the reigning comedian. Their first picture together amounted to a duel before the assembled professionals. Sterling, by no means untalented, was a big man with a florid Teutonic style which, under this special pressure, he turned on full blast. Chaplin defeated him within a few minutes with a wink of the mustache, a hitch of the trousers, a quirk of the little finger.

With *Tillie's Punctured Romance*, in 1914, he became a major ¶20 star. Soon after, he left Sennett when Sennett refused to start a landslide among the other comedians by meeting the raise Chaplin demanded. Sennett is understandably wry about it in retrospect, but he still says, "I was right at the time." Of Chaplin he says simply, "Oh well, he's just the greatest artist that ever lived." None of Chaplin's former rivals rate him much lower than that; they speak of him no more jealously than they might of God. We will try here only to suggest the essence of his supremacy. Of all comedians he worked most deeply and most shrewdly within a realization of what a human being is, and is up against. The Tramp is as centrally representative of humanity, as many-sided and as mysterious, as Hamlet, and it seems unlikely that any dancer or actor can ever have excelled him in eloquence, variety or poignancy of motion. As for pure motion, even if he had never gone on to make his magnificent feature-length comedies, Chaplin would have made his period in movies a great one singlehanded even if he had made nothing except *The Cure*, or *One A.M.* In the latter, barring one immobile taxi driver, Chaplin plays alone, as a drunk trying to get upstairs and into bed. It is a sort of inspired elaboration on a soft-shoe dance, involving an angry stuffed wildcat, small rugs on slippery floors, a Lazy Susan table, exquisite footwork on a flight of stairs, a contretemps with a huge, ferocious pendulum and the funniest and most perverse Murphy bed in movie history—and, always made physically lucid, the delicately weird mental processes of a man ethereally sozzled.

¶21 Before Chaplin came to pictures people were content with a couple of gags per comedy; he got some kind of laugh every second. The minute he began to work he set standards—and continually forced them higher. Anyone who saw Chaplin eating a boiled shoe like brook trout in *The Gold Rush*, or embarrassed by a swallowed whistle in *City Lights*, has seen perfection. Most of the time, however, Chaplin got his laughter less from the gags, or from milking them in any ordinary sense, than through his genius for what may be called *inflection*—the perfect, changeful shading of his physical and emotional attitudes toward the gag. Funny as his bout with the Murphy bed is, the glances of awe, expostulation and helpless, almost whimpering desire for vengeance which he darts at this infernal machine are even better.

A painful and frequent error among tyros is breaking the comic line with a too-big laugh, then a letdown; or with a laugh which is out of key or irrelevant. The masters could ornament the main line beautifully; they never addled it. In *A Night Out* Chaplin, passed out, is hauled along the sidewalk by the scruff of his coat by staggering Ben Turpin. His toes trail; he is as supine as a sled. Turpin himself is so drunk he can hardly drag him. Chaplin comes quietly to, realizes how well he is being served by his struggling pal, and with a royally delicate gesture plucks and savors a flower. ¶22

The finest pantomime, the deepest emotion, the richest and most poignant poetry were in Chaplin's work. He could probably pantomime Bryce's *The American Commonwealth* without ever blurring a syllable and make it paralyzingly funny into the bargain. At the end of *City Lights* the blind girl who has regained her sight, thanks to the Tramp, sees him for the first time. She has imagined and anticipated him as princely, to say the least; and it has never seriously occurred to him that he is inadequate. She recognizes who he must be by his shy, confident, shining joy as he comes silently toward her. And he recognizes himself, for the first time, through the terrible changes in her face. The camera just exchanges a few quiet close-ups of the emotions which shift and intensify in each face. It is enough to shrivel the heart to see, and it is the greatest piece of acting and the highest moment in movies. ¶23

Harold Lloyd worked only a little while with Sennett. During most of his career he acted for another major comedy producer, Hal Roach. He tried at first to offset Chaplin's influence and establish his own individuality by playing Chaplin's exact oppo- ¶24 site, a character named Lonesome Luke who wore clothes much too small for him and whose gestures were likewise as unChaplinesque as possible. But he soon realized that an opposite in itself was a kind of slavishness. He discovered his own comic identity when he saw a movie about a fighting parson: a hero who wore glasses. He began to think about those glasses day and night. He decided on horn rims because they were youthful, ultravisible on the screen and on the verge of becoming fashionable (he was to make them so). Around these large lensless horn rims he began to develop a new character, nothing grotesque or eccentric, but a fresh, believable young man who could fit into a wide variety of stories.

¶25 Loyd depended more on story and situation than any of the other major comedians (he kept the best stable of gagmen in Hollywood, at one time hiring six); but unlike most "story" comedians he was also a very funny man from inside. He had, as he has written, "an unusually large comic vocabulary." More particularly he had an expertly expressive body and even more expressive teeth, and out of his thesaurus of smiles he could at a moment's notice blend prissiness, breeziness and asininity, and still remain tremendously likable. His movies were more extroverted and closer to ordinary life than any others of the best comedies: the vicissitudes of a New York taxi driver; the unaccepted college boy who, by desperate courage and inspired ineptitude, wins the Big Game. He was especially good at putting a very timid, spoiled or brassy young fellow through devastating embarrassments. He went through one of his most uproarious Gethsemanes as a shy country youth courting the nicest girl in town in *Grandma's Boy*. He arrived dressed "strictly up to date for the Spring of 1862," as a subtitle observed, and found that the ancient colored butler wore a similar flowered waistcoat and moldering cutaway. He got one wandering, nervous forefinger dreadfully stuck in a fancy little vase. The girl began cheerfully to try to identify that queer smell which dilated from him;

Grandpa's best suit was rife with mothballs. A tenacious litter of kittens feasted off the goose grease on his home-shined shoes.

Lloyd was even better at the comedy of thrills. In *Safety* ¶26
Last, as a rank amateur, he is forced to substitute for a human fly and to climb a medium-sized skyscraper. Dozens of awful things happen to him. He gets fouled up in a tennis net. Popcorn falls on him from a window above, and the local pigeons treat him like a cross between a lunch wagon and St. Francis of Assisi. A mouse runs up his britches-leg, and the crowd below salutes his desperate dance on the window ledge with wild applause of the dare-devil. A good deal of this full-length picture hangs thus by its eyelashes along the face of a building. Each new floor is like a new stanza in a poem; and the higher and more horrifying it gets, the funnier it gets.

In this movie Lloyd demonstrates beautifully his ability to ¶27
do more than merely milk a gag, but to top it. (In an old, simple example of topping, an incredible number of tall men get, one by one, out of a small closed auto. After as many have clambered out as the joke will bear, one more steps out: a midget. That tops the gag. Then the auto collapses. That tops the topper.) In *Safety Last* Lloyd is driven out to the dirty end of a flagpole by a furious dog; the pole breaks and he falls, just managing to grab the minute hand of a huge clock. His weight promptly pulls the hand down from IX to VI. That would be more than enough for any ordinary comedian, but there is further logic in the situation. Now, hideously, the whole clockface pulls loose and slants from its trembling springs above the street. Getting out of difficulty with the clock, he makes still further use of the instrument by getting one foot caught in one of these obstinate springs.

A proper delaying of the ultrapredictable can of course be ¶28
just as funny as a properly timed explosion of the unexpected. As Lloyd approaches the end of his horrible hegira up the side of the building in *Safety Last*, it becomes clear to the audience, but not to him, that if he raises his head another couple of inches

he is going to get murderously conked by one of the four arms of a revolving wind gauge. He delays the evil moment almost interminably, with one distraction and another, and every delay is a suspense-tightening laugh; he also gets his foot nicely entangled in a rope, so that when he does get hit, the payoff of one gag sends him careening head downward through the abyss into another. Lloyd was outstanding even among the master craftsmen at setting up a gag clearly, culminating and getting out of it deftly, and linking it smoothly to the next. Harsh experience also taught him a deep and fundamental rule: never try to get "above" the audience.

¶29 Lloyd tried it in *The Freshman*. He was to wear an unfinished, basted-together tuxedo to a college party, and it would gradually fall apart as he danced. Lloyd decided to skip the pants, a low-comedy cliché, and lose just the coat. His gagmen warned him. A preview proved how right they were. Lloyd had to reshoot the whole expensive sequence, build it around defective pants and climax it with the inevitable. It was one of the funniest things he ever did.

¶30 When Lloyd was still a very young man he lost about half his right hand (and nearly lost his sight) when a comedy bomb exploded prematurely. But in spite of his artificially built-out hand he continued to do his own dirty work, like all of the best comedians. The side of the building he climbed in *Safety Last* did not overhang the street, as it appears to. But the nearest landing place was a roof three floors below him, as he approached the top, and he did everything, of course, the hard way, that is, the comic way, keeping his bottom stuck well out, his shoulders hunched, his hands and feet skidding over perdition.

¶31 If great comedy must involve something beyond laughter, Lloyd was not a great comedian. If plain laughter is any criterion —and it is a healthy counterbalance to the other—few people have equaled him, and nobody has ever beaten him.

¶32 Chaplin and Keaton and Lloyd were all more like each other, in one important way, than Harry Langdon was like any of them. Whatever else the others might be doing, they all used more or less elaborate physical comedy; Langdon showed how little of that one might use and still be a great silent-screen comedian. In his screen character he symbolized something as deeply and centrally human, though by no means as rangily so, as the Tramp. There was, of course, an immense difference in inventiveness and range of virtuosity. It seemed as if Chaplin could do literally anything, on any instrument in the orchestra. Langdon had one queerly toned, unique little reed. But out of it he could get incredible melodies.

Like Chaplin, Langdon wore a coat which buttoned on his ¶33
wishbone and swung out wide below, but the effect was very different: he seemed like an outsized baby who had begun to outgrow his clothes. The crown of his hat was rounded and the brim was turned up all around, like a little boy's hat, and he looked as if he wore diapers under his pants. His walk was that of a child which has just gotten sure on its feet, and his body and hands fitted that age. His face was kept pale to show off, with the simplicity of a nursery-school drawing, the bright, ignorant, gentle eyes and the little twirling mouth. He had big moon cheeks, with dimples, and a Napoleonic forelock of mousy hair; the round, docile head seemed large in ratio to the cream-puff body. Twitchings of his face were signals of tiny discomforts too slowly registered by a tinier brain; quick, squirty little smiles showed his almost prehuman pleasures, his incurably premature trustfulness. He was a virtuoso of hesitations and of delicately indecisive motions, and he was particularly fine in a high wind, rounding a corner with a kind of skittering toddle, both hands nursing his hatbrim.

He was as remarkable a master as Chaplin of subtle emo- ¶34
tional and mental process and operated much more at leisure. He once got a good three hundred feet of continuously bigger laughs out of rubbing his chest, in a crowded vehicle, with Lim-

burger cheese, under the misapprehension that it was a cold salve. In another long scene, watching a brazen showgirl change her clothes, he sat motionless, back to the camera, and registered the whole lexicon of lost innocence, shock, disapproval and disgust, with the back of his neck. His scenes with women were nearly always something special. Once a lady spy did everything in her power (under the Hays Office) to seduce him. Harry was polite, willing, even flirtatious in his little way. The only trouble was that he couldn't imagine what in the world she was leering and pawing at him for, and that he was terribly ticklish. The Mata Hari wound up foaming at the mouth.

¶35 There was also a sinister flicker of depravity about the Langdon character, all the more disturbing because babies are premoral. He had an instinct for bringing his actual adulthood and figurative babyishness into frictions as crawley as a fingernail on a slate blackboard, and he wandered into areas of strangeness which were beyond the other comedians. In a nightmare in one movie he was forced to fight a large, muscular young man; the girl Harry loved was the prize. The young man was a good boxer; Harry could scarcely lift his gloves. The contest took place in a fiercely lighted prize ring, in a prodigious pitch-dark arena. The only spectator was the girl, and she was rooting against Harry. As the fight went on, her eyes glittered ever more brightly with blood lust and, with glittering teeth, she tore her big straw hat to shreds.

¶36 Langdon came to Sennett from a vaudeville act in which he had fought a losing battle with a recalcitrant automobile. The minute Frank Capra saw him he begged Sennett to let him work with him. Langdon was almost as childlike as the character he played. He had only a vague idea of his story or even of each scene as he played it; each time he went before the camera Capra would brief him on the general situation and then, as this finest of intuitive improvisers once tried to explain his work, "I'd go into my routine." The whole tragedy of the coming of dialogue, as far as these comedians were concerned—and one reason for the increasing rigidity of comedy every since—can be epitomized in the mere thought of Harry Langdon confronted with a script.

Langdon's magic was in his innocence, and Capra took beautiful care not to meddle with it. The key to the proper use of Langdon, Capra always knew, was "the principle of the brick." "If there was a rule for writing Langdon material," he explains, "it was this: his only ally was God. Langdon might be saved by the brick falling on the cop, but it was *verboten* that he in any way motivate the brick's fall." Langdon became quickly and fantastically popular with three pictures, *Tramp, Tramp, Tramp, The Strong Man* and *Long Pants*; from then on he went downhill even faster. "The trouble was," Capra says, "that high-brow critics came around to explain his art to him. Also he developed an interest in dames. It was a pretty high life for such a little fellow." Langdon made two more pictures with high-brow writers, one of which (*Three's a Crowd*) had some wonderful passages in it, including the prize-ring nightmare; then First National canceled his contract. He was reduced to mediocre roles and two-reelers which were more rehashes of his old gags; this time around they no longer seemed funny. "He never did really understand what hit him," says Capra. "He died broke [in 1944]. And he died of a broken heart. He was the most tragic figure I ever came across in show business." ¶37

Buster Keaton started work at the age of three and one-half with his parents in one of the roughest acts in vaudeville ("The Three Keatons"); Harry Houdini gave the child the name Buster in admiration for a fall he took down a flight of stairs. In his first movies Keaton teamed with Fatty Arbuckle under Sennett. He went on to become one of Metro's biggest stars and earners; a Keaton feature cost about $200,000 to make and reliably grossed $2,000,000. Very early in his movie career friends asked him why he never smiled on the screen. He didn't realize he didn't. He had got the dead-pan habit in variety; on the screen he had ¶38 merely been so hard at work it had never occurred to him there was anything to smile about. Now he tried it just once and never again. He was by his whole style and nature so much the most deeply "silent" of the silent comedians that even a smile was as deafeningly out of key as a yell. In a way his pictures are like a transcendent juggling act in which it seems that the whole universe is in exquisite flying motion and the one point of repose is the juggler's effortless, uninterested face.

¶39 Keaton's face ranked almost with Lincoln's as an early American archetype; it was haunting, handsome, almost beautiful, yet it was irreducibly funny; he improved matters by topping it off with a deadly horizontal hat, as flat and thin as a phonograph record. One can never forget Keaton wearing it, standing erect at the prow as his little boat is being launched. The boat goes grandly down the skids, and, just as grandly, straight on to the bottom. Keaton never budges. The last you see of him, the water lifts the hat off the stoic head and it floats away.

¶40 No other comedian could do as much with the dead pan. He used this great, sad, motionless face to suggest various related things: a one-track mind near the track's end of pure insanity; mulish imperturbability under the wildest of circumstances; how dead a human being can get and still be alive; an awe-inspiring sort of patience and power to endure, proper to granite but uncanny in flesh and blood. Everything that he was and did bore out this rigid face and played laughs against it. When he moved his eyes, it was like seeing them move in a statue. His short-legged body was all sudden, machinelike angles, governed by a daft aplomb. When he swept a semaphorelike arm to point, you could almost hear the electrical impulse in the signal block. When he ran from a cop his transitions from accelerating walk to easy jogtrot to brisk canter to headlong gallop to flogged-piston sprint—always floating, above this frenzy, the untroubled, untouchable face—were as distinct and as soberly in order as an automatic gearshift.

Keaton was a wonderfully resourceful inventor of mechanistic gags (he still spends much of his time fooling with Erector sets); as he ran afoul of locomotives, steamships, prefabricated and over-electrified houses, he put himself through some of the hardest and cleverest punishment ever designed for laughs. In *Sherlock Jr.*, boiling along on the handlebars of a motorcycle quite unaware that he has lost his driver, Keaton whips through city traffic, breaks up a tug-of-war, gets a shovelful of dirt in the face from each of a long line of Rockette-timed ditch-diggers, approaches a log at high speed which is hinged open by dynamite precisely soon enough to let him through and, hitting an obstruction, leaves the handlebars like an arrow leaving a bow, whams through the window of a shack in which the heroine is about to be violated, and hits the heavy feet-first, knocking him through the opposite wall. The whole sequence is as clean in motion as the trajectory of a bullet. ¶41

Much of the charm and edge of Keaton's comedy, however, lay in the subtle leverages of expression he could work against his nominal dead pan. Trapped in the side-wheel of a ferryboat, saving himself from drowning only by walking, then desperately running, inside the accelerating wheel like a squirrel in a cage, his only real concern was, obviously, to keep his hat on. Confronted by Love, he was not as dead-pan as he was cracked up to be, either; there was an odd, abrupt motion of his head which suggested a horse nipping after a sugar lump. ¶42

Keaton worked strictly for laughs, but his work came from so far inside a curious and original spirit that he achieved a great deal besides, especially in his feature-length comedies. (For plain hard laughter his nineteen short comedies—the negatives of which have been lost—were even better.) He was the only major comedian who kept sentiment almost entirely out of his work, and he brought pure physical comedy to its greatest heights. Beneath his lack of emotion he was also uninsistently sardonic; deep below that, giving a disturbing tension and grandeur to ¶43 the foolishness, for those who sensed it, there was in his comedy a freezing whisper not of pathos but of melancholia. With the humor, the craftsmanship and the action there was often, besides, a fine, still and sometimes dreamlike beauty. Much of his Civil War picture *The General* is within hailing distance of Mathew Brady. And there is a ghostly, unforgettable moment in *The Navigator* when, on a deserted, softly rolling ship, all the pale doors along a deck swing open as one behind Keaton and, as one, slam shut, in a hair-raising illusion of noise.

¶44 Perhaps because "dry" comedy is so much more rare and odd than "dry" wit, there are people who never much cared for Keaton. Those who do cannot care mildly.

¶45 As soon as the screen began to talk, silent comedy was pretty well finished. The hardy and prolific Mack Sennett made the transfer; he was the first man to put Bing Crosby and W. C. Fields on the screen. But he was essentially a silent-picture man, and by the time the Academy awarded him a special Oscar for his "lasting contribution to the comedy technique of the screen" (in 1938), he was no longer active. As for the comedians we have spoken of in particular, they were as badly off as fine dancers suddenly required to appear in plays.

¶46 Harold Lloyd, whose work was most nearly realistic, naturally coped least unhappily with the added realism of speech; he made several talking comedies. But good as the best were, they were not so good as his silent work, and by the late thirties he quit acting. A few years ago he returned to play the lead (and play it beautifully) in Preston Sturges's *The Sin of Harold Diddlebock*, but this exceptional picture—which opened, brilliantly, with the closing reel of Lloyd's *The Freshman*—has not yet been generally released.

¶47 Like Chaplin, Lloyd was careful of his money; he is still rich and active. Last June, in the presence of President Truman, he became Imperial Potentate of the A.A.O.N.M.S. (Shriners). Harry Langdon, as we have said, was a broken man when sound came in.

Up to the middle thirties Buster Keaton made several ¶48
feature-length pictures (with such players as Jimmy Durante, Wallace Beery and Robert Montgomery); he also made a couple of dozen talking shorts. Now and again he managed to get loose into motion, without having to talk, and for a moment or so the screen would start singing again. But his dark, dead voice, though it was in keeping with the visual character, tore his intensely silent style to bits and destroyed the illusion within which he worked. He gallantly and correctly refuses to regard himself as "retired." Besides occasional bits, spots and minor roles in Hollywood pictures, he has worked on summer stages, made talking comedies in France and Mexico and clowned in a French circus. This summer he has played the straw hats in *Three Men on a Horse*. He is planning a television program. He also has a working agreement with Metro. One of his jobs there is to construct comedy sequences for Red Skelton.

The only man who really survived the flood was Chaplin, ¶49
the only one who was rich, proud and popular enough to afford to stay silent. He brought out two of his greatest nontalking comedies, *City Lights* and *Modern Times*, in the middle of an avalanche of talk, spoke gibberish and, in the closing moments, plain English in *The Great Dictator*, and at last made an all-talking picture, *Monsieur Verdoux*, creating for that purpose an entirely new character who might properly talk a blue streak. *Verdoux* is the greatest of talking comedies though so cold and savage that it had to find its public in grimly experienced Europe.

Good comedy, and some that was better than good, outlived ¶50
silence, but there has been less and less of it. The talkies brought one great comedian, the late, majestically lethargic W. C. Fields, who could not possibly have worked as well in silence; he was the toughest and the most warmly human of all screen comedians, and *It's A Gift* and *The Bank Dick*, fiendishly funny and incisive white-collar comedies, rank high among the best comedies (and best movies) ever made. Laurel and Hardy, the only comedians who managed to preserve much of the large, low style of silence

and who began to explore the comedy of sound, have made nothing since 1945. Walt Disney, at his best an inspired comic inventor and teller of fairy stories, lost his stride during the war and has since regained it only at moments. Preston Sturges has made brilliant, satirical comedies, but his pictures are smart, nervous comedy-dramas merely italicized with slapstick. The Marx Brothers were side-splitters but they made their best comedies years ago. Jimmy Durante is mainly a nightclub genius; Abbott and Costello are semiskilled laborers, at best; Bob Hope is a good radio comedian with a pleasing presence, but not much more, on the screen.

¶51 There is no hope that screen comedy will get much better than it is without new, gifted young comedians who really belong in movies, and without freedom for their experiments. For everyone who may appear we have one last, invidious comparison to offer as a guidepost.

¶52 One of the most popular recent comedies is Bob Hope's *The Paleface*. We take no pleasure in blackening *The Paleface*; we single it out, rather, because it is as good as we've got. Anything that is said of it here could be said, with interest, of other comedies of our time. Most of the laughs in *The Paleface* are verbal. Bob Hope is very adroit with his lines and now and then, when the words don't get in the way, he makes a good beginning as a visual comedian. But only the beginning, never the middle or the end. He is funny, for instance, reacting to a shot of violent whisky. But he does not know how to get still funnier (*i.e.*, how to build and milk) or how to be funniest last (*i.e.*, how to top or cap his gag). The camera has to fade out on the same old face he started with.

¶53 One sequence is promisingly set up for visual comedy. In it, Hope and a lethal local boy stalk each other all over a cow town through streets which have been emptied in fear of their duel. The gag here is that through accident and stupidity they keep just failing to find each other. Some of it is quite funny.

But the fun slackens between laughs like a weak clothesline, and by all the logic of humor (which is ruthlessly logical) the biggest laugh should come at the moment, and through the way, they finally spot each other. The sequence is so weakly thought out that at that crucial moment the camera can't afford to watch them; it switches to Jane Russell.

Now we turn to a masterpiece. In *The Navigator* Buster ¶54 Keaton works with practically the same gag as Hope's duel. Adrift on a ship which he believes is otherwise empty, he drops a lighted cigarette. A girl finds it. She calls out and he hears her; each then tries to find the other. First each works purposefully down the long, vacant starboard deck, the girl, then Keaton, turning the corner just in time not to see each other. Next time around each of them is trotting briskly, very much in earnest; going at the same pace, they miss each other just the same. Next time around each of them is going like a bat out of hell. Again they miss. Then the camera withdraws to a point of vantage at the stern, leans its chin in its hand and just watches the whole intricate superstructure of the ship as the protagonists stroll, steal and scuttle from level to level, up, down and sidewise, always managing to miss each other by hair's-breadths, in an enchantingly neat and elaborate piece of timing. There are no subsidiary gags to get laughs in this sequence and there is little loud laughter; merely a quiet and steadily increasing kind of delight. When Keaton has got all he can out of this fine modification of the movie chase he invents a fine device to bring the two together: the girl, thoroughly winded, sits down for a breather, indoors, on a plank which workmen have left across sawhorses. Keaton pauses on an upper deck, equally winded and puzzled. What follows happens in a couple of seconds at most: air suction whips his silk topper backward down a ventilator; grabbing frantically for it, he backs against the lip of the ventilator, jacknifes and falls in backward. Instantly the camera cuts back to the girl. A topper falls through the ceiling and lands tidily, right side up, on the plank beside her. Before she can look more than startled, its owner follows, head between his knees, crushes the topper, breaks the plank with the point of his spine and proceeds to the floor. The breaking of the plank smacks Boy and Girl together.

¶55 It is only fair to remember that the silent comedians would have as hard a time playing a talking scene as Hope has playing his visual ones, and that writing and directing are as accountable for the failure as Hope himself. But not even the humblest journeymen of the silent years would have let themselves off so easily. Like the masters, they knew, and sweated to obey, the laws of their craft.

For Greater Insight

1. One of the remarkable features of this essay is its spate of colorful language, of precisely chosen words, of vivid figurative writing, and of fresh, sparkling ideas. The third paragraph is a good place to begin observing these qualities. What does Agee mean by the sentence "He realized . . . within that license"? What does the silence of the silent films require of the comedian? Agee says, ". . . figure of speech, or rather of vision, for loss of consciousness." Explain "figure of speech" and "figure of vision." Why is "cadenza" exactly the right word?
2. An artist recently said, in reference to painting, "Language is at best an imperfect medium for conveying emotion." Read Par. 5 carefully. Does Agee agree with the artist's statement? Do you agree? Why? Which is likely to be more vivid, more clearly understood—words, a picture, or an action? Why?
3. Justify Agee's use of "cliché."
4. In Par. 6, in the sentence "They [laughs] never build . . . of a roller coaster," Agee is using metaphorical writing in a description of the "boffo." Explain the metaphor, and explain why it is effective.
5. How do you know that Par. 9 is a transitional paragraph?
6. Par. 18 is also a transitional paragraph. What is the subject of Pars. 10–17? What subject is begun in Par. 19? (If you had to

read anything but Par. 18 to answer that question, you were not reading well, because Agee says as plainly as possible "I have been talking about ———, and in a moment I am going to be speaking in detail of ———." In what words does Agee make this clear?)

7. In Par. 18, note that Agee tells what Lloyd, Keaton, and Langdon looked like. What did Chaplin look like? What does Agee's statement tell you about his feeling for Chaplin?
8. One of the delightful aspects of Agee's writing is his brilliant choice of the correct word, and his frequent pairing of words in strange but effective combinations. (Some of these combinations are identifiable as special figures of speech; Miss Groby would have admired them excessively. We can enjoy them, however, without trying to classify them.)
   Note the following: Par. 3: with tallow knees, vortex of his dizziness; Par. 10: as jazzily as a convention of water bugs, fantastically adroit clumsiness, lampshade mustache, like Paderewski assaulting a climax, his Adam's apple, an orange in a Christmas stocking; Par. 20: physically lucid, delicately weird, ethereally sozzled. Choose several of these phrases, and explain why they are effective and unusual. Keep your eyes open for similar expressions. They will add to your enjoyment.
9. Explain the first sentence in Par. 28. Can you think of an example of either technique in any movie you have seen? Which technique is illustrated in Par. 28?
10. What was Langdon's "unique little reed"?
11. The arrangement of details in climactic order is always an interesting device. In Par. 40, in the last sentence, Agee uses the device. Explain the terms in the series and comment on their effectiveness. Why is the final simile a good one?
12. Study the accounts of similar incidents in *Paleface* and *The Navigator*. Why does Agee believe one comedy routine to have been successful and the other a failure? What part does hyperbole play in the successful routine?
13. Portions of reviewers' comments about Agee's writing are quoted below. None refer directly and specifically to the essay you have just read, although many are applicable. Comment on them, saying why you agree with some and not with others.
    a. "A vocabulary at once personal to the poet [Agee] and appropriate to the intention."

b. ". . . superior, highly original, accurately poetic writing."
c. ". . . the reader [of Agee's writing] would curse the author as a confused adolescent, an Ezra Pound in Wolfe's clothing, a shocking snob, or a belligerent mystic posing with a purple pencil on the Left Bank of *Fortune*."
d. "Agee steadily retains the artist's supreme gift: he can bring even a reluctant reader into the heart of his own experience."
e. "With his words he could evoke a wonderfully precise impression of the littlest things."
f. "Some consider them [Agee's film reviews] the only body of criticism in this field worthy of permanent recording."

Word Study

steadily *deteriorated*:
happy *atavists*:
realized a broad *license*:
ruthless discipline within that license:
make a *cadenza* of it:
down the *vortex* of his dizziness:
signified *nirvana*:
accomplishments of the *mime*:
deeper uses for the *idiom*:
something *quaintly archaic*:
a sort of *pot-pourri* variety show:
parody laced with *slapstick*:
a *gaggle* of . . . policemen:
equally *certifiable* male civilians:
caromed about the *pristine* world:
fantastically *adroit* clumsiness:
wandlike old Ben Turpin:
for a *Renunciation* Scene:
the *incarnation* of *rampant gullibility*:
a *myopic* and *inebriated* walrus:
ambidextrous:
megalomaniacally scrolled iron beds:
Grand Rapids in extremis:
the *squalid braggadocio*:
reacting like *dervishes*:
it was *Armageddon*:

fizzier than life:
majestic trajectory of pure *anarchic* motion:
searing *redolence*:
demirep perfumery:
pipeline of *horsing* and *miming*:
as *fecund* of talent:
uninhibited imagination:
relatively *rational* others:
weird and *amorphous*:
sad as a *daguerreotype*:
poignancy of motion:
a *contretemps* with a . . . pendulum:
perverse Murphy bed:
physically *lucid*:
ethereally sozzled:
glances of . . . *expostulation*:
among *tyros*:
they never *addled* it:
supine as a sled:
thesaurus of smiles:
prissiness, breeziness, and *asininity*:
vicissitudes of a . . . taxi driver:
his horrible *hegira*:
skidding over *perdition*:
sinister flicker of *depravity*:
babies are *premoral*:
a *recalcitrant* automobile:
intuitive improvisers:
can be *epitomized*:
transcendent juggling act:
early American *archetype*:
mulish *imperturbability*:
a *daft aplomb*:
his *nominal* dead pan:
he was *uninsistently sardonic*:
not of *pathos* but of *melancholia*:
majestically *lethargic*:
funny and *incisive*:
invidious comparison:
lethal local boy:

Language and Literature

Ladies' and Gentlemen's Guide to Modern English Usage

Inspired by Mr. H. W. Fowler's excellent *Dictionary of Modern English Usage.*

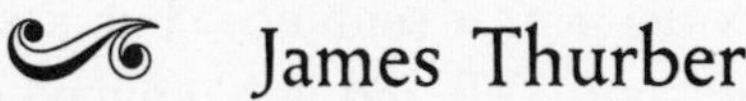

James Thurber

The essay which follows is made up of three parts chosen from "Ladies' and Gentlemen's Guide to Modern English Usage." This "Guide" appears in the Thurber collection, *Owl in the Attic*, first published in 1931.

Humor is of many kinds—humor of situation, of the unexpected, of exaggeration, of the ridiculous, of the pun, the play on words—the list is nearly endless. Here Thurber is having fun with language, deliberately sounding like a solemn lecturer, and at the same time making the most absurd statements.

You will be well advised to avoid the use of *who, which,* and *whether* for several days, for Thurber will have confused you thoroughly—as doubtless he intended to!

I. *Who and Whom*

The number of people who use "whom" and "who" wrongly is appalling. The problem is a difficult one and it is complicated by the importance of tone, or taste. Take the common expression, "Whom are you, anyways?" That is of course, strictly speak- ¶1 ing, correct—and yet how formal, how stilted! The usage to be preferred in ordinary speech and writing is "Who are you, anyways?" "Whom" should be used in the nominative case only when a note of dignity or austerity is desired. For example, if a writer is dealing with a meeting of, say, the British Cabinet, it would be better to have the Premier greet a new arrival, such as an under-secretary, with a "Whom are you, anyways?" rather than a "Who are you, anyways?"—always granted that the Premier is sincerely unaware of the man's identity. To address a person one knows by a "Whom are you?" is a mark either of incredible lapse of memory or inexcusable arrogance. "How are you?" is a much kindlier salutation.

¶2 The Buried Whom, as it is called, forms a special problem. This is where the word occurs deep in a sentence. For a ready example, take the common expression: "He did not know whether he knew her or not because he had not heard whom the other had said she was until too late to see her." The simplest way out of this is to abandon the "whom" altogether and substitute "where" (a reading of the sentence that way will show how much better it is). Unfortunately, it is only in rare cases that "where" can be used in place of "whom." Nothing could be more flagrantly bad, for instance, than to say "Where are you?" in demanding a person's identity. The only conceivable answer is, "Here I am," which would give no hint at all as to whom the person was. Thus the conversation, or piece of writing, would, from being built upon a false foundation, fall of its own weight.

¶3 A common rule for determining whether "who" or "whom" is right is to substitute "she" for "who," and "her" for "whom," and see which sounds the better. Take the sentence, "He met a woman who they said was an actress." Now if "who" is correct then "she" can be used in its place. Let us try it. "He met a woman she they said was an actress." That instantly rings false. It can't be right. Hence the proper usage is "whom."

¶4 In certain cases grammatical correctness must often be

subordinated to a consideration of taste. For instance, suppose that the same person had met a man whom they said was a street-cleaner. The word "whom" is too austere to use in connection with a lowly worker, like a street-cleaner, and its use in this form is known as False Admiration or Pathetic Fallacy.

You might say: "There is, then, no hard and fast rule?" ¶5 ("was then" would be better, since "then" refers to what is past). You might better say, then (or have said): "There was then (or is now) no hard and fast rule?" Only this, that it is better to use "whom" when in doubt, and even better to re-word the statement, and leave out all the relative pronouns, except ad, ante, con, in, inter, ob, post, prae, pro, sub, and super.

II. *Which*

The relative pronoun "which" can cause more trouble than ¶6 any other word, if recklessly used. Foolhardy persons sometimes get lost in which-clauses and are never heard of again. My distinguished contemporary, Fowler, cites several tragic cases, of which the following is one: "It was rumored that Beaconsfield intended opening the Conference with a speech in French, his pronunciation of which language leaving everything to be desired . . ." That's as much as Mr. Fowler quotes because, at his age, he was afraid to go any farther. The young man who originally got into that sentence was never found. His fate, however, was not as terrible as that of another adventurer who became involved in a remarkable which-mire. Fowler has followed his devious course as far as he safely could on foot: "Surely what applies to games should also apply to racing, the leaders of which being the very people from whom an example might well be looked for . . ." Not even Henry James could have successfully emerged from a sentence with "which," "whom," and "being" in it. The safest way to avoid such things is to follow in the path of the American author, Ernest Hemingway. In his youth he was trapped in a which-clause one time and barely escaped with his mind. He was going along on solid ground until he got into this: "It was the one thing of which, being very much afraid—for whom has not been warned to fear such things—he . . ." Being a young and powerfully built man, Hemingway was able to fight his way back to where he had started, and begin again. This time he skirted the treacherous morass in this way: "He was afraid of one thing. This was the one thing. He had been warned to fear such things. Everybody has been warned to fear such things." Today Hemingway is alive and well, and many happy writers are following along the trail he blazed.

¶7 What most people don't realize is that one "which" leads to another. Trying to cross a paragraph by leaping from "which" to "which" is like Eliza crossing the ice. The danger is in missing a "which" and falling in. A case in point is this: "He went up to a pew which was in the gallery, which brought him under a colored window which he loved and always quieted his spirit." The writer, worn out, missed the last "which"—the one that should come just before "always" in that sentence. But supposing he had got it in! We would have: "He went up to a pew which was in the gallery, which brought him under a colored window which he loved and which always quieted his spirit." Your inveterate whicher in this way gives the effect of tweeting like a bird or walking with a crutch, and is not welcome in the best company.

¶8 It is well to remember that one "which" leads to two and that two "whiches" multiply like rabbits. You should never start out with the idea that you can get by with one "which." Suddenly they are all around you. Take a sentence like this: "It imposes a problem which we either solve, or perish." On a hot night, or after a hard day's work, a man often lets himself get by with a monstrosity like that, but suppose he dictates that sentence bright and early in the morning. It comes to him typed out by his stenographer and he instantly senses that something is the matter with it. He tries to reconstruct the sentence, still clinging to the "which," and gets something like this: "It imposes a problem which we either solve, or which, failing to solve, we must perish on account of." He goes to the water-cooler, gets a drink, sharpens his pencil, and grimly tries again. "It imposes a problem which we either solve or which we don't solve and . . ." He begins once more: "It imposes a problem which we either solve, or which we do not solve, and from which . . ." The more times he does it the more "whiches" he gets. The way out is simple: "We must either solve this problem, or perish." Never monkey with "which." Nothing except getting tangled up in a typewriter ribbon is worse.

V. *Whether*

A certain type of person is wont to let "whether" get him down. For one thing, he will wear himself out doubling the alternative. That is, he will write some such clause as "Whether or not the birds will or will not come north this year." Either "or not" or "or will not" should be dropped. If one or the other isn't dropped, an ornithologist can get into all sorts of trouble, such as "Whether or not the nuthatch will or will not hatch, is not known." If the thing goes as far as that, a person should drop ornithology too. A good ornithologist doesn't need "whethers." He should know whether or not the bird will hatch, and say so. ¶9

The use of "whether" after "doubt" is another troublesome matter. Yet the rule is simple. When the sentence is affirmative, use "whether"—"I doubt whether he will go." When the sentence is negative, use "that"—"I do not doubt that he will go." Practically nobody remembers this rule, however, and the best thing to do is carry it on a little slip of paper in your pocket and refer to it when needed. In great crises, it is well not to ¶10 bother with either one. For example, if a gentleman wishes to address a lady as follows, "I no longer doubt whether (that) I love you," the best modern usage is simply to place his arms around her waist. In this case her arms should go around his shoulders. Occasionally a gentleman will put his arms around a lady's shoulders and expect her to put hers around his waist. Since this is contrary to accepted custom, the result often is that both parties reach for the same place, i.e., waist or shoulders, at the same time, and thus appear to be boxing. Nothing can end a courtship any faster than to appear to be boxing. If a gentleman is going to depart from the common practice he should give warning.

¶11 The question of when to use "whether or no" instead of "whether or not" will likely never be decided now. Grammarians have avoided the subject since the deplorable experience of Dr. Amos Crawley, M.A., L.L.D., who, in his invaluable but, alas, uncompleted monograph, "Clarified Expression," unaccountably got involved, while his wife and servants were away and he was alone in the house, in a construction beginning: "Whether or not 'whether or no' is ever preferable to 'whether or not' depends on whether or not . . ." at which point he was stricken. The best advice is make up your mind and avoid doubt-clauses.

For Greater Insight

1. Can you pick out the one form which Thurber recommends that is right? Can you point out the deliberate errors in the first paragraph?
2. Actually, Thurber's idea of the Buried Whom is a problem. There are times when we get the "whom" so far away from its grammatical relatives that we are almost unable to trace those relations. However, you might try deliberately to create such a sentence. You'll know why Thurber rewrote ten times!
3. Why do you suppose Thurber put "a reading of the sentence that way will show how much better it is" in parentheses? Why didn't he write the sentence again, using "where"?

4. Is there a rule about substituting "she" for "who" and "her" for "whom"? If you think there is, can you explain how Thurber has purposely misled you, and has apparently proved his point?
5. In the piece about "which" there is just enough sense mixed up with the nonsense to make the material sound straightforward. Can you separate the two? (If you've never written a sentence with a troublesome set of "whiches," you won't really appreciate this.)
6. Your attention has been called elsewhere to the fact that essay style permits a certain amount of pleasant dalliance with ideas as they come to the essayist. He may pursue the idea in writing, much as you pursue a thought. In the piece on "Whether," Thurber has pursued a new idea in one paragraph. Which paragraph? Explain the digression.
7. You will profit by taking some point of usage or grammar and trying to write about it with a mixture of sense and nonsense. Try "and" and "but," "well" as an introductory word, "swell" as a term of general approbation, or any one of dozens. It can be almost guaranteed that you will find it very hard to make mistakes deliberately.

Word Study

is *appalling*:
how *stilted*:
austerity is desired:
flagrantly bad:
devious course:
treacherous *morass*:
inveterate whicher:
a *monstrosity* like that:
is *wont* to let:
an *ornithologist*:
uncompleted *monograph*:

How to Read a Dictionary

Mortimer Adler

Dr. Adler's long history of interest in words, language, philosophy, and education has led to a brilliant career in university and administrative positions. Working with Robert Maynard Hutchins, he revolutionized the educational program at the University of Chicago. He founded the Great Books Program. In all his work he has been controversial and vigorous.

Dr. Adler is currently Director of the Institute for Philosophical Research in Chicago, Illinois.

If you expect to find in Adler's essay a cold, factual set of directions for the use of a dictionary—something like an exposition on "How to Recognize a Genuine Antique"—you are mistaken. He begins by pointing out that you can read a dictionary for the fun of it, discovering fascinating bits of trivia. At the end of this section he says it is hard to stop writing in that vein, hints that he should get on with the "how to" section, but then invites us to follow him in another pleasant digression before he touches the main purpose.

This kind of intellectual sauntering is one facet of the essay style, and a delightful one, provided you do not let your practical, demanding mind become impatient with attractive bypaths. Plan to read this essay when you are not rushing to complete a heavy homework assignment. You should read leisurely, and look for the end of Adler's introduction about the amusing little things one finds in the dictionary. Then you need to read more seriously what he says about use and misuse of a dictionary, a section which really deals with our general literary levels and the history of dictionaries. In Par. 15 Adler gets down to the business of stating the rules, and here you need to read with care.

The dictionary invites a playful reading. It challenges anyone to sit down with it in an idle moment only to find an hour gone by without being bored. Recently I noticed an advertisement for a dictionary as a wonder book. "Astonished Actually Means Thunderstruck" was the headline, written obviously in the hope that the prospective buyer would be thunderstruck, or wonder-struck, enough to look further. And the rest of the ad listed such tidbits as . . . "*disaster* literally means 'the stars are against you!' " or "to tantalize is to torment with the punishment of Tantalus as told in Greek mythology." ¶1

While I do not think astonishment is the dictionary's main mission in life, I cannot resist reporting some of the things I learned accidentally while thumbing its pages, in the course of writing this article. I discovered that the word "solecism" derives from Soli, the name of a Greek colony in Cilicia, whose inhabitants were thought by the Athenians to speak bad Greek; hence, "solecism" was probably the equivalent in Greek slang for a Bostonian's contemptuous reference to "New Yorkese." I learned that "coal" originally meant charred wood. It was then applied to mineral coal when this was first introduced, under such names as "sea-coal" and "pit-coal." Now that mineral coal is the more common variety, we redundantly refer to charred wood as "charcoal." I was edified by the fact that the drink "Tom and Jerry" derives its name from the two chief characters in Egan's "Life of London" (1821), that in England a low beer joint is called a "Tom and Jerry Shop," and that indulgence in riotous behavior is called "to tom and jerry." I had always thought that a forlorn hope was really a hope on the verge of turning into despair, but it seems that it isn't a hope at all. "Hope" here is a misspelling of the Dutch word "hoop" meaning heap. A forlorn hope is a ¶2 storming party, a band of heroes who are willing to end up in a heap for their country's cause. And most shocking of all was the discovery that one theory about the origin of the magician's "hocus pocus" accounts for it as a corruption of "*hoc est corous*" —the sacred words accompanying the sacrament of the Eucharist. This, together with the reversal in meaning of "dunce"—from the proper name of Duns Scotus, the subtlest doctor of the Church, to naming a numbskull—provides a two word commentary on the transition from the Middle Ages to modern times.

¶3 The staid modern dictionary is full of such wit even when it doesn't try to be funny, as Dr. Johnson did when he defined "oats" as "a grain which in England is generally given to horses, but in Scotland supports the people." Look up "Welsh rabbit," for example, or "scotch capon" or "swiss steak," and you will discover gentle jokes about national shortcomings in diet.

¶4 I find that what interests me most of all are the shifts in meaning of common words in daily use. From meaning an attendant on horses, "marshall" has come to mean a leader of men; though also originating in the stable, "constable" has gone in the reverse direction from signifying an officer of highest rank to denoting a policeman; "boon" has done an about-face by becoming the gift which answers a petition, having been the prayer which asked for it; "magistrate" and "minister" have changed places with each other in the ups and downs of words, for in current political usage, "magistrate" usually names a minor official, whereas "minister" refers to a *major* diplomatic or cabinet post. It is often hard to remember that a minister is a *servant* of the people, and harder still to recall the precise point of religious controversy which caused the substitution of "minister" for "priest" as the name for one who served in the performance of sacerdotal functions. And readers of our Constitution should have their attention called to a shift in the word "citizen" from meaning any one who, by birth or choice, owes allegiance to the state, to the narrower designation of those who are granted the right to vote. Similarly, "commerce" has narrowed in meaning; like "trade," it once meant every dealing in merchandise, but now is distinguished from industry according to the difference between distributing commodities and producing them.

The word "commerce" reminds me of one other sort of incidental inquiry the dictionary lures you into. You discover that "commerce" and "mercenary" have the same root in "*mercis*," wares, and that leads you to the closely related root "*merces*," pay or reward, which is embodied in the word "mercy." If you start this game of research, you will find such roots as "*spec*" from "*spectare*" meaning to look at or see, which generates a family of 246 English words (species, speculate, specimen, specify, spectacle, inspect, respect, aspect, etc.); or "*press*" from "*primo*" meaning to squeeze, which has an equally large family (impress, repress, pressing, compress, surpress, oppress, depress, express, etc.). ¶5

It is almost as hard to stop writing about the dictionary in this way as to stop reading one when you are in hot pursuit of the mysteries of human speech. But, over and above such fascinations, the dictionary has its sober uses. To make the most of these one has to know how to read the special sort of book a dictionary is. But, before I state the rules, let me see if I can explain why most people today don't use dictionaries in a manner befitting the purpose for which they were originally created. ¶6

In its various sizes and editions, the dictionary is an unlisted best-seller on every season's list. To be able to get along without one would be a sign of supreme literacy—of complete competence as a reader and writer. The dictionary exists, of course, because there is no one in that condition. But, if the dictionary is the necessity we all acknowledge, why is it so infrequently used by the man who owns one? And, even when we do consult it, why do most of us misuse the dictionary or use it poorly? ¶7

¶8 The answer to both questions may be that few of us make efforts at reading or writing anything above the present level of our literary competence. The books—or maybe it is just the newspapers and magazines—we read, and the things we write, don't send us to the dictionary for help. Our vocabularies are quite adequate, because the first rule in most contemporary writing is the taboo against strange words, or familiar words in strange senses.

¶9 Of course, there are always people (not excluding college graduates) who have difficulty with spelling or pronouncing even the common words in daily discourse. That, by the way, is the source of the most frequent impulse to go to the dictionary. There is nothing wrong about this. The dictionary is there to render this simple service—in fact, Noah Webster began his career as the compiler of a spelling book which sold in the millions. But my point remains—the dictionary has other and more important uses, and the reason we do not generally avail ourselves of these services is not our superiority, but rather our lack of need as the life of letters is currently lived.

¶10 The history of dictionaries, I think, will bear me out on this point. The Greeks did not have a dictionary, even though "lexicon" is the Greek word for it. They had no need for foreign language dictionaries because there was no literature in a foreign language they cared to read. They had no need for a Greek word-book because the small educated class already knew what such a book would contain. This small group of literate men would have been, like the modern French Academy, the makers of the dictionary, the arbiters of good usage. But at a time when so sharp a line separated the learned from the lewd (which, in an obsolete usage, means *unlettered*), there was no occasion for the few men who could make a dictionary to prepare one for the others.

¶11 George Santayana's remark about the Greeks—that they were the only uneducated people in European history—has a double significance. The masses were, of course, uneducated, but even the learned few were not educated in the sense that they had to sit at the feet of foreign masters. Education, in that sense, begins with the Romans, who went to school to Greek pedagogues, and became cultivated through contact with Greek culture. It is not surprising, therefore, that the first dictionaries were glossaries of Homeric words. The earliest lexicon which is still extant is such a glossary, prepared by a Greek, Apollonius, in the fifth century of our era, obviously intended to help Romans read the "Iliad" and "Odyssey" of Homer, as well as other Greek literature which employed the Homeric vocabulary. Most of us today need similar glossaries to read Shakespeare well.

There were dictionaries in the Middle Ages—a famous Latin ¶12
one by the Spaniard, Isidore of Seville, which was really a philosophical work, a sort of encyclopedia of worldly knowledge accomplished by discussions of the most important technical terms occurring in learned discourse. There were foreign-language dictionaries in the Renaissance (both Latin and Greek) made necessary by the fact that the *humane letters* which dominated the education of the period were from the ancient languages. Even when the vulgar tongues—English, French, or Italian—gradually displaced Latin as the language of learning, the pursuit of learning was still the privilege of the few. Under such circumstances, dictionaries were intended for a limited audience, mainly as an aid to reading the most worthy literature. In attempting to compile a standard dictionary, Dr. Johnson derived his norms from the usage of the best writers, on the theory that this would furnish a guide to others who tried to read them, or who tried to write as well.

We see, then, that from the beginning the educational motive ¶13
dominated the making of dictionaries, though, as in the case of Dr. Johnson, and the work of the French and Italian Academies, there was also an interest in preserving the purity and order of the language. As against the latter interest, the Oxford English

Dictionary, begun in 1857, was a new departure, in that it did not try to dictate the best usage, but rather to present an accurate historical record of every type of usage—the worst as well as the best, taken from popular as well as stylish writing. But this conflict between the mission of the lexicographer as self-appointed arbiter and his function as historian can be regarded as a side-issue, for the dictionary, however constructed, is primarily an educational instrument. And the problem is whether that instrument is currently well used.

¶14 Our own Noah Webster is in a sense the hero of the story. Alarmed by the state into which learning had fallen after the Revolutionary War, Webster sought to make a one volume dictionary which would serve in the self-education of the semi-literate masses. He was concerned with the masses, not the elite, and with self-education, at a time when this country had not yet become democratic enough to regard the public education of all its children as a primary obligation of the state. The Webster dictionary was probably one of the first self-help books to become a popular best-seller. And the paradox is that now, with public education widely established in this country, with "literacy" as universal as suffrage, the self-help potentialities of a dictionary are seldom realized by the millions who own one. I am not thinking merely of children from progressive schools who cannot use a dictionary because they do not know the alphabet. I am thinking of all the products of contemporary education who, not being taught or inspired to read the great and difficult books, have little use for the dictionary. *How much better educated was the self-read man whom Webster helped!*

¶15 This brief history of dictionaries is relevant to the rules for reading and using them well. One of the first rules as to how to read a book is to know what sort of book it is. That means knowing what the author's intention was and what sort of thing you can expect to find in his work. If you look upon a dictionary merely as a spelling book or a guide to pronunciation, you will use it accordingly. If you realize that it contains a wealth of historical information, crystallized in the growth of language, you will pay attention, not merely to the variety of meanings which are listed under each word, but to their order.

And above all if you are interested in advancing your own education, you will use a dictionary according to its primary intention—as a help in reading books that might otherwise be too difficult because their vocabulary includes technical words, archaic words, literary allusions, or even familiar words used in now obsolete senses. The number of words in a man's vocabulary is as definite as the number of dollars he has in the bank; equally definite is the number of senses in which a man is able to use any given word. But there is this difference: a man cannot draw upon the public treasury when his bank-balance is overdrawn, but we can all draw upon the dictionary to get the coin we need to carry on the transaction of reading anything we want to read. ¶16

Let me be sure that I am not misunderstood. I am not saying that a dictionary is all you need in order to move anywhere in the realms of literature. There are many problems to be solved, in reading a book well, other than those arising from the author's vocabulary. And even with respect to vocabulary, the dictionary's primary service is on those occasions when you are confronted with a technical word or with a word that is wholly new to you—such as "costard" (an apple), or "hoatzin" (a South American bird), or "rabato" (a kind of flaring collar). More frequently the problem of interpretation arises because a relatively familiar word seems to be used in a strange sense. Here the dictionary will help, but it will not solve the problem. The dictionary may suggest the variety of senses in which the troublesome word can be used, but it can never determine how the author you are reading used it. That you must decide by wrestling with the context. More often than not, especially with distinguished writers, the word may be given a special, an almost unique, shade of meaning. The growth of your own vocabulary, in the ¶17 important dimension of multiple meanings as well as in mere quantity of words, will depend, first of all, upon the character of the books you read, and secondly, upon the use you make of the dictionary as a guide. You will misuse it—you will stultify rather than enlighten yourself—if you substitute the dictionary for the exercise of your own interpretative judgment in reading.

¶18 This suggests several other rules as to how *not* to read a dictionary. There is no more irritating fellow than the man who tries to settle an argument about communism, or justice, or liberty, by quoting from Webster. Webster and all his fellow lexicographers may be respected as authorities on word-usage, but they are not the ultimate founts of wisdom. They are no Supreme Court to which we can appeal for a decision of those fundamental controversies which, despite the warnings of semanticists, get us involved with abstract words. It is well to remember that the dictionary's authority can, for obvious reasons, be surer in the field of concrete words, and even in the field of the abstract technical words of science, than it ever can be with respect to philosophical words. Yet these words are indispensable if we are going to talk, read, or write about the things that matter most.

¶19 Another negative rule is: Don't swallow the dictionary. Don't try to get word-rich quick, by memorizing a lot of fancy words whose meanings are unconnected with any actual experience. Merely verbal knowledge is almost worse than no knowledge at all. If learning consisted in nothing but knowing the meanings of words, we could abolish all our courses of study, and substitute the dictionary for every other sort of book. But no one except a pedant or a fool would regard it as profitable or wise to read the dictionary from cover to cover.

¶20 In short, don't forget that the dictionary is a book about words, not about things. It can tell you how men have used words, but it does not define the nature of the things the words name. A Scandinavian university undertook a "linguistic experiment" to prove that human arguments always reduce to verbal differences. Seven lawyers were given seven dictionary definitions of truth and asked to defend them. They soon forgot to stick to the "verbal meanings" they had been assigned, and became vehemently involved in defending or opposing certain fundamental views about the nature of truth. The experiment showed that discussions may start about the meanings of words, but that, when interest in the problem is aroused, they seldom end there. Men pass from words to things, from names to natures. The dictionary can start an argument, but only thought or research can end it.

If we remember that a dictionary is a book about words, we can derive from that fact all the rules for reading a dictionary intelligently. Words can be looked at in four ways. ¶21

(1) *Words are physical things*—writable marks and speakable sounds. There must, therefore, be uniform ways of spelling and pronouncing them, though the uniformity is often spoiled by variations. ¶22

(2) *Words are parts of speech.* Each single word plays a grammatical role in the more complicated structure of a phrase or a sentence. According to the part it plays, we classify it as a certain part of speech—noun or verb, adjective or adverb, article or preposition. The same word can vary in different usages, shifting from one part of speech to another, as when we say "Man the boat" or "Take the jump." Another sort of grammatical variation in words arises from their inflection, but in a relatively uninflected language like English, we need pay attention only to the conjugation of the verb (infinitive, participle, past tense, etc.), the case of the noun (singular and plural), and the degree of the adjective (especially the comparative and superlative). ¶23

(3) *Words are signs.* They have meanings, not one but many. These meanings are related in various ways. Sometimes they shade from one into another; sometimes one word will have two or more sets of totally unrelated meanings. Through their ¶24

meanings words are related to one another—as synonyms sharing in the same meaning even though they differ in its shading; or as antonyms through opposition or contrast of meanings. Furthermore, it is in their capacity as signs that we distinguish words as proper or common names (according as they name just one thing or many which are alike in some respect); and as concrete or abstract names (according as they point to some thing which we can sense, or refer to some aspect of things which we can understand by thought but not observe through our senses).

¶25 Finally, (4) *words are conventional.* They mean or signify natural things, but they themselves are not natural. They are man-made signs. That is why every word has a history, just as everything else man makes has a time and place of origin, and a cultural career, in which it goes through certain transformations. The history of words is given by their etymological derivation from original word-roots, prefixes, and suffixes; it includes the account of their physical change, both in spelling and pronunciation; it tells of their shifting meanings, and which among them are archaic and obsolete, which are current and regular, which are idiomatic, colloquial, or slang.

¶26 A good dictionary will answer all your questions about words under these four heads. The art of reading a dictionary (as any other book) consists in knowing what questions to ask about words and how to find the answers. I have suggested the questions. The dictionary itself tells you how to find the answers. In this respect, it is a perfect self-help book, because it tells you what to pay attention to and how to interpret the various abbreviations and symbols it uses in giving you the four varieties of information about words. Anyone who fails to consult the explanatory notes and the list of abbreviations at the beginning of a dictionary can blame only himself for not being able to read the dictionary well. Unfortunately, many people fail here, as in the case of other books, because they insist upon neglecting the prefatory matter—as if the author were just amusing himself by including it.

I think these suggestions about how to read, and how not to misuse, a dictionary are easy to follow. But like all other rules they will be followed well only by the man who is rightly motivated in the first place. And, in the last place, they will be wisely applied only by the man who remembers that we are both *free* and *bound* in all our dealing with language, whether as writers or readers. ¶27

> "When I use a word," Humpty-Dumpty said in a rather scornful tone, "it means just what I choose it to mean—neither more nor less."
>
> "The question is," said Alice, "whether you can make words mean so many different things."
>
> "The question is," said Humpty-Dumpty, "which is to be master—that's all."

For Greater Insight

1. Adler says, in Par. 7, "The dictionary exists . . . because there is no one in that condition." Describe in your own words the condition he refers to. Is he correct when he says that there is no one in that condition?
2. Explain what Adler means by "level of our literary competence." Is he right about "few of us"? What is your personal reaction to a book or a speaker using words just a little beyond your knowledge? Do you rise to the challenge? Or yield to the frustration?
3. Compare Dr. Johnson's procedure (Par. 12) with what is said about *Webster's Third New International Dictionary* in Par. 20 of *Will Strunk* (p. 152). Was Dr. Johnson descriptive or prescriptive?
4. How did Noah Webster's purpose differ from the purposes of other lexicographers? Has that purpose any relation to the modern use of dictionaries? A positive or negative relation?
5. Explain the meaning of the italicized sentence at the end of Par. 14. Why was the contemporary of Webster better educated? Was he, really? Better educated than who was? Who or what may be at fault?
6. Is Adler encouraging the use of the dictionary as an end or goal, or as a means to an end? What would he like to accomplish?

7. In Par. 17 Adler points out a situation in which the dictionary won't solve a problem. What is the problem, and what does he mean by "wrestling with the context"? Can you supply an illustration? Find Adler's use of "the vulgar tongues," look up *vulgar* in the dictionary, and from the dictionary and from context, decide what Adler meant.
8. In Par. 18 Adler uses the terms *concrete* and *abstract*. Explain both in such a way that you make Adler's point clear.
9. You should be able to carry on a discussion about any of Adler's four ways of looking at words.
10. Which is correct, Humpty-Dumpty or Alice?

Word Study

we *redundantly* refer:
was *edified* by:
sacerdotal functions:
the *taboo* against strange words:
is still *extant*:
the *vulgar* tongues:
derived his *norms*:
self-appointed *arbiter*:
the *paradox* is:
wrestling with the *context*:
you will *stultify*:
warnings of *semanticists*:
except a *pedant*:
their *etymological* derivation:
the *prefatory* matter:

In Defense of Editing

Norman Podhoretz

Mr. Podhoretz has been since 1959 editor of *Commentary*, a publication devoted to nonpartisan appraisal of social, economic, and political problems besetting the world today. His success is attested to by the fact that under his editorship the price of the magazine has risen from 40¢ to 75¢, the circulation from 14,000 to 57,000, and the annual deficit has been reduced from $100,000 to $30,000 in 1966, with the expectation of its being wiped out entirely.

Commentary attracts some of the finest thinkers and writers, and some of the most discerning readers.

To students who are learning that, for a writer, the best he can do is the least he should do, and that perfection is the only really acceptable goal, some of Podhoretz' points will be revealing —and encouraging. His essay first appeared in *Harper's Magazine* in October 1965.

It seems to have become the fashion lately for writers who have ¶1
had difficulties with one magazine or another to complain in public about the terrible treatment they have received at the hands of insensitive editors. B. H. Haggin not long ago voiced such a complaint in *Partisan Review* against Robert Hatch of *The Nation;* more recently, in the *Hudson Review*, Hans J. Morgenthau had a go at me. As it happens, both Haggin and Morgenthau were speaking out of what might easily be regarded as

personal pique, but the question they raised—Are editors necessary?—is nevertheless an interesting one, touching as it does on the general state of discourse in America and the whole issue of the maintenance of standards. To take up that question, one has to discuss aspects of the editorial process that were perhaps better kept private, but now that they are being made public from the point of view of the aggrieved author, they might just as well be talked about from the point of view of the working editor as well. And the only way for a working editor to begin talking honestly about them is to attempt an answer to the question as it was put in more positive form by John Fischer in the June *Harper's:* What do editors do?

¶2 Most people, I imagine, if they think about it at all, think that the job of an editor is to pick and choose among finished pieces of work which have been submitted to him and deliver them to the printer; that is to say, he acts as a middleman between individual authors and an expectant public. In the six years that I have been editing *Commentary,* there have indeed been occasions when my job corresponded roughly to that conception of it. But the editorial process is usually far more complicated. Typically, between the receipt of a manuscript at the offices of almost any magazine and the dispatch of a publishable article to the printer fall the shadows—of *doubt,* of *deliberation,* of *labor,* of *negotiation.*

¶3 *Doubt:* Every magazine that deserves the name has a character, a style, a point of view, a circumscribed area of concern, a conception of how discourse ought to be conducted; if it lacks these things, it is not a magazine but a periodical anthology of random writings. Obviously the editor's personality, his cast of mind, his biases, his interests are crucial to the formation of this character. Yet once it has been formed—if it has been truly formed—it takes on an independent existence of its own, resisting even the editor's efforts to change or qualify it. It is enormously important for him to fight his own magazine, to keep it from becoming hardened and predictable, to keep it open and mobile. Yet if he whores too avidly after strange gods, desiring this man's art and that man's scope, the magazine will avenge itself by refusing to assimilate the foreign substance. Instead of achieving surprise, he will achieve a tasteless incongruity, like a woman with the wrong hairdo; instead of looking more flexible and lively, his magazine will take on an uncertain and affected air. This is why phrases like "Not for us" or "Unsuitable" so often accompany rejected manuscripts. They are used partly to soothe the wounded feeling of authors, but there is a truth in them by which magazines live or die.

Rites of Commissioning

To understand that magazines have their own insistent characters is to understand why the vast majority of the articles they publish are likely to be commissioned. (The strictly literary magazines are an exception, for the obvious reason that poems and stories, unlike articles, are not as a rule written to order. But even a literary magazine can only become a real magazine —that is, acquire a character—by going after particular writers whom the editor values more highly than others; that, too, may perhaps be regarded as a form of commissioning.) ¶4

If an established writer or a regular contributor comes to a magazine with a proposal that the editor likes, he will naturally be told to go ahead. But before he is told to go ahead, the editor will indicate to him how he thinks the subject ought properly to be handled: "properly," of course, meaning the editor's conception of how the intrinsic demands of the subject can best be reconciled with the demands of the magazine's character. ¶5

The other, more common, form of commissioning follows not upon the writer's initiative but upon the editor's. The editor —or, mysteriously, the magazine itself—decides that an article is needed on a given subject and he looks for someone who can ¶6 do it as far as possible in the "right" way. This search for the right writer sets what is one of the editor's most interesting problems, but it can be exhausting; often the writer he wants is a busy man who must be cajoled, flattered, harassed, nagged. And even with cajolery, flattery, harassment, and nagging, the search ends half the time in failure, either because no one can be found, or because the person who eventually is found never delivers, or worse, turns out to be the wrong writer. With enough experience, however, an editor will know where to go, and with enough luck he will snare his man. Still, he has to be very lucky indeed or very inspired in his choice of the writer to get the piece *he* is dreaming of (and almost miraculously lucky to get it on the promised date). It happens once in a great while. But the typical conclusion to this phase of the editorial process is the delivery of a manuscript which only faintly approximates the editor's ideal conception, or else differs radically from it. Thus *Doubt*, and then . . .

¶7 *Deliberation:* Is it right for *us*? Can it be made right for us? How? Will the author be willing to revise it? Can he revise it on time? Will he let *us* revise it? Are we willing to risk offending a valuable contributor by pushing very hard? Are we being unfair or too rigid? Should we perhaps publish the piece more or less as it is? Are we perhaps a little crazy?

¶8 Such are the questions that are struggled with at editorial conferences or via inter-office memos. Finally, when the manuscript may have gone the rounds of the editorial staff a second time (the conference having left everyone thoroughly uncertain) a decision, enthusiastic or grudging, is reached. A letter is written or a telephone conversation held or a lunch date arranged. "This is what we think still needs to be done. Will you do it?" If yes, the whole process is repeated when the revised version comes in. Or, if no: "Will you let us do it, then? Naturally you'll have an opportunity to check the edited version." If yes to that, the phase of deliberation gives way to . . .

Labor: One edits a manuscript by trying to correct the flaws ¶9
that inevitably appear when it is subjected to the minutest scrutiny of which the editor is capable. In America (and indications are that this is beginning to happen in England, too), the overwhelming majority of the flaws to be corrected are either technical or minimally aesthetic: flaws of grammar, flaws of syntax, flaws of structure, flaws of rhetoric, flaws of taste.

But the deficiencies that tend to show up on a ruthlessly ¶10
close study of a manuscript may be substantive too. Under the editorial microscope things that were not visible to the naked eye—neither the editor's nor the author's—suddenly make an unexpected appearance. One sentence does not logically follow from the next; the paragraph on page 8 only makes sense if it is transposed to page 6 and stitched in with a clever transition to cover the seam; a point which seemed persuasive on a first reading turns out to need bolstering with more documentation (or the irrelevancies surrounding it have to be peeled away); an argument which looked reasonable before is now revealed as contradicting another argument elsewhere in the piece, or to have ignored or distorted the evidence on the other side of the case.

Some of these deficiencies—the logical and structural ones ¶11
—can be remedied by the editor himself if he has acquired a truly inward grasp of what the author is trying to say and show and evoke. But it must be left to the author to fill in gaps, to add further information, to take up new questions that have arisen, to shore up weaknesses that have become evident. Accordingly the edited version of his article will be sent to him with a letter explaining what has been done to the manuscript and why, asking him to make sure that no inaccuracies have crept in through the editing, and requesting that he deal with the substantive problems which have emerged upon careful scrutiny. The phase of *Labor* has come to a close, and what remains is . . .

Negotiation: Seeing the edited manuscript, the author, as ¶12 likely as not, is more than a little outraged. This is, after all, *his* article; he takes responsibility for it; it is to appear under his name. By what right does anyone presume to tamper with it? (On the other hand, some authors, curiously enough including many who write very well, are often grateful for editing.) When the outrage subsides, however, he will begin to wonder whether there might not perhaps be a certain justice in the criticisms reflected in the editing; not all, of course, but some. Adjustments will naturally have to be made here and there, but on the whole the edited version will do.

Clash of Vanities

¶13 Just as the editor may have been worrying about the possibility of losing both article and author by pressing too hard on the manuscript, so on his side the author may be worried lest he lose his chance of publishing the piece and disaffect the editor. There is a clash of interests and vanities here which does not differ greatly in principle from the clash of opposing groups in politics, and it is ordinarily settled in much the same way as political struggles are—by negotiation. The author accepts most of the editing but insists on certain points (the restoration of a passage that has been cut or of a formulation that has been changed), the editor agrees, and the piece is at long last sent to the printer.

¶14 Thus is the editorial process completed—so far as this one article is concerned. There may be as many as fifteen or twenty other pieces in the same issue. Not all of them will have involved so much effort. Two or three will have required only a little touching up or none at all; several others will have needed considerable editing but not in every sentence; still others will have needed more editing than the editor—knowing the author would object, and on balance wanting the piece even in an imperfect state—dared to do. (Reading such pieces in proof, or even in print, the editor can hardly control his pencil.)

It takes, then, a great deal of work, an enervating concentration on detail, and a fanatical concern with the bone and sinew of the English language to edit a manuscript—to improve an essentially well-written piece or to turn a clumsily written one into, at the very least, a readable and literate article, and, at the very most, a beautifully shaped and effectively expressed essay which remains true to the author's intention, which realizes that intention more fully than he himself was able to do. In addition to work, manuscript editing takes time—and time is critical to an enterprise that lives under the pressure of deadlines. And in addition to time, it takes a combination of sympathy—getting inside someone else's mind—and rigor—resistance to being swallowed up by that other mind, once inside—that is extremely difficult to maintain. ¶15

Who Cares?

Is it all worth it? Over and over again one asks oneself that question, tempted as one is to hoard some of the energy that goes into editing for thinking one's own thoughts or doing one's own writing. One asks oneself whether anyone would know the difference if one simply sent all those pieces to the printer after a perfunctory reading. And one asks oneself whether anyone really cares about writing of this kind *as* writing. For all editors have had the experience of publishing inadequately edited pieces that were praised beyond their deserts, and articles they knew to be classics of their type that were scarcely noticed and certainly not valued at their proper worth. If such articles (which are not edited—one has no impulse to tamper with perfection) are not appreciated, what hope is there that lesser (edited) pieces will be? ¶16

In the end an editor is thrown back, as any man doing any job faithfully must be, on the fact that *he* cares and that he can therefore do no other. He cares about the English language; he cares about clarity of thought and grace of expression; he ¶17 cares about the traditions of discourse and of argument. It hardly needs to be said that even good editors will sometimes bungle a job and that bad editors invariably will, but it nevertheless remains true that the editorial process is a necessity if standards are to be preserved and if the intellectual life in America is not to become wholly compartmentalized and ultimately sterile in spirit.

¶18 Apocalyptic as this may sound, I believe it to be an accurate statement of the case. It is no secret that the number of people in this country who can write an acceptable piece of exposition in literate English is astoundingly low. But if one goes beyond that minimal requirement and asks for a piece of exposition whose virtues include clarity, economy, coherence, and grace, one is hard put to find it even among professional journalists or professors of English, let alone professors of economics or sociology. (One is, however, rather more likely to find it among the professors of history, who as a class are for some reason the best writers in the academy today.) Whatever the causes of this sorry condition may be, the fact is that it exists, and until it is remedied the only alternative to (competent) editing must be a further debasement of our language and a further loosening of our already tenuous hold on the traditions of civilized public discourse.

¶19 In our culture—I exaggerate only slightly—those who know cannot write, and those who can write do not know. An editor who wants an article on a given subject which seems important to him at a given time has very little trouble locating people with impeccable credentials and unquestionable authority. Since such people are rarely good writers, however, he has three choices as an editor: he can decide not to get a piece on the subject at all; he can resign himself to publishing one that is gratuitously unreadable and guilty of grave offenses against the art of exposition; or he can edit. To opt for the first choice is to lose opportunities; to opt for the second is to behave irresponsibly both toward the readers of his magazine and toward the standards of his profession; to opt for the third is to risk error and arrogance for the sake of creating the monthly illusion that we live in a world where a certain mode of serious discussion can still take place. What is today an illusion was once a reality; but without the illusion—that is, the sense of what is possible—before our eyes, how will we ever make it a reality again?

Apart from standards, there is also the matter of American ¶20
intellectual life itself. Once upon a time—or so it now seems—all educated men spoke the same language and therefore were able to communicate with one another. They strolled together in marketplaces or ate together at High Table conversing all the while, wittily, on all manner of things. These educated men were all equally philosophers, equally theologians, equally scientists. But then one day, in the very midst of a conversation, they suddenly discovered that something strange had happened: they could no longer understand one another. They all wondered why they had been punished in this mysterious way by the multiplication of tongues (which soon came to be known as "disciplines"). Some blamed it on the growth of an idolatrous cult of Science among their fellows; others blamed it on the laziness and complacency of the *littérateurs*. The argument still rages today, but the "disciplines" are if anything further apart than they were in that far-off time when the common language was first shattered into a hundred isolated fragments.

Finding the Language

In my view, the primary responsibility of the magazine ¶21
editor is to participate in the struggle to reconstruct that shattered common language. There *must* be a language in which all but the most highly technical matters can be discussed without distortion or falsification or watering-down; there *must* be a language impartially free of all the various jargons through which

the "disciplines" maintain their proud and debilitating isolation; there *must* be a language in which the kinship of these disciplines is expressed and revealed and reaffirmed.

¶22 A man who does not believe in the possibility of such a language cannot edit a magazine (though he may be able to edit a specialized journal of one kind or another). For from the belief in the possibility of such a language everything else that makes an editor follows: the conception of a culture as organic—as one and not many—and therefore accessible in all its modalities to the general intelligence; the correlative conviction that by the exercise of his general intelligence a man can determine what the important issues are even in areas in which he has no special training; the arrogance to assert that *this* is the relevant point rather than *that;* the nerve to tell others how to discuss things which they know more about than he does.

¶23 And so we come back to where we began: to manuscript editing. Mr. Fischer is right in stressing qualities like intuition, curiosity, and enthusiasm when he talks about the process by which an editor decides on subjects to be covered, problems to be investigated, issues to be raised. But it is manuscript editing and manuscript editing alone that makes it possible for these subjects to be covered properly, these problems to be investigated adequately, these issues to be raised incisively.

¶24 (I should add that the article you have just read was commissioned and deliberated upon, but not edited. Perhaps—I hope not—it should have been.)

For Greater Insight

1. What is a hypothetical question? In the first paragraph Podhoretz asks two such questions. What are they? How do they help the author indicate the purpose of his essay? How do they help the reader?
2. What was your idea of the task of the editor before you read this essay?

3. At the end of the second paragraph Podhoretz uses the expression "fall the shadows." What does he mean by "shadows"? Why is the word a good one?
4. Explain what Podhoretz means by *doubt, deliberation, labor,* and *negotiation.*
5. Does Podhoretz believe that a periodical must develop a "character" and stick to it, or does he believe there should be change and variety? Explain.
6. When he names the four "shadows," Podhoretz tells us that his essay will have at least four parts. He also uses four section headings in larger type. What is the function of these headings in relation to the four "shadows"? How do they serve a transitional purpose?
7. Explain how Podhoretz has made completely clear the divisions between his explanations of the four "shadows." Look at the end of Par. 6 and the beginning of Par. 7, the end of 8 and the beginning of 9, and the end of 11 and the beginning of 12. This is unusual; is it effective?
8. Students who think that an established professional writer simply sits down at the typewriter and dashes off deathless prose effortlessly the first time around should study carefully the sections on *deliberation, labor,* and *negotiation,* and then Par. 18. The questions to be thought about are simple, but perhaps you'd better keep the answers to yourself!
9. For students using this text, the sections "Who Cares?" and "Finding the Language" may well be the most important. Do you agree or disagree? Why?
10. What does the editor (Podhoretz) care about? Explain all terms used—"grace of expression," for example.
11. According to Par. 20, what happened to the language of educated men? Why did it happen? Is it good or bad? Why?
12. In Par. 21, Podhoretz says three times, "There *must* be a language . . ." Does he mean that there is such a language, and that someone must discover it, or that such a language must be created? In any event, why must there be such a language? What would it accomplish?
13. Many authors enjoy using fragments and paraphrases from other pieces of literature—*allusions* to them. Podhoretz is no exception. In Pars. 2 and 3 he has allusions to T. S. Eliot's *The Hollow Men,* to the Bible, and to Shakespeare. Can you locate them?

Word Study

personal *pique*:
aggrieved authors:
a *circumscribed* area:
his *biases*:
assimilate the foreign substance:
tasteless incongruity:
intrinsic demands:
minimally aesthetic:
may be *substantive*:
irrelevancies surrounding it:
disaffect the editor:
an *enervating* concentration:
a *perfunctory* reading:
sterile in spirit:
Apocalyptic as this may sound:
debasement of our language:
tenuous hold:
impeccable credentials:
gratuitously unreadable:
opt for the first:
idolatrous cult:
complacency of the *littérateurs*:
debilitating isolation:
in all its *modalities*:

British and American English

Simeon Potter

Although basically the languages are the same, there are so many differences between British English and American English that often natives of Great Britain and the United States are unable to communicate with each other without serious problems. The major problems are of two kinds: (1) the different pronunciations of words common to both British English and American English, and (2) the use of different words for the same thing. It is with the nature and history of the differences that the present essay is concerned.

The essay is Chapter 13 of *Our Language*, a book written and published in Great Britain for British readers.

Simeon Potter is a Londoner by birth, and has taught English in Czechoslovakia, Denmark, and England, where he has held the Baines Chair of English in the University of Liverpool. He is the author of several books on the English language and on linguistics, including *Language in the Modern World.*

The language taken by John Smith to Virginia in 1607 and by ¶1
the Pilgrim Fathers to Massachusetts in 1620 was the English of Shakespeare and Milton. During the following century and a half most of the colonists who reached the shores of New England were British, but the Dutch founded New Amsterdam and held it until it was seized by the British in 1664 and renamed after the King's brother, the Duke of York. When, in

1790, the thirteen colonies on the Atlantic seaboard ratified the Federal Constitution, they comprised four million English-speaking people, most of whom still dwelt to the east of the Appalachian Mountains. From the linguistic point of view this was the first and decisive stage in the history of United States English, which, by universal consent but less accurately, we call American English for short.

¶2 During the period from 1790 to the outbreak of the Civil War in 1860, new States were created west of the Appalachians and the Alleghenies and fresh immigrants arrived in large numbers from Ireland and Germany. The Irish potato famine of 1845 drove one and a half million Irishmen to seek a home in the New World and the European revolution of 1848 caused as many Germans to settle in Pennsylvania and the Middle West.

¶3 The third period, from the end of the Civil War in 1865 to the present day, was marked ethnographically by the arrival of Scandinavians, Slavs and Italians. During the closing decades of the nineteenth century one million Scandinavians, or one fifth of the total population of Norway and Sweden, crossed the Atlantic Ocean and settled, for the most part, in Minnesota and in the Upper Mississippi Valley. They were followed by millions of Czechs, Slovaks, Poles, Yugoslavs, and Italians, whose numbers were still further augmented by refugees in flight from the dire political persecutions which degraded Europe in the first half of the twentieth century. As the great American Republic took shape with the attachment of French and Spanish populations, with the addition of native Indian tribes in the Middle West, and with the absorption of Chinese and Japanese who landed on the Pacific Coast, so the cosmopolitan character of the United States became more accentuated. Further, the African Negroes have come to number over ten millions. Never, however, has the language of Washington and Lincoln been in jeopardy. At no time has there threatened any real danger that English might not be capable of completely assimilating the immigrant tongues or that the children of the French in Louisiana, the Germans in Pennsylvania, the Scandinavians in Minnesota, or the Slavs and Italians in Michigan might not all be able to understand, speak, read, and write English in the third and fourth generations.

The literary language, indeed, has seldom diverged percep- ¶4
tibly from that of the homeland. Washington Irving, Edgar Allan Poe and Nathaniel Hawthorne spared no pains in their day to write impeccable standard English. Henry James, Logan Pearsall Smith and Thomas Stearns Eliot were born in America but found an intellectual home in Europe. Edmund Wilson, Elmer Edgar Stoll, George Sherburn, Douglas Bush, and other eminent American critics write not unlike their British models, George Saintsbury, Andrew Cecil Bradley, Oliver Elton, and Sir Herbert Grierson. English literature is now cosmopolitan and worldwide: no sea or ocean bounds can be set to its domain. Henceforth English literature must include all excellent and memorable writing in the English language, regardless of political and geographical boundaries.

In spelling, vocabulary, and pronunciation, and in the syntax ¶5
of the lower levels of speech, divergences remain. The distinctive features of American spelling are mainly a legacy bequeathed by that energetic little pale-faced man Noah Webster (1758–1843), whose *American Spelling Book* appeared in 1783 and whose *American Dictionary of the English Language,* the ancestor of all later Webster Dictionaries, was published in 1828. Webster would have liked to effect more drastic reforms in spelling, but he was restrained by necessity. 'Common sense and convenience', he averred, 'would lead me to write *public, favor, nabor, hed, proov, flem, hiz, giv, det, ruf,* and *wel* instead of *publick, favour, neighbour, head, prove, phlegm, his, give, debt, rough,* and *well.*' The practical man of business, however, prevailed over the theoretical reformer. Webster sought a market for his new book on both sides of the Atlantic and he was advised to modify his drastic changes considerably. Today the second

unabridged edition (1934) of Webster's *New International Dictionary* is the official spelling guide of the Government Printing Office and the accepted authority in all American courts. It sanctions such spellings as *-or* for *-our* in *favor, honor, humor, labor, odor,* and *valor* for English *favour, honour, humour, labour, odour,* and *valour; -er* for *-re* in *caliber, center, fiber, meter,* and *theater* for English *calibre, centre, fibre, metre,* and *theatre;* one consonant for two in *traveler, traveling, traveled, jewelry,* and *wagon* for English *traveller, travelling, travelled, jewellery,* and *waggon; -s-* for *-c-* in the substantives *defense, offense,* and *practise* for English *defence, offence,* and *practice;* various simplifications such as *ax, catalog, check, forever, jail, mask, medieval, program, story, tho, thoro, thru,* and *today* for English *axe, catalogue, cheque, for ever, gaol, masque, mediaeval, programme, storey* (of a building), *though, thorough, through,* and *to-day.* On the analogy, as he thought, of *affection, collection,* and *direction,* Noah Webster clung to *connection* and *reflection* and these spellings are still favoured in America instead of the preferable forms *connexion* and *reflexion.* In general, however, the modified spellings of Webster's Dictionary are sound and sensible. Hundreds of American spellings have won acceptance in England, not only *public* for *publick, jail* for *gaol, cider* for *cyder, asphalt* for *asphalte,* and the like, but also the *-or* spellings for all agent substantives—*author, censor, conqueror, donor, juror, tailor, tutor,* and *visitor*—all, in fact, except *paviour* and *saviour.* The schoolchildren of England are no longer penalized for spelling in the American way and in recent years certain American publishers have deliberately restored a more old-fashioned English spelling.

¶6 On arriving in the United States for the first time the Englishman is made unduly aware of differences in vocabulary because these differences happen to loom exceptionally large in the language of travel and transport. Let us assume, by way of illustration, that he decides to continue his journey by rail, that is, by *railroad.* He does not register his luggage but he *checks* his *baggage,* which is then placed, not in the luggage van, but in the *baggage car;* perhaps he must first rescue it from the left-luggage office, which, he discovers, is called the *checkroom.* A goods train is referred to as a *freight train* and a brake-van becomes a *caboose.* He looks for the inquiry office in order to corroborate details and he finds that it is called the *information bureau;* or he may decide to consult a *bulletin-board,* in England a notice-board, or a *schedule,* in England a time-table, on his own account. He is surprised to learn that a season ticket is a *commutation ticket* and that a season-ticket holder is a plain *commuter.* The driver of his train is the *engineer* and the guard is the *conductor.* He hears someone refer to a *switch,* which turns out to be a *point,* and he soon discovers that a *grade crossing* is merely a level crossing. When he reaches his destination he finds an *automobile* waiting for him at the *railroad depot.* He cannot help noticing that the windscreen is called the *windshield,* the bonnet the *hood,* and that petrol is alluded to as *gasoline* or plain *gas.* That explains why the filling station is named the *gas station* and why *accelerating* is described as *stepping on the gas.* On his way through the town he passes trams or *street cars* with their trolley-poles or *contact rods.* He observes cyclists, *cyclers* or *wheelmen,* riding near the pavement or *sidewalk.* One of them has just stopped to mend a puncture or *fix a flat.* Not far away a lorry or *truck* is in difficulties and the breakdown gang or *wrecking crew* is getting to work. Having alighted at his hotel, he finds that it has no personal lift or *elevator* to take him up to his room on the *fifth floor* (which, luckily for him, turns out to be only what he calls the fourth), but that a service lift or *dumbwaiter* may be used for luggage or *baggage.*

At no point is the intelligent traveller inconvenienced by ¶7
these hitherto unfamiliar, but easily assimilable, expressions. The more difficult task is to understand the living and everchanging

idioms of American slang. Much may be learnt about colloquial and slang idioms from the pages of that intermittent journal *Dialect Notes,* which began its career as long ago as 1890; and from numerous articles appearing in *American Speech,* which was founded as a monthly in 1925, and which now continues to thrive as a quarterly publication of the Columbia University Press. Much, too, may be learnt from the large fourth edition (1936) of Henry Louis Mencken's *The American Language* and its two copious *Supplements* of 1945 and 1948. From *A Dictionary of American English on Historical Principles* (1938–44), by Sir William Craigie and James R. Hulbert, much may be learnt about the 'more serious and solid elements of American English' and about those 'speechways' which mirror the American life of the past. Here, naturally, information may be gleaned about those many trees, shrubs, animals, birds, and reptiles which are rare or unknown in Europe. The countless new arts and techniques of a highly developed civilization figure prominently in its pages, but slang and dialect are restricted to expressions of early date or of special prominence. Twentieth-century neologisms do not appear in it at all, for the editors set the year 1900 as their arbitrary time-limit. Since that date many thousands of new words have become current American and have made their way up from slang to the more respectable levels of colloquial speech. 'Today', wrote the Baltimore journalist H. L. Mencken in 1945 (*The American Language Supplement One,* p. 323), 'it is no longer necessary for an American writer to apologize for writing American. He is not only forgiven if he seeks to set forth his notions in the plainest and least pedantic manner possible; he is also sure of escaping blame (save, of course, by an Old Guard of English reviewers) if he makes liberal dips into the vocabulary of everyday, including its most plausible neologisms. Indeed, he seems a bit stiff and academic if he doesn't make some attempt, however unhappy, to add to the stock of such neologisms himself. How many are launched in this great Republic every year I do not know, but the number must be formidable. . . . So many novelties swarm in that it is quite impossible for the dictionaries to keep up with them; indeed, a large number come and go without the lexicographers so much as hearing of them. At least four-fifths of those which get any sort of toe-hold in the language originate in the United States, and most of the four-fifths remain here. We Americans live in an age and society given over to enormous and perhaps even excessive word-making —the most riotous seen in the world since the break-up of Latin. It is an extremely wasteful process, for with so many newcomers to choose from it is inevitable that large numbers of pungent and useful words and phrases must be discarded and in the end forgotten by all save linguistic paleontologists. But we must not complain about that, for all the great processes of nature are wasteful, and it is by no means assured that the fittest always survive.' Such neologisms are clipped words like *lube* for *lubricating oil* and *co-ed* for *co-educational;* back-formations like *to televise* (1931) from *television* and *to propagand* (1939) from *propaganda;* blends like *cablegram* from *cable* and *telegram, Aframerican* from *African* and *American, radiotrician* from *radio* and *electrician, sportcast* from *sport* and *broadcast,* and *sneet* from *snow* and *sleet;* artificial or made-up formations like *carborundum, cellophane,* and *pianola;* and acronyms or telescoped names like *nabisco* from *National Biscuit Company* or *socony* from *Standard Oil Company.* Hundreds of new expressions have also arisen by a revival and extension of grammatical conversion or the free interchange of function among parts of speech. When we *park* our cars we are using the substantive *park* as a verb in a particular sense. Shakespeare, it is true, used *to park* as a verb in the sense 'to confine or enclose as in a park' in I *Henry the Sixth,* IV. ii. 45: 'How are we park'd and bounded in a pale!' But *to park* in the sense 'to place compactly in a park' was a new conversion made by the British Army in 1812 at the time of the Napoleonic Wars. Nearly one hundred years later, in

1910, it was adopted by British chauffeurs and by American automobilists into their vocabulary. Since then *to park* has come to mean 'to leave or keep other things and persons in a suitable place until required' and Americans park not only their automobiles but also their children, their dogs, and their chewing-gum (P. G. Wodehouse, *The Inimitable Jeeves*). *Stream-line* was first recorded in 1873 in the highly technical language of hydrodynamics. Later, in 1907, it was applied in aerodynamics to the shape given to cars and aircraft offering the minimum resistance to the air. Later still, in 1913, it was converted into the verb *to streamline,* which has recently become a vogue-word in America and has been extended to mean any attempt whatever at simplification. That 'nasty newcomer' *to panic* was used by Thomas Hood in 1827, but apparently by no other writer until it was re-invented in the United States in 1910. To-day Americans no longer hesitate to *loan* (as well as to *lend*), to *audition* (grant a hearing or audition to), to *accession* (new library-books), to *remainder* (unsold and unsalable books), to *service* (a car or an automobile), to *blueprint* (to make any plan of any thing), to *contact* (to get into touch with), to *deadhead* (to admit as a 'deadhead' without payment), to *highlight* (to bring out the brightest parts or chief features of a subject), to *research* (to make researches), to *wastebasket* (to cast as rubbish into the wastepaper-basket), to *air* (to disseminate by radio), to *wax* (to record for the phonograph), and to *brain-trust* (to participate in what we English prefer to call a brains-trust). A bargain is a *good buy,* articles of food are *eats,* and technical skill is the *know-how.*

¶8 We refer quite naturally in everyday English to 'children and *grown-ups*' without realizing, perhaps, what an interesting linguistic form the word *grown-ups* is. It is the second or past participle of the intransitive durative verb *grow* (the past participle of which, because durative, has present signification) + the adverb *up;* compounded, converted into a substantive, and given the plural inflexion *-s*. This precise form is not old. It is first recorded in a letter penned by Jane Austen in 1813, although *grown-up* had been used as an epithet adjective in the seventeenth century. When we speak of giving our friends a good *send-off* we are employing an expression first used in this sense of 'a good-will demonstration' by Mark Twain in 1872. Hitherto this verb-adverb substantive had referred to the sending off or starting of contestants in a race. Many other substantives of this type have since found favour in America. A place of concealment is a *hide-out,* a drop in social esteem a *come-down,* a re-organization of staff a *shake-up,* and a free lunch a *hand-out.* Any arrangement or establishment is a *set-up,* a meeting of any kind is a *get-together,* and an escape is a *get-away.* Any action which brings matters to an issue or forces men to disclose their plans is a *show-down* as, at card-games, the players suddenly lay cards on the table. The Americans have a liking, too, for picturesque and vivid verb-phrases, both old and new: *to cut a shine, go the whole hog, shell out, go for, go in for, rope in, go him one better, go it blind, face the music, go it alone, stand from under, do the square thing, knock the spots off, spread it on thick, shinny on one's own side, get away with it,* and *paint the town red.* Journalists, gossip-columnists, makers of film and radio scripts, song writers and advertising agents are busy coining new turns of speech day by day. Some of these are literally ephemeral. They do not 'catch on'; they have their day and they are forgotten. Others live on and eventually, perhaps, they are tacitly adopted by the whole English-speaking world.

Suffixes may be resuscitated and multiplied by analogy. In ¶9
conformity with *mathematician* and *electrician* the old *undertaker,* itself shortened from *funeral undertaker,* becomes *mortician* (1923), not to mention *beautician.* Cafeteria in Spanish is a 'coffee-house': in American English it is extended to mean a 'help-yourself restaurant' and thence proceed *caketeria, fruiteria, groceteria, smoketeria,* and a host of others, some accepted,

others transitory, if not merely facetious. On the basis of *sanatorium,* other institutions are named *healthatorium, restatorium,* and *shavatorium.* Thomas Carlyle and others sought to revive the suffix *-dom,* corresponding to German *-tum,* in the nineteenth century and among their creations that survived were *boredom, officialdom,* and *serfdom.* Hundreds of new *-dom* compounds—*filmdom, stardom, crosswordpuzzledom, dictatordom, gangsterdom,* and *slumdom*—are now fashionable in America. The ancient agent suffixes, Greek *-ist* and Germanic *-ster,* have likewise come to life again in *vacationist* (holiday-maker, 1888), *manicurist* (1889), *behaviorist* (coined by John B. Watson in 1913), *receptionist* (1923), *blurbist* (concoctor of blurbs or slip-cover encomiums, 1925), and *editorialist* (1944); *ringster* (1879), *gangster* (1896), *roadster* (1910), and *speedster* (1918).

¶10 Among the more outstanding features of American pronunciation a few may here be noted. In words like *for, door, farm,* and *lord* the *r* is still sounded as a fricative, whereas in English it is silent except in expressions like *far away* and *the door opens* where a linking *r* is naturally inserted. In most dialects of Southern England the rolled or trilled *r* sound was weakened in pronunciation in the seventeenth century and lost in the eighteenth. Americans pronounce words like *dance, fast, grass, half,* and *path* with a low front *a* sound [æ] as in *cat,* which is still heard in the northern counties of England and which persisted in the southern counties until the end of the eighteenth century. Americans pronounce words like *dock, fog, hot,* and *rod* with a low back *a* sound [ɑ] like the vowel sound in *car* and *father* shortened. They pronounce words like *dew, duke, new,* and *steward* with the [ju:] sound reduced to [u:] so that *dew* and *duke* sound like *do* and *dook.* Just as in Spanish, Portuguese and Provençal, the Latin and Italian *armata,* past participle feminine, 'armed (force)', has become *armada,* so in present-day American *-t-* is often voiced, so that *beating* sounds very much like *beading, matter* like *madder,* and *metal* like *medal.* The plosion, however, is softer and less aspirated than in English.

Further, it may be noted that both word-stress and sentence-stress are weaker in American than in British English and intonation is more level. Consequently American speech is more monotonous, but at the same time it is generally more distinct. It is, as Mencken puts it, 'predominantly *staccato* and *marcato*', whereas British English, like Russian, 'tends towards *glissando*'. Unstressed syllables are pronounced with more measured detachment and therefore with greater clarity. There is less variety of tone and the customary tempo is slower. Many speakers have fallen into a habit which they have unconsciously inherited from seventeenth-century East Anglian Puritans. They allow the soft palate or velum to droop while speaking, and as a result part of the breath stream passes through the nose giving a certain nasalized quality or 'nasal twang' to vowel sounds which may vary considerably in degree from individual to individual. ¶11

Compare the way in which a New Yorker says *extraordinary, supernumerary, temporary,* and *unexceptionable* with the pronunciation of a Londoner. The American invariably gives to the unstressed syllables in these words greater 'prominence' (to use the technical term in phonetics) and, consequently, greater audibility. In words like *dormitory, monastery, necessary,* and *secretary* he habitually places a not unpleasing secondary stress upon the penult or last syllable but one. Some words he stresses differently from us. He stresses *aristocrat, detail, eczema, frontier, harass, primarily,* and *subaltern* on the second syllable whereas we stress them on the first. Conversely, he stresses *address, alloy, ally, corollary, defect, idea, inquiry, opponent, quinine, recess, recourse, redress, research, resource* and *romance* on the first syllable whereas we English stress them on the second. Other words, like *advertisement* and *financier,* are stressed on the second syllable in London but on the third syllable in New York. ¶12

Now these observations apply not only to the speech of New York City but also to the so-called General American dialect as a whole, which includes the Middle Atlantic States, that is, New Jersey, Pennsylvania and the whole of New York State west ¶13 of the Hudson River, as well as all the Middle and Western States. General American thus comprises two-thirds of the whole population and four-fifths of the land surface of the United States reaching from the Atlantic Ocean in the east to the Pacific Ocean in the west. The other two dialects, New England and Southern, are important and significant, but they are much more limited. The dialect of New England is spoken in Maine, New Hampshire, Vermont, Massachusetts, Rhode Island, Connecticut, and the strip of New York State lying to the east of the Hudson River. It is nearer British English in many respects. For example, the rounded vowel is retained in *dock,* the long low back *a* is heard in *dance* and the *r* is dropped in *far* and *farm.* At the same time, it is less homogeneous than General American. Even within its narrower confines the New England dialect has far more social and regional variations. The Southern dialect includes the States of Maryland, Virginia, North and South Carolina, Georgia, Florida, Kentucky, Tennessee, Alabama, Mississippi, Arkansas, and Louisiana, as well as a great part of Missouri, Oklahoma, and Texas. In other words, it is spoken in all the States, except Delaware and West Virginia, lying south of Pennsylvania and the Ohio River and east of a line running from St Louis to the middle waters of the Colorado River and thence down that river to its mouth in the Gulf of Mexico. Many people in these parts speak with a drawl. They speak with slow enunciation and they frequently drag out and diphthongize stressed vowels, saying [jeīs], or even [jeíjəs], for *yes,* and [klæīs], or even [klæjəs], for *class.*

¶14 In spite of countless smaller variations in pronunciation, vocabulary, and idiom, the three American dialects do not greatly differ from one another. For two centuries and more American families have been constantly on the move: speech communities have seldom been isolated for more than one generation. It would be no exaggeration to say that greater differences in pronunciation are discernible among the speech-forms of Northern England between Trent and Tweed than among the dialects of the whole of North America.

It is now customary for American and British scholars and scientists to co-operate in the writing of composite books addressed to the whole English-speaking world and the councils of learned societies have taken steps to standardize technical nomenclature. Other potent forces are now at work bringing the two main streams of English more closely together. Future historians of our language, with their longer perspective in looking back, may well record that it was during the century and a quarter from 1800 to 1925 that British and American English showed the greatest divergence and that, after 1925, unifying factors—the ubiquity of radio and the interchange of films, novels, journals, and plays—all worked in one and the same direction to make that divergence narrower and narrower. Films and newspapers bring the latest American slang to England, so that even a trained observer may no longer differentiate with certainty between native and imported neologisms. Such a highly expressive phrase as *It's up to us* sounds so very American. We take it for granted that it *is* American. But who could be really certain about its provenance without looking a little more closely into the matter, without consulting Mencken, Horwill and *American Speech* on the one hand, and Partridge and the Supplement to *The Oxford English Dictionary* on the other? In 1942 the United States War Department furnished men and women serving in Europe with *A Short Guide to Great Britain* which included a long list of American and English variants. It was a painstaking, if over-elaborate, publication: its aim—to obviate every conceivable occasion of misapprehension—was entirely meritorious. This aim was shared by H. W. Horwill in his two careful studies which had appeared a few years previously and which have already acquired historical value: *A Dictionary of Modern American Usage* (1935) and *An Anglo-American Interpreter* (1939). In his Preface to the last-mentioned book the author quotes the ¶15 statement of a 'distinguished journalist' that 'an American, if taken suddenly ill while on a visit to London, might die in the street through being unable to make himself understood. . . . He would naturally ask for the nearest drugstore, and no one would know what he meant.' Everyone would now know the meaning of this and hundreds of other expressions marked American in Horwill's *Interpreter* and in the War Department's *Short Guide.* Indeed, they may now be heard from the lips of English children every day. The most fashionable American locution of the hour may be heard all over England within the space of a few weeks and then, perhaps, heard no more.

For Greater Insight

1. Potter reviews the waves of immigration that have occurred in the United States since colonial days. The total number of such immigrants has been far in excess of the four million people who lived in the United States in 1790. In spite of this, what has never been seriously threatened?
2. In what four respects do American and British English differ? (It may interest you to know that an American teacher in England was asked what he taught. "English," he replied. "But surely you don't call it English?" "Of course. What else would I call it?" "Why, American, I should think.")
3. Study Webster's list of words he wanted to change, and discover how many actually have changed. It is interesting to observe the contrasts and similarities between Webster's suggestions and Edwards.' ("Meihem in ce Klasrum," pp. 260ff.)
4. Some indication of the constantly changing standards in language may be found by looking in *Webster's Third New International Dictionary,* or *Webster's Seventh New Collegiate Dictionary,* for some of the words Potter lists in Par. 5. Try *practice, thoro, thru.* Does what you find support Potter, or has American English undergone some change since he wrote?
5. Although the subject of paragraphing does not come up in Potter's essay, it can be pointed out that a great many American writers would think Par. 7 of his essay too long. Where would you break it up? Justify each choice.

6. What does Potter mean in Par. 7 by "vogue-word"? Does he mention here any word or expression you are not familiar with? If so, look it up to see whether it is still part of American English.
7. In speaking of the suffix *ist* (Par. 9), Potter has missed one word common in England but quite unknown here. *Stockist*, according to the *Oxford English Dictionary*, means "One who stocks certain goods for sale." What word would an American use for this? The word *blurb*, by the way, was coined by Gelett Burgess, an American, and if you know what the word means you may be able to guess that a *slipcover* is a book jacket or dust jacket.
8. In two places—Pars. 1 and 11—Potter refers to the fact that the first permanent settlers in American spoke the language of Shakespeare and Milton. In Par. 12 he speaks of the difference in stress on syllables in words like *secretary* and *necessary*. In England, the latter would be pronounced *neh'-suh-sree*. In Shakespeare's *Julius Caesar*, Act II, scene 2, you will find the lines

   "Seeing that death, a necessary end
   Will come, when it will come."

   Read these aloud, pronouncing "necessary" as you normally would, and as the English do. Which way do you think it was pronounced in Shakespeare's time? Why?
9. If you can, listen to radio or television or a movie in which British people speak. Do not judge from some dialect in a movie, but try to listen to an announcer or some well-educated person. Can you identify some of the sounds described in Par. 13? Identify your own section of the United States, and test Potter's analysis. Have you ever tried exchanging tape recordings with people your own age in various parts of your own country?

Word Study

comprised four million . . . people:
was marked *ethnographically*:
numbers were . . . *augmented*:
dire . . . persecutions:
assimilating the . . . tongues:
has seldom *diverged*:
impeccable standard English:

in the *substantives*:
to *corroborate*:
Twentieth-century *neologisms*:
pungent and useful words:
linguistic paleontologists:
are literally *ephemeral*:
are *tacitly* adopted:
slip-cover *encomiums*:
the *plosion*:
the *ubiquity* of radio:
about its *provenance*:
was . . . *meritorious*:
American *locution*:

The Perilous Labor of Prince Thag

James Thurber

"The Perilous Labor of Prince Thag" is a portion of *The White Deer*, a book which is described on the jacket as a tale "of kings and princes and enchanted deer, of Thurber wizards and dwarfs, of perilous labors, of dark enchantment, of rhymed riddles, of false love and true. His story is a fairy tale for grown-ups . . . a story funny, wise, and absurd."

The white deer is a lovely princess on whom a magic spell has been cast, to be broken only when the three sons of a king follow a magic pattern. Prince Thag is the first to set out on the quest.

The section included here has been chosen not because it is an essay, for it is not. It was not chosen because it has contemporary thought, for it has none. It was chosen because it is simply gorgeous use and misuse of language. With a misplaced consonant or a wrong vowel or a likely but meaningless combination of letters, Thurber creates wonderful nonsense that comes close to making sense.

The first paragraph is straightforward and clear. The second will catch you if you don't watch carefully, so do watch out, and enjoy yourself—and for the best effect read this piece aloud.

The road that Prince Thag followed dwindled to a zigzag path ¶1
that zigzagged through a growth of gnarled and toppling trees like figures frozen in a dance. From all the trees a sticky thickish

liquid dripped and oozed and gave or rather lent the air a heavy sweetish fragrance, for the sweetish heavy fragrance died and rose and died again and rose and died and rose again.

¶2 "This heavish sweety fragrance," Thag muttered to himself, "that rises, or that roses, isn't fit for human noses, and it tricks the minds of men. Three times two is eight," he said, "and one is ten."

¶3 A furry bluish smoke came drifting through the trees in rings and hoops and collars.

¶4 "I distrust this stickish thicky stuff—" The tall Prince bit his lip. "Hag's thad enough."

¶5 "A lozy moon globbers in the pipe trees," said a voice in a tone which for one reason or another thaggravated Had. "I'm up here in the crouch of the tree," the voice continued.

¶6 "Crotch, you mean," said Thag, catching sight of a roundish balding man a few feet above him.

¶7 "On the contrary," said the man, "crunch is what you meet in aching."

¶8 "That's wince," said Thag angrily.

¶9 "Mince is what you do to words," the round man retorted.

¶10 "It's glibbers, in any case," said Thag haughtily, "not globbers, as you said. The word is in the pleasant trense."

¶11 "Ah, but you speak of mood," said the round man. "I was referring to the moon. It is important to mind your D's and N's in these particular woods, which are not *too* particular, if you grasp *me*."

¶12 "Nobody's grabbing *you*," said Thag. He showed his upper teeth. "Furthermore, I resent your preferring to it as a 'peasant trench.' "

¶13 The other stared down at Thag. "I don't care what you say," he said coldly. "I say glibbers."

¶14 High up in a tree, a chock climbed slowly.

¶15 "I wonder what type it is?" said Thag.

¶16 "It's sick thirsty," said the man, "or half past hate or a quarter to fight. I'm in no moon for questions."

"You're in no *mood*," said Thag. ¶17

"First he accosts me, then he tells me what I'm not in," said the man. "I crutch in the crouch of this tree to avoid troublemakers like you, riding on their nagamuffins." ¶18

"You are thinking of ragmudgeons," said Thag with dignity. ¶19

"Now he tells me what I'm thinking of," said the man. ¶20

"And crouch is what you do, not where you are," said Thag. ¶21

"How can I do anything where I am not?" asked the man. "I have half a mind to come down and trounce you." ¶22

Thag laughed. ¶23

"That's right," whined the man, "laugh at a man with only half a mind." He sniffled. "A man with a crutch." ¶24

"You crouch in a crotch, but you have no crutch," said Thag. ¶25

The man burst into tears. "That's right," he bawled, "laugh at a man because he has no crutch." He shook his fist at Thag and cried, "A plague on both your horses!" ¶26

Four redbirds in a tangle bush sang "verti verti verti go" as Thag closed his mouth and held his breath and shut his eyes and galloped on through the stingish ringy smoke and the trickish sicky smell, and after a long moment he rode out of the growth of gnarled and toppling trees, and beheld before his eyes the shining Valley of Euphoria. ¶27

For Greater Insight

If you've read the interview with Sir Laurence Olivier, you'll remember the story about Margot Fonteyn (p. 176). She said she had explained what she was doing in the ballet while she was doing it. This Thurber fragment is like that—it explains itself; no one else can do it.

No questions!

Word Study

vertigo:
Valley of *Euphoria*:

Meihem In Ce Klasrum

Dolton Edwards

Please don't read this essay until you are asked to, and then read it straight through from the beginning to the end. To do otherwise will spoil much of the pleasure.

The strange and awesome complexities of the English language have been the basis for a good many essays. These vary from solemn suggestions about our pronunciation of combinations like *ough* to even more learned suggestions about grammatical structure, and to humor like that of Mark Twain in "English As She Is Taught."

As you read this essay you will meet a great many new ideas and new spellings. If you follow the instructions at the top of this page, you will understand each new section as you continue, and you will find yourself able to read even the final paragraph smoothly. You will also have demonstrated a principle of the psychology of the learning process, but of that more later.

¶1 Because we are still bearing some of the scars of our brief skirmish with II-B English, it is natural that we should be enchanted by Mr. George Bernard Shaw's current campaign for a simplified alphabet.

¶2 Obviously, as Mr. Shaw points out, English spelling is in much need of a general overhauling and streamlining. However, our own resistance to any changes requiring a large expenditure of mental effort in the near future would cause us to view with some apprehension the possibility of some day receiving a morning paper printed in—to us—Greek.

Our own plan would achieve the same end as the legislation ¶3
proposed by Mr. Shaw, but in a less shocking manner, as it consists merely of an acceleration of the normal processes by which the language is continually modernized.

As a catalytic agent, we would suggest that a National Easy ¶4
Language Week be proclaimed, which the President would inaugurate, outlining some short cut to concentrate on during the week, and to be adopted during the ensuing year. All school children would be given a holiday, the lost time being the equivalent of that gained by the spelling short cut.

In 1946, for example, we would urge the elimination of the ¶5
soft "c," for which we would substitute "s." Sertainly, such an improvement would be selebrated in all sivic-minded sircles as being suffisiently worth the trouble, and students in all sities in the land would be reseptive toward any change eliminating the nesessity of learning the differense between the two letters.

In 1947, sinse only the hard "c" would be left, it would be ¶6
possible to substitute "k" for it, both letters being pronounsed identikally. Imagine how greatly only two years of this prosess would klarify the konfusion in the minds of students. Already we would have eliminated an entire letter from the alphabet. Typewriters and linotypes kould all be built with one less letter, and all the manpower and materials previously devoted to making "c's" kould be turned toward raising the national standard of living.

In the fase of so many notable improvements, it is easy to ¶7
foresee that by 1948, "National Easy Language Week" would be a pronounsed sukses. All skhool tshildren would be looking forward with konsiderable exsitement to the holiday, and in a blaze of national publisity it would be announsed that the double konsonant "ph" no longer existed, and that the sound would hense-

forth be written "f" in all words. This would make sutsh words as "fonograf" twenty persent shorter in print.

¶8 By 1949, publik interest in a fonetik alfabet kan be expekted to have inkreased to the point where a more radikal step forward kan be taken without fear of undue kritisism. We would therefore urge the elimination at that time of al unesesary double leters, whitsh, although quite harmles, have always ben a nuisanse in the language and a desided deterent to akurate speling. Try it yourself in the next leter you write, and se if both writing and reading are not fasilitated.

¶9 With so mutsh progres already made, it might be posible in 1950 to delve further into the posibilities of fonetik speling. After due konsideration of the reseption aforded the previous steps, it should be expedient by this time to spel al difthongs fonetikaly. Most students do not realize that the long "i" and "y," as in "time" and "by," are aktualy the difthong "ai," as it is writen in "aisle," and that the long "a" in "fate," is in reality the difthong "ei" as in "rein." Although perhaps not imediately aparent, the saving in taime and efort wil be tremendous when we leiter elimineite the sailent "e," as meide posible bai this last tsheinge.

¶10 For, as is wel known, the horible mes of "e's" apearing in our writen language is kaused prinsipaly bai the present nesesity of indikeiting whether a vowel is long or short. Therefore, in 1951 we kould simply elimineit al sailent "e's," and kontinu to read and wrait merily along as though we wer in an atomik ag of edukation.

¶11 In 1951 we would urg a greit step forward. Sins bai this taim it would have ben four years sins anywun had usd the leter "c," we would sugest that the "National Easy Languag Wek" for 1951 be devoted to substitution of "c" for "th." To be sur it would be som taim befor peopl would bekom akustomd to reading ceir newspapers and buks wic sutsh sentenses in cem as "Ceodor caught he had cre cousand cistls crust crough ce cik of his cumb."

In ce seim maner, bai meiking eatsh leter hav its own ¶12
sound and cat sound only, we kould shorten ce language stil mor. In 1952 we would elimineit ce "y"; cen in 1953 we kould us ce leter to indikeit ce "sh" sound, cerbai klarifaiing words laik yugar and yur, as wel as redusing bai wun mor leter al words laik "yut," "youre," and so forc. Cink, cen, of al ce benefits to be geind bai ce distinktion whitsh wil cen be meid between words laik:

ocean now writen oyean
machine " " mayin
racial " " reiyial

Al sutsh divers weis of wraiting wun sound would no longer ¶13
exist, and whenever wun keim akros a "y" sound he would know exaktli what to wrait.

Kontinuing cis proses, year after year, we would eventuali ¶14
hav a reali sensibl writen langug. By 1975, wi ventyur tu sei, cer wud bi no mor uv ces teribli trublsum difikultis, wic no tu leters usd to indikeit ce seim nois, and laikwais no tu noises riten wic ce seim leter. Even Mr. Yaw, wi beliv, wud be hapi in ce noleg cat his drims fainali keim tru.

For Greater Insight

1. What does "streamlining" in Par. 2 mean? (See "British and American English," Par. 7, p. 248.)
2. You probably know that George Bernard Shaw was an advocate—and a learned one—of changes in the writing of English. Is Edwards serious, or is he "pulling your leg"? Where do you find your first clue?
3. Why is Edwards' suggestion about making changes a year at a time a good one? Does it have some drawbacks? What are they?
4. In Par. 12, Edwards' first sentence states a truth that is the basis for nearly all changes recommended in the English alphabet. Edwards hasn't solved his problem consistently, because he uses "sound," "would," and "kould." What other faults can you find?
5. How did u get along wic ce last paragraf? Did u find cat u kud understand it kwait wel? I cot u wud be suksesful!

Actually, besides having been entertained by some delightfully clever nonsense, you have found—if you read this as you were asked to—that learning a little bit at a time and using at once what you learned, you learned a good deal quite rapidly. This is an oversimplification of the psychological principle behind programmed learning.

6. If someone in your class knows phonetics, or the new types of alphabet being developed to aid in teaching young children to read, you could spend a profitable hour discussing them. Just to point up the problem, in how many ways can you spell the sound made by the "oo" in a word like "roof" or "wood"?
7. As a final task, explain what Edwards has failed to do in Par. 14 with "langug." And what is sensible about "yugar" and "yur"? If "sugar" is pronounced "shugar," why isn't "sum" pronounced "shum"? The list is endless!

Word Study

brief *skirmish*:
a *catalytic* agent:
the *ensuing* year:
fonetik (*phonetic*) alphabet:
desided deterent (*deterrent*):
fasilitated (*facilitated*):
should be *expedient*:
difthong (*diphthong*):

Literature and Values

Walden

E. B. White

E. B. White, well-known writer of the *New Yorker* staff, received the Gold Medal for Essays and Criticism from the National Institute of Arts and Letters in May 1960. Here he tells of a visit to Walden Pond. All of us have made at some time or other a pilgrimage to a place we have known. Sometimes it is a neighborhood, sometimes a city, a vacation spot vivid with memories, or a house once familiar.

This essay is an account of such a pilgrimage, but to a place —Walden Pond—that the author knew only through the writing of Henry David Thoreau.

You will find that the author has remembered his reading well, that he observes details vividly, and that he reports his observations effectively. In his unhurried, leisurely way, he will take you with him.

Miss Nims, take a letter to Henry David Thoreau. Dear Henry: ¶1
I thought of you the other afternoon as I was approaching Concord doing fifty on Route 62. That is a high speed at which to hold a philosopher in one's mind, but in this century we are a nimble bunch.

On one of the lawns in the outskirts of the village a woman ¶2
was cutting the grass with a motorized lawn mower. What made me think of you was that the machine had rather got away from

her, although she was game enough, and in the brief glimpse I had of the scene it appeared to me that the lawn was mowing the lady. She kept a tight grip on the handles, which throbbed violently with every explosion of the one-cylinder motor, and as she sheered around bushes and lurched along at a reluctant trot behind her impetuous servant, she looked like a puppy who had grabbed something that was too much for him. Concord hasn't changed much, Henry; the farm implements and the animals still have the upper hand.

¶3 I may as well admit that I was journeying to Concord with the deliberate intention of visiting your woods; for although I have never knelt at the grave of a philosopher nor placed wreaths on moldy poets, and have often gone a mile out of my way to avoid some place of historical interest, I have always wanted to see Walden Pond. The account which you left of your sojourn there is, you will be amused to learn, a document of increasing pertinence; each year it seems to gain a little headway, as the world loses ground. We may all be transcendental yet, whether we like it or not. As our common complexities increase, any tale of individual simplicity (and yours is the best written and the cockiest) acquires a new fascination; as our goods accumulate, but not our well-being, your report of an existence without material adornment takes on a certain awkward credibility.

¶4 My purpose in going to Walden Pond, like yours, was not to live cheaply or to live dearly there, but to transact some private business with the fewest obstacles. Approaching Concord, doing forty, doing forty-five, doing fifty, the steering wheel held snug in my palms, the highway held grimly in my vision, the crown of the road now serving me (on the righthand curves), now defeating me (on the lefthand curves), I began to rouse myself from the stupefaction which a day's motor journey induces. It was a delicious evening, Henry, when the whole body is one sense, and imbibes delight through every pore, if I may coin a phrase. Fields were richly brown where the harrow, drawn by the stripped Ford, had lately sunk its teeth; pastures were green; and overhead the sky had that same everlasting great look which you will find on Page 144 of the Oxford pocket edition. I could feel the road entering me, through tire, wheel, spring, and cushion; shall I not have intelligence with earth too? Am I not partly leaves and vegetable mold myself—a man of infinite horsepower, yet partly leaves.

Stay with me on 62 and it will take you into Concord. As ¶5
I say, it was a delicious evening. The snake had come forth to die in a bloody S on the highway, the wheel upon its head, its bowels flat now and exposed. The turtle had come up too to cross the road and die in the attempt, its hard shell smashed under the rubber blow, its intestinal yearning (for the other side of the road) forever squashed. There was a sign by the wayside which announced that the road had a "cotton surface." You wouldn't know what this is, but neither, for that matter, did I. There is a cryptic ingredient in many of our modern improvements—we are awed and pleased without knowing quite what we are enjoying. It is something to be traveling on a road with a cotton surface.

The civilization round Concord today is an odd distillation of ¶6
city, village, farm, and manor. The houses, yards, fields look not quite suburban, not quite rural. Under the bronze beech and the blue spruce of the departed baron grazes the milch goat of the heirs. Under the porte-cochère stands the reconditioned station wagon; under the grape arbor sit the puppies for sale. (But why do men degenerate ever? What makes families run out?)

It was June and everywhere June was publishing her im- ¶7
memorial stanza; in the lilacs, in the syringa, in the freshly edged paths and the sweetness of moist beloved gardens, and the little wire wickets that preserve the tulips' front. Farmers were already moving the fruits of their toil into their yards, arranging the rhubarb, the asparagus, the strictly fresh eggs on the painted stands under the little shed roofs with the patent shingles. And though it was almost a hundred years since you had taken your

ax and started cutting out your home on Walden Pond, I was interested to observe that the philosophical spirit was still alive in Massachusetts: in the center of a vacant lot some boys were assembling the framework of the rude shelter, their whole mind and skill concentrated in the rather inauspicious helter-skeleton of studs and rafters. They too were escaping from town, to live naturally, in a rich blend of savagery and philosophy.

¶8 That evening, after supper at the inn, I strolled out into the twilight to dream my shapeless transcendental dreams and see that the car was locked up for the night (first open the right front door, then reach over, straining, and pull up the handles of the left rear and the left front till you hear the click, then the handle of the right rear, then shut the right front but open it again, remembering that the key is still in the ignition switch, remove the key, shut the right front again with a bang, push the tiny keyhole cover to one side, insert key, turn, and withdraw). It is what we all do, Henry. It is called locking the car. It is said to confuse thieves and keep them from making off with the laprobe. Four doors to lock behind one robe. The driver himself never uses a laprobe, the free movement of his legs being vital to the operation of the vehicle; so that when he locks the car it is a pure and unselfish act. I have in my life gained very little essential heat from laprobes, yet I have ever been at pains to lock them up.

¶9 The evening was full of sounds, some of which would have stirred your memory. The robins still love the elms of New England villages at sundown. There is enough of the thrush in them to make song inevitable at the end of day, and enough of the tramp to make them hang round the dwellings of men. A robin, like many another American, dearly loves a white house with green blinds. Concord is still full of them.

¶10 Your fellow-townsmen were stirring abroad—not many afoot, most of them in their cars; and the sound which they made in Concord at evening was a rustling and a whispering. The sound lacks steadfastness and is wholly unlike that of a train. A train, as you know who lived so near the Fitchburg line, whistles once or twice sadly and is gone, trailing a memory in smoke, soothing to ear and mind. Automobiles, skirting a village green, are like flies that have gained the inner ear—they buzz, cease, pause, start, shift, stop, halt, brake, and the whole effect is a nervous polytone curiously disturbing.

As I wandered along, the toc toc of ping pong balls drifted ¶11
from an attic window. In front of the Reuben Brown house a Buick was drawn up. At the wheel, motionless, his hat upon his head, a man sat, listening to Amos and Andy on the radio (it is a drama of many scenes and without an end). The deep voice of Andrew Brown, emerging from the car, although it originated more than two hundred miles away, was unstrained by distance. When you used to sit on the shore of your pond on Sunday morning, listening to the church bells of Acton and Concord, you were aware of the excellent filter of the intervening atmosphere. Science has attended to that, and sound now maintains its intensity without regard for distance. Properly sponsored, it goes on forever.

A fire engine, out for a trial spin, roared past Emerson's ¶12
house, hot with readiness for public duty. Over the barn roofs the martins dipped and chittered. A swarthy daughter of an asparagus grower, in culottes, shirt, and bandanna, pedalled past on her bicycle. It was indeed a delicious evening, and I returned to the inn (I believe it was your house once) to rock with the old ladies on the concrete veranda.

Next morning early I started afoot for Walden, out Main ¶13
Street and down Thoreau, past the depot and the Minuteman Chevrolet Company. The morning was fresh, and in a bean field along the way I flushed an agriculturalist, quietly studying his beans. Thoreau Street soon joined Number 126, an artery of the State. We number our highways nowadays, our speed being so great we can remember little of their quality or character and are

lucky to remember their number. (Men have an indistinct notion that if they keep up this activity long enough all will at length ride somewhere, in next to no time.) Your pond is on 126.

¶14 I knew I must be nearing your woodland retreat when the Golden Pheasant lunchroom came into view—Sealtest ice cream, toasted sandwiches, hot frankfurters, waffles, tonics, and lunches. Were I the proprietor, I should add rice, Indian meal, and molasses—just for old time's sake. The Pheasant, incidentally, is for sale: a chance for some nature lover who wishes to set himself up beside a pond in the Concord atmosphere and live deliberately, fronting only the essential facts of life on Number 126. Beyond the Pheasant was a place called Walden Breezes, an oasis whose porch pillars were made of old green shutters sawed into lengths. On the porch was a distorting mirror, to give the traveler a comical image of himself, who had miraculously learned to gaze in an ordinary glass without smiling. Behind the Breezes, in a sun-parched clearing, dwelt your philosophical descendants in their trailers, each trailer the size of your hut, but all grouped together for the sake of congeniality. Trailer people leave the city, as you did, to discover solitude and in any weather, at any hour of the day or night, to improve the nick of time; but they soon collect in villages and get bogged deeper in the mud than ever. The camp behind Walden Breezes was just rousing itself to the morning. The ground was packed hard under the heel, and the sun came through the clearing to bake the soil and enlarge the wry smell of cramped housekeeping. Cushman's bakery truck had stopped to deliver an early basket of rolls. A camp dog, seeing me in the road, barked petulantly. A man emerged from one of the trailers and set forth with a bucket to draw water from some forest tap.

¶15 Leaving the highway I turned off into the woods toward the pond, which was apparent through the foliage. The floor of the forest was strewn with dried old oak leaves and *Transcripts.* From beneath the flattened popcorn wrapper (*granum explosum*) peeped the frail violet. I followed a footpath and descended to the water's edge. The pond lay clear and blue in the morning light, as you have seen it so many times. In the shallows a man's waterlogged shirt undulated gently. A few flies came out to greet me and convoy me to your cove, past the No Bathing signs on which the fellows and the girls had scrawled their names. I felt strangely excited suddenly to be snooping around your premises, tiptoeing along watchfully, as though not to tread by mistake upon the intervening century. Before I got to the cove I heard something which seemed to me quite wonderful: I heard your frog, a full, clear *troonk*, guiding me, still hoarse and solemn, bridging the years as the robins had bridged them in the sweetness of the village evening. But he soon quit, and I came on a couple of young boys throwing stones at him.

Your front yard is marked by a bronze tablet set in a stone. ¶16
Four small granite posts, a few feet away, show where the house was. On top of the tablet was a pair of faded blue bathing trunks with a white stripe. Back of it is a pile of stones, a sort of cairn, left by your visitors as a tribute I suppose. It is a rather ugly little heap of stones, Henry. In fact the hillside itself seems faded, browbeaten; a few tall skinny pines, bare of lower limbs, a smattering of young maples in suitable green, some birches and oaks, and a number of trees felled by the last big wind. It was from the bole of one of these fallen pines, torn up by the roots, that I extracted the stone which I added to the cairn—a sentimental act in which I was interrupted by a small terrier from a nearby picnic group, who confronted me and wanted to know about the stone.

I sat down for a while on one of the posts of your house to ¶17
listen to the bluebottles and the dragonflies. The invaded glade sprawled shabby and mean at my feet, but the flies were tuned to the old vibration. There were the remains of a fire in your ruins, but I doubt that it was yours; also two beer bottles trodden into the soil and become part of earth. A young oak had

taken root in your house, and two or three ferns, unrolling like the ticklers at a banquet. The only other furnishings were a DuBarry pattern sheet, a page torn from a picture magazine, and some crusts in wax paper.

¶18 Before I quit I walked clear round the pond and found the place where you used to sit on the northeast side to get the sun in the fall, and the beach where you got sand for scrubbing your floor. On the eastern side of the pond, where the highway borders it, the State has built dressing rooms for swimmers, a float with diving towers, drinking fountains of porcelain, and rowboats for hire. The pond is in fact a State Preserve, and carries a twenty-dollar fine for picking wild flowers, a decree signed in all solemnity by your fellow-citizens Walter C. Wardwell, Erson B. Barlow, and Nathaniel I. Bowditch. There was a smell of creosote where they had been building a wide wooden stairway to the road and the parking area. Swimmers and boaters were arriving; bodies plunged vigorously into the water and emerged wet and beautiful in the bright air. As I left, a boatload of town boys were splashing about in mid-pond, kidding and fooling, the young fellows singing at the tops of their lungs in a wild chorus:

> Amer-ica, Amer-ica, God shed his grace on thee,
> And crown thy good with brotherhood
> From sea to shi-ning sea!

¶19 I walked back to town along the railroad, following your custom. The rails were expanding noisily in the hot sun, and on the slope of the roadbed the wild grape and the blackberry sent up their creepers to the track.

¶20 The expense of my brief sojourn in Concord was:

Canvas shoes	$1.95	
Baseball bat	.25	gifts to take back to a boy
Left-handed fielder's glove	1.25	
Hotel and meals	4.25	
In all	$7.70	

As you see, this amount was almost what you spent for food for eight months. I cannot defend the shoes or the expenditure for shelter and food: they reveal a meanness and grossness in my nature which you would find contemptible. The baseball equipment, however, is the kind of impediment with which you were never on even terms. You must remember that the house where you practiced the sort of economy which I respect was haunted only by mice and squirrels. You never had to cope with a short-stop.

For Greater Insight

1. You probably already know who Henry David Thoreau was, and understand the meaning of Walden in his life. If not, your first task is to find out. He is far more important to our contemporary society than most people realize. Why?
2. How is the leisurely style of the essay shown in the second paragraph? What part of the paragraph seems to you the best descriptive detail?
3. Why should Thoreau's account be a "document of increasing pertinence"? What does White mean by "The world loses ground"?
4. Explain the last sentence in the third paragraph, especially from "as our goods accumulate . . ."
5. Explain the relationship between "the cotton surface"—and White's comments on it—and the advertisements which shout "It's new! It's improved! It has not one, but three active ingredients!"
6. In Par. 7, what were the boys doing who were "escaping from town"? Are savagery and philosophy appropriate words here? Why? Do we all "escape from town"? How?
7. Why does White go into such detail about locking the car?
8. In Par. 11, what is White really saying in the last sentence?
9. In Par. 14, White is critical, sarcastic, ironic, and cynical. Some of his observations are hard to understand, but once understood, very worth the effort.
    a. What is White saying in the sentence, "On the porch . . . without smiling"?
    b. What were trailer people trying to discover? What had they discovered?

10. A good deal of the keenness of White's observations is apparent in the way he has put the unchanged aspects of Walden Pond beside some contemporary disfigurement. Pick out several of these contrasts for comment. Explain the irony in the song the young fellows were singing.

Word Study

her *impetuous* servant:
your *sojourn* there:
of increasing *pertinence*:
be *transcendental* yet:
from the *stupefaction*:
imbibes delight:
a *cryptic* ingredient:
under the *porte-cochère*:
inauspicious helter-skeleton:
a nervous *polytone*:
barked *petulantly*:
meanness and *grossness*:
kind of *impediment*:

The Retort Transcendental

E. B. White

It is clear from the previous essay that White has been reliving in his imagination the experiences recounted in Thoreau's *Walden*. The New England Transcendentalists, of whom Thoreau was one, were known for their "plain living and high thinking," and the thinking could be on a very high level indeed. Now in "The Retort Transcendental," White makes fun of himself a bit, showing what droll situations would result if one replied to the questions and comments of everyday life on the level—and in the language—of *Walden*.

In May of the year 1927 I bought a World's Classics edition of "Walden" for, I think, ninety cents and slipped it in my pocket for convenient reading. Since then I have carried it about with me on the cars and in buses and boats, as it is the most amusing detective story I possess. There is, however, a danger in rereading a book, or rather in dipping frequently into the same book: the trouble is you begin to learn some of the lines. In my case, with "Walden," I have recently found that when someone asks me a simple question I reply with a direct quote. ¶1

I go into a restaurant, we'll say, at the lunch hour, and the headwaiter approaches me, accusingly. ¶2

"All alone?" he asks. ¶3

¶4 "I feel it wholesome to be alone the greater part of the time," I reply. "To be in company, even with the best, is soon wearisome and dissipating. I love to be alone." Then I glare triumphantly at the waiter and snatch the napkin from the plate.

¶5 Or I am walking along the street and meet an acquaintance —someone I haven't seen in a long time and don't care if I never see again.

¶6 "Where y'been all this time?" he demands.

¶7 "If a man does not keep pace with his companions," I retort, "perhaps it is because he hears a different drummer."

¶8 Actually, I suppose, I don't say that at all; yet it often seems to me as though I were saying it. More and more I find it difficult to distinguish clearly between what I am saying and what I might easily be saying. Maybe it's the times. At any rate, Thoreau answers a surprisingly large number of the commonest questions that get thrown at me these days. He is a Johnny-on-the-spot for all ordinary occasions and situations.

¶9 I enter a room.

¶10 "Won't you sit down?" asks my hostess, indicating a vacancy.

¶11 "I would rather sit on a pumpkin and have it all to myself," I reply, accepting the velvet cushion with weary resignation.

¶12 "What would you like to drink?" she continues.

¶13 "Let me have a draught of undiluted morning air," I snarl. "If men will not drink of this at the fountainhead of the day, why, then, we must even bottle up some and sell it in the shops, for the benefit of those who have lost their subscription ticket to morning time in the world." Then I slump into my cushion and wait for the clear amber liquor and the residual olive.

¶14 "Know any good books?" my partner asks at dinner. Slowly I swing my head around, bruising my chin on the hard, rough wing of my collar, my eyes glazed with the strain of evening. I place my lips to her ear.

¶15 "Much is published," I whisper, cryptically, "but little printed. We are in danger of forgetting the language which all things and events speak without metaphor, which alone is copious and standard."

Or I am at home, getting ready, perhaps, to escort my wife ¶16
to a soirée.

"What's it like out tonight?" she asks, glancing anxiously at ¶17
her rubbers in the corner of the closet.

"This is a delicious evening," I hear my voice saying, "when ¶18
the whole body is one sense, and imbibes delight through every pore."

Next morning, seeing my suit lying rumpled and mussed on ¶19
the chair beside the bed, she will inquire, "You got anything to go to the presser's?"

"No, my dear," I reply. "Every day our garments become ¶20
more assimilated to ourselves, receiving the impress of the wearer's character. If you have any enterprise before you, try it in your old clothes." (I am glad to say my wife doesn't mind Thoreau any more and simply calls the presser.)

The situations are endless, the answers inexhaustible. I recall ¶21
that one of my angriest and boldest retorts was made on a day when a couple of silly, giggling girls arrived at our house and began effervescing.

"Isn't this an attractive place?" they squealed. ¶22

"On the contrary," I snapped, "I sometimes dream of a larger ¶23
and more populous house, standing in a golden age, of enduring materials, and without gingerbread work, which shall consist of only one room, a vast, rude, substantial primitive hall, without ceiling or plastering, with bare rafters and purlins supporting a sort of lower heaven over one's head—useful to keep off rain and snow; where the king and queen posts stand out to receive your homage, when you have done reverence to the prostrate Saturn of an older dynasty on stepping over the sill; a cavernous house, wherein you must reach up a torch upon a pole to see the roof . . . a house whose inside is as open and manifest as a bird's nest."

The girls sobered up instantly and were quiet and tractable ¶24 the rest of their visit. But I don't know—I'm afraid I shall have to put "Walden" away and buy another book to travel with. Or possibly a link puzzle. One doesn't remember anything much from long association with a link puzzle.

For Greater Insight

1. The quotation about the man who does not keep pace has been used again and again in a great variety of situations. What specific instances can you name in which the quotation would be appropriate?
2. What is a circumlocution? What is "the clear amber liquid and the residual olive"? Why doesn't he use the right word?
3. Read again the whole comment "Much is published . . . copious and standard." Thoreau was suggesting that observation of things and events, that thinking, was as important as printed books. On page 202 an artist is quoted as saying, "Language is at best an imperfect medium for conveying emotion." Michelangelo's Pietà, for example, transcends mere language. Is there a relation between Thoreau's thought and that of the artist? Explain.
4. A link puzzle is one of those sets of heavy wire bent into a shape which permits their being linked and unlinked in only one way. Why is White going to buy one?
5. How would you describe this essay?

Word Study

Retort *Transcendental*:
wearisome and *dissipating*:
fountainhead of the day:
is *copious*:
to a *soirée*:
imbibes delight:
assimilated to ourselves:
began *effervescing*:
quiet and *tractable*:

Out for Stars:
A Meditation on Robert Frost

George Frisbie Whicher

George Frisbie Whicher taught at Columbia University, the University of Illinois, Amherst, the University of Hawaii, Johns Hopkins, and in Istanbul, Turkey. He wrote widely in verse, fiction, essays, and scholarly reviews.

The essay here is subtitled "Meditation on Robert Frost." The word "meditation" is wholly appropriate, for what Whicher has given us is part analysis, part interpretation, and part recollection.

As you read, find the analysis, the interpretation, and the recollection; and observe over it all, the meditative mood. This is an essayist thoroughly familiar with his subject, appreciating the subject in proportion to his familiarity with it, and sharing with us his ideas and his enthusiasm.

Streamlining is one of the most popular fallacies of our time. ¶1
If you apply streamlining to poetry the argument runs about as follows: Since the chief aim of poetry is to bring about a formal ordering or integration of the feelings, communication cannot be its main purpose. Consequently poetry that eliminates communication is purer, and hence better, than poetry that admits a "message." The poem should not attempt to rival the scientific textbook; or as Archibald MacLeish has so incisively put it, "A poem should not mean but be."

¶2 With the modernist poet's fastidious avoidance of meaning (once he has stated his *ars poetica*), it is instructive to compare the practice of a great poet like Dante, who seems curiously unaware of how much he might have improved his *Commedia* if he had not sought to use it as an instrument of communication. Instead of reducing the element of meaning to the lowest possible terms, Dante appears almost avid to multiply meanings, to double and redouble the implications of his thought. Can it be that disdain of meaning is a symptom of the poverty of poetry in a time of failing convictions?

¶3 A renewed perception of the many levels of implication beneath the innocent-looking surfaces of Robert Frost's poems reminded me recently of the manifold harmonies of Dante's great poetic instrument. Reading again in Mr. Untermeyer's expert selection, *Come In*, the lyric that so happily lends its title to the book, I became aware that the words of the poem were opening vistas in several directions, as from one spot in the forest the eye may fancy that it discerns colonnaded aisles leading off ahead, behind, and on either hand.

¶4 Particularly in the last two stanzas I thought I could detect an effect like "underpainting," layer upon layer, beneath the plain intent of the words:

> Far in the pillared dark
> Thrush music went—
> Almost like a call to come in
> To the dark and lament.
>
> But no, I was out for stars:
> I would not come in.
> I meant not even if asked,
> And I hadn't been.

¶5 Here is a poem which, though it does not shirk the obligation of lucid statement, is not exhausted when its surface meaning has been communicated. Instead the simplicity and clearness of the incident recorded leave the reader unimpeded by verbal perplexities, not to turn away satisfied unless he is a singularly obtuse reader, but to look further into these limpid depths and perceive what he can, whether of cloudy reflections of his own mind or of ultimate intentions lurking in the poet's.

After the labor of assimilating to our being much poetry ¶6
that aims not to mean but to be, the pleasure of encountering a poem that actually conveys a well-defined reading of experience is enormous.

Taken literally, the lines I have quoted record a very ordi- ¶7
nary incident of a walk at twilight. A man with an eye for the first stars is distracted momentarily by the poignant beauty of the thrush's song, but he refuses to follow its lure into the darkening woods or to accept its mood of lamentation. The laconic last two lines confirm the New England setting of the poem.

Indeed, the intonations are so characteristic that they can ¶8
hardly fail to recall to the many persons who have listened to Robert Frost's remarkable readings from his poems the voice of the poet himself. Every other part of the poem is equally authentic. Much that Frost has written attests his intimate acquaintance with country things: he can be trusted to select the moment of the day when the wood-thrush's song sounds clearest. His reference to stars is no casual literary gesture, but a tribute to a lifelong passion for astronomy, amply confirmed in other poems.

Not only the person speaking, but the setting of the poem ¶9
is utterly true to life. It might be any one of the New Hampshire or Vermont farms where Frost has lived, since he has seldom lodged far from the edge of the woods and the companionship of trees. I do not know where this poem was written, or what landscape was present to the writer's mind, but to me it seems to fit perfectly the region of Ripton, Vermont, where he has latterly spent his summers.

The dark woods might be the half-mile stretch of state ¶10

forest, largely pine, between his cottage on the Homer Noble place and "Iry" Dow's, the homeplace of his current venture in farming. To get from one property to the other by road is a matter of several miles, and it is natural, therefore, to cut through the woods. But if one were going nowhere in particular it would be easy to refuse the walk beneath the trees for a climb to upland pastures, whence as from a shelf hung high on the slope of the Green Mountains one may look off westward across a narrow strip of Lake Champlain to tumbled Adirondack masses on the rim of the world and above them the evening star.

¶11 Ripton is typical "Frost Country," though the bulk of his writing was done before he came to live in this neighborhood. It reached the height of its prosperity about the time of the Civil War. The mounting tide of human settlement then flowed up to the higher clearings; since then it has mostly receded, leaving behind a sparse population on "marginal" land and many cellar holes. Among the people are some whom Frost might name along with the best he has encountered anywhere in rural New England. Others are not to be clearly distinguished from the oddments on any beach at low tide.

¶12 There was "Iry" Dow, for example, now departed, who for upward of forty years professed to make his living as a blacksmith, though prevented by a weak heart from making any strenuous exertions. Consequently a great deal of conversation flowed between blows on the anvil. "That Iry Dow," said one irritated customer, "is as much slower'n stock-still's stock-still is slower'n greased lightnin'." The year before he died, the village elected him to the legislature so that he might continue his endless talk without the bother of now and then pretending to beat on a horseshoe. Nothing that Frost found among these people would have suggested any need of revising what he had previously written of other little towns north of Boston.

¶13 The surrounding country, dominated by the ridge of the mountains, once partly settled, then unsettled again, is full of the wild things, both animals and plants, that the poet has so often observed and described. A great lover of woodlands and Morgan horses, the late Joseph Battell, once possessed much of Ripton, and his will is still reflected in the quantity of standing timber. So bold and numerous are the deer that vegetable gardens need the protection of an electrically charged wire. Overgrown roads follow the brooks and lead to abandoned mowings high on the ridges.

In one respect, however, Ripton is peculiar. It contains ¶14
Bread Loaf, the summer school of English which Frost helped to found some twenty-five years ago and which he still benevolently frequents. Frost, in fact, would not be fully himself unless there were an educational project somewhere in the offing for him to cherish and humorously despair of, for he is a born teacher with a knack of charging dry subjects with intellectual excitement and a large patience for struggling learners.

Teaching to him is a natural extension of his unfeigned ¶15
interest in people. I have seen him ask friendly, insistent questions about the little country town where a man was born and brought up, and have watched the man, at first answering with diffidence because for years he had been apologetic about his simple beginnings and anxious to live them down, gradually warm to his memories, discover a fresh respect for the sources of his being, and go out from the interview (as he said later) with a new dimension added to his personality. I doubt if Frost knew how much that conversation meant to the other man. He was just expressing an interest in the ways of little towns.

It is against the background of Ripton, then, that I picture ¶16
Frost hearing thrush music, as it is there that I recall him in many other postures: a stocky figure but alert in motion, wearing an old suit and scuffed shoes, freshly laundered soft shirt open at his throat, his white hair tousled in the wind, his seafarer's blue eyes twinkling. One would find him skirting a mowing

field, crossing a stone wall to a pasture where blueberries grew, measuring the water in the spring, or playing softball with young friends on a diamond wrung from the hayfield, where running for a fly was an adventure. Then would come hours of such converse as I never expect to repeat.

¶17 For me the poem I have quoted is inseparably bound up with these personal memories of the man and the region. But for anyone, even for anyone ages hence, it is marked with authentic traits of individuality, images to the ear and to the eye, that distinguish it from conventionalized writing just as readily as a portrait can be told from an idealized face when archaeologists study the sculptures found in the buried cities of Yucatan.

¶18 In the first instance, then, the poem is justified by its absolute integrity of substance. Whatever it speaks of is something that the poet has absorbed completely into himself, generally by seeing it, hearing it, living through it—less frequently by imaginative reading. But though the poem may appear simple and complete on the literal level, its texture may be dense with implied cross-references. In such poetry it is not inappropriate to look for undermeanings, at one's own risk, of course. The meanings may be all in the reader's eye, or again they may attain to a certain significance if they are confirmed by what the poet has elsewhere written.

¶19 Frost himself may be held responsible if readers persist in looking in his poems for more meaning than meets the casual eye. Though he denies a didactic intent, he is not unwilling to have his poetic records of experience flower in explicit apothegm. Only there is seldom or never any indication of his writing for the sake of the moral. In that respect he differs completely from makers of fables. La Fontaine, as Mr. Untermeyer claims, might conceivably have shaped the substance of Frost's "At Woodward's Gardens" into an apologue entitled "The Boy, the Monkeys, and the Burning-Glass," ending with the epigram: "It's knowing what to do with things that counts." But Frost's first instinct is to make sure of the reality of his material; nine-tenths of his poem is painstakingly devoted to picturing his monkeys, not as actors in a fable, but as actual monkeys. He calls our attention to their "purple little knuckles" and condenses all the confusion of the simian brain into one delicious line:

> They bit the glass and listened for the flavor.

Not until that has been fully done does he turn to the moral as a means of rounding the poem. To call such a piece of writing a fable, as at least two good critics have recently chosen to do, is to label it as something less than it actually is. Except where Frost has completed his poem by attaching an abstract meaning to it—not necessarily a statement of the poem's whole meaning—he is entitled to insist that his intention has been to present, not the symbol of a thought, but an image of an experience. To this there is only one answer: that experience as Frost absorbs and interprets it often spreads out into so many ramifications that thoughts get tangled in it like stars seen through tree branches.

To consider now more searchingly the stanzas that I have ¶20
quoted about the thrush, would it not be possible to read the episode as a literary parable? A poet of our time hears a bird-like voice from the dark wood (ancient symbol of error) singing of irremediable ills. The call to "come in to the dark and lament" awakens an impulse to become a modernist poet of the decadent school, to take the veil (or, as Frost once put it, "take the blanket") of calculated obscurity and imitate the fashionable lead of the French Symbolistes. The summons, however sweetly conveyed, can be resisted by a poet who has long considered it inappropriate "to write the Russian novel in America," and who prefers to keep on in the way he was going.

To place this interpretation on the poem (and I do not ¶21

imply that the poem demands it) is to emphasize Frost's remarkable independence of the contemporary note in letters. Though he has studied the experimental poetry of recent years with attention—and some amusement—he has never felt called to share in any experiments except his own, which have been more far-reaching in their metrical subtlety than many readers realize. Ever since as a young poet barely out of his teens Frost was advised by a New York editor to try to write like Sidney Lanier, he has been set in his determination to write like no one but Robert Frost.

¶22 His aloofness has been held against him. It has been asserted that any sensitive spirit of our time must be wounded by the spectacle of the world as it exists and must respond by exhibiting his mutilations in public. Frost's obvious cultivation of soundness and balance, therefore, has been taken as indicative of a refusal to face the bitter realities that really matter, of a retreat to a protected backwater safe from the storm. This to a man who, unlike many of his critics, has worked in the factory and on the farm, who has known poverty as well as grief, and who has waited twenty years for recognition of his work to overtake him!

¶23 If Frost has not been willing to come in to the dark and lament, it has not been because he was unacquainted with the night, but because he had something to do that pleased him better. Perhaps he has felt that the business of putting love in order, of creating form out of the formless, can be better done by a poet who declined to be warped by the pressures of modern living. At any rate he has been unwavering in his allegiance to an Emersonian conception of human wholeness.

¶24 His deep-seated instinct for centrality and balance brings us back to the poem of the thrush to discover its meaning as ethical symbol. We are not disappointed. What else does the poem portray but one of the familiar dilemmas of man's existence? His walk lies between the two extremes represented by the dark woods and the stars. To the heavenly extreme he can never attain, to the other he is unwilling to let himself descend, but he may be aware of both and may on occasion incline a little one way or the other. That is what our living is, discovering where the extremes lie and where we belong on a sort of scale drawn between them.

There are innumerable such scales in politics, in religion, ¶25
in education. If we do not complete the scale, we risk falling into the illusion of progress—that is, of supposing that we are drifting inevitably toward a far-off divine event—or we are conscious only of what we have fallen from and invent the myth of original sin. Looking toward one extreme only, we commonly speak of savagery in contrast to civilization. Frost recently made us aware of the other end of the scale when he declared, "The opposite of civilization is Utopia." Thus the scale is completed, and man is put back between the poles—where he belongs.

One result of thinking of the normal human position as ¶26
somewhere midway between two extremes is to awaken a fierce distrust of extremists and totalitarians, no matter how high-minded they may be. Once we are forced as far as we can go toward either extreme, we are committed, we lose our power to maneuver, we must adopt the party line. Only from a central position can we be said to have the ability to choose that makes life dramatic. Frost would not trade the freedom of his material in the world as he finds it for any number of freedoms in Utopia. What he holds precious is the privilege of meeting the exigencies of life by apt recalls from past experience, with only enough newness to freshen thought.

But what if the world's crisis is so desperate as to justify ¶27
a concerted movement to one extreme or the other in the attempt to alleviate it? Are we always to see life waste away into war, insanity, poverty, and crime and do nothing about it? Here indeed we touch on ultimate values. In an address to Amherst seniors a few years ago Frost declared that the thought of coming to condone the world's sorrow is terrible to contemplate. It is our

darkest concern. Yet unless I misread the poem, Frost has indicated the inevitable response of a wise man in the poem we have been discussing. To be resolutely "out for stars" is not to be concerned overmuch with the still, sad music of humanity.

¶28 The poet must nerve himself to say with Housman, "Be still, my soul, and see injustice done." It is his function to realize the millennium, not in terms of social adjustments, but either

> right beside you book-like on the shelf,
> Or even better god-like in yourself.

Frost has spoken with deep compassion of the Shelleyan natures who insist on bearing their share, or more than their share, of the world's miseries, but he has not hesitated to proclaim that the call to struggle for society's betterment is "poetry's great anti-lure." He is not attracted by

> the tenderer-than-thou
> Collectivistic regimenting love
> With which the modern world is being swept.

The poet, in so far as he is a poet, must not be too cognizant of mankind's wounds or his own. His business is not to make humanity whole, but to explore the uses of wholeness. It is naïve to hang the class struggle on his shoulders. In the American tradition one does not have to join the army to be a good citizen.

¶29 If anyone still should ask, Why is the function that the poet performs so important that he may seek exemption from duties incumbent on his fellows? the best answer is, Read once again the lovely stanzas of "Come In" or the poem "Choose Something Like a Star" that stands as an afterword in the anthology of Frost's writings compiled by Mr. Untermeyer. Is it nothing to us that someone should be out for stars? Is it nothing in a universe where every star we can examine seems to be engaged in radiating incredible light and heat—is it nothing, in our preoccupation with war and wages and prices, to be reminded of the sense in which a star by its mere existence can "ask a little of us here?"

> It asks of us a certain height,
> So when at times the mob is swayed
> To carry praise or blame too far,
> We may choose something like a star
> To stay our minds on and be staid.

For Greater Insight

1. What are the two points of view concerning poetry presented in the first two paragraphs? On what side is Whicher? What is the relationship here to Margot Fonteyn's comment on page 176? Or to Question 3 on p. 280?
2. Par. 7 explains Frost's poem. Is "out for stars" to be taken literally or symbolically? Or perhaps in both senses?
3. Pars. 9–17 describe "Frost Country"—people, places, institutions—as Whicher knows it. The paragraphs are full of detail. They are also the kind of "intellectual sauntering" which is one of the hallmarks of the essay. At the end of this section, in Par. 17, the last sentence merits study. If you know many others of Frost's poems you can answer this question. What is there in Frost's poems which makes the reader feel that they come from real experience, that he has lived those moments, known those emotions, and walked in those places? Illustrate your answer by reference to poems you know.
4. How does Whicher, in Par. 19, justify the examination of Frost's poems for their hidden meaning?
5. Pars. 20–23 offer an interpretation of the two stanzas. Is this a narrow interpretation, or a broad, general one? Do you agree with it? Why? Does Whicher? How do you know?
6. Pars. 24 to the end of the essay offer another interpretation of the two stanzas. Is this a narrow interpretation, or a broad, general one? Do you agree with it? Why? Does Whicher? How do you know?
7. Consider carefully what Whicher says in Par. 25 about savagery, civilization, and Utopia. Explain the scale, and where mankind is.
8. Read again carefully the last paragraph, beginning with the words "Is it nothing to us . . ." Although you may not be reading these essays in the order in which they are presented here, this essay

is the last in the book. In conclusion, may you all have both the enormous satisfaction and the equally enormous frustration of being "out for stars."

Word Study

popular *fallacies*:
incisively put it:
fastidious avoidance:
appears almost *avid*:
disdain of meaning:
a renewed *perception*:
levels of *implication*:
manifold harmonies:
colonnaded aisles:
shirk the obligation of *lucid* statement:
unimpeded by verbal *perplexities*:
obtuse reader:
limpid depths:
ultimate intentions *lurking* in the poet's (mind):
assimilating to our being:
poignant beauty:
laconic last two lines:
from the *oddments*:
benevolently frequents:
in the *offing*:
unfeigned interest:
answering with *diffidence*:
a *didactic* intent:
in *explicit apothegm*:
of *irremediable* ills:
the *decadent* school:
their *metrical subtlety*:
familiar *dilemmas*:
exigencies of life:
to *alleviate* it:
realize the *millennium*:
cognizant of mankind's wounds:
It is *naïve*: